FINAL DESTINATION:
DISASTER

FINAL DESTINATION:
DISASTER

GEORGE JEHN

WHAT *REALLY*
HAPPENED TO
EASTERN
AIRLINES

CHANGING LIVES PRESS

CHANGING LIVES PRESS
50 Public Square #1600
Cleveland, OH 44113
www.changinglivespress.com

Library of Congress Cataloging-in-Publication Data is available
through the Library of Congress.

ISBN: 978-0-9894529-6-0

Cover design by Michael Short
Author photo courtesy of John H. Taylor
Color Photography by Allen Gerber
Interior layout by Gary A. Rosenberg • www.thebookcouple.com

Printed in the United States of America

10 9 8 7 6 5 4 3 2 1

CONTENTS

*To the many thousands
of former Eastern employees
who never knew the complexity
of events surrounding them,
but who paid dearly.*

PROLOGUE

On January 1, 1985, at approximately 8:38 p.m., an Eastern Airlines Boeing 727 Flight 980 piloted by Captain Larry Campbell on a routine flight from Asuncion, Paraguay, to La Paz, Bolivia, crashed into the Andes Mountains outside the La Paz, Bolivia John F. Kennedy International Airport. All twenty-nine souls on board were killed.

Normally, following any airliner crash, an extensive probe to determine the cause would be undertaken by the investigative agencies of the countries involved—in this case, the United States and Bolivia—as well as Eastern Airlines and other interested parties. But this time, no timely inquiry was ever launched, even though public statements to the contrary emanating from the highest government and Eastern sources were widely—and, as I subsequently discovered, deceptively—circulated.

Some victims' relatives, frustrated by this inaction, wanted to embark on their own trek to the crash site. They were eventually dissuaded by one Eastern pilot who mounted his own expedition to try to get some answers. Meanwhile, the U.S. government's and Eastern's delaying tactics helped insure that the reasons for the crash would remain forever buried on a barren and bleak South American mountainside.

Eleven months later, winter had again arrived in the northeast, and while sitting in the cozy warmth of my study in front of a blazing fire on a bitter cold December evening, I delved into the United States National Transportation Safety Board (NTSB) papers that were finally issued on the Flight 980 crash. The more I read, the more troubled I became. I envisioned the pitch black sky on that fateful night, only illuminated intermittently by lightning crackling from a thunderstorm visible on the jet's radar directly ahead, and pictured the frigid snow swirling beneath the 727 like a stealthy whirlwind in a silent, desolate landscape more than nineteen-thousand feet above sea level. The closest bastion of warmth was the flight's next stopover, La Paz, a little over fifty miles away and closing fast. But Flight 980 never made it there, its final and silent tomb instead a windswept ridge in the Bolivian Andes. I wondered what might have transpired in the final moments between the pilots' acknowledgment of a descent clearance to 18,000 feet in preparation for landing at La Paz and the jet's devastating impact with Mount Illimani.

At the time, as a sixteen-year veteran Eastern pilot, I was very troubled, first by the NTSB's initial refusal to conduct *any* investigation, then after they were forced to do so, their inexplicable delay of over ten months to even send an expedition to the crash site. I had just finished poring over the partially redacted NTSB "after action" report on this useless trek, which raised more questions than any it possibly answered. Never before had I witnessed so many uninvestigated possible causes and unanswered questions in light of such a serious disaster. There were too many contradictions, too much information that was conveniently ignored, overlooked, or simply cast aside, never to be examined by that U.S. government agency, at least not publicly.

No one had lifted a finger to discover what had *really* caused this crash.

Deepening the mystery, this was the only time since the founding of the NTSB that the cause of a crash of a United States commercial jet airliner had not undergone intense scrutiny. In addition, other Eastern pilots had subsequently reported a number of close calls on their South American flights. Although it was these items that originally aroused my interest, I discovered that indeed there was more: something was *very* different about the manner in which the Flight 980 disaster was handled—or mishandled—which set it apart from every other airliner crash. So much so that I subsequently launched my own in-depth investigation, pondering why only the union that represented the pilots wanted to uncover what caused this disaster.

Just then, my private phone line unexpectedly rang. At the time I had no idea this was a call that would ultimately change the destinies of hundreds of thousands of people. I picked up the telephone, unaware that *nothing* would ever be the same again.

PART I

THE BACKGROUND

CHAPTER ONE

Larry Schulte, the lanky, gray-haired chairman of the Eastern Airlines Master Executive Council (MEC) unit of the Air Line Pilots Association (ALPA), the latter the national union that represented the Eastern pilots, was on the other end of the line. I had worked with Larry a number of years prior when he was an elected representative from Eastern's Washington pilot base and I was the same from New York. After exchanging pleasantries, he stated that he wanted to meet with me the following evening in Miami where the Eastern ALPA unit was headquartered. I informed him I had to fly a three-day trip, but he insisted that I call crew scheduling and have them remove me to conduct ALPA business, meaning ALPA would pick up the tab for my salary and expenses. Without further explanation, I did as requested.

I took an Eastern nonstop New York-to-Miami flight the next day to meet with Schulte over dinner. I had been away from MEC work for some time, a time-consuming, mostly thankless job that had almost cost me my marriage, given that even though I was an elected representative, a complete month of flying was required most of the time. Then, upon my arrival back home, there were normally a dozen or more phone calls awaiting me that had to be returned. There were over fifteen hundred pilots based in Eastern's New York domicile, meaning something was always happening that required my attention.

As former MEC members, Schulte and I were rarely, if ever, on the same wavelength. I was more of a hardliner, while he was more willing to cede to management demands. As a result I believed he was inadequate for the grueling chairman's job. During the flight I pondered why he wanted to meet. Did he do an abrupt about-face? What was this all about?

After checking into the Miami Airport Marriott hotel, I quickly showered and hailed a cab for the approximate ten-minute cab ride to Mancini's
restaurant, a small, gaudy Coral Gables Italian bistro located just outside
of Miami where we had agreed to meet. As I entered, the stench of garlic
and the restaurant décor made me a bit queasy. I had dined there before;
the joint was ostensibly designed to resemble a New York City Little Italy
eatery, but the food didn't come close. It was a place whose fare usually
awoke you in the middle of the night with a bad case of indigestion or
agida, as Italians call it. As it turned out, I'd be awake all night feeling like
acid was burning a hole through my stomach lining, wishing it were caused
by something as simple as *agida.* Another item contributing to my queasi-
ness was Schulte's high-pitched tone of voice, which didn't inspire the confidence expected of a pilot leader. We shook hands, and he immediately
got to the business at hand.

"I can't comprehend the situation," he began. "It's as though management is trying to provoke a pilot strike, cause problems and undo all of the
good from the recent past."

I figured his concerns referenced the ongoing Eastern pilot contract
negotiations. "I only have a limited knowledge," I replied, "mostly scuttle-
butt picked up while flying. We don't discuss contract negotiations at the
Employee Involvement committee meetings, so clue me in. What's going
on in the negotiations that has you so upset?"

Past practices normally dictated that the give and take during negotiations was a well-kept secret between the negotiators for both sides, along
with the union hierarchy and Eastern's top management and advisors.
There was good reason for this because there was usually lots of give and
take, meaning movement from opening positions, with the final outcome
a mutually acceptable, middle-ground deal of some type. This way both
parties could claim a victory of sorts. There was no need to include the
pilots in these daily events, unless it became clear that no agreement could
possibly be reached and a strike vote appeared inevitable. But this critical
action would not normally be undertaken until well beyond the contract's
amendable date when talks became hopelessly deadlocked. In this case,
the current pilot contract still had over two months to run until even one

sentence in it could be changed. I had *suspected* something might be amiss from the tone of discussions at the Employee Involvement Committee meetings, where I was the sole pilot member, when brusque comments "slipped" from the lips of some management personnel. Despite public statements to the contrary, I saw signs that told me the time of harmonious labor management relationships might inexplicably be coming to an abrupt end. I wished that wasn't the case, but after an approximate four-year hiatus, these conflicting signals had led me to run for another two-year term on the MEC from the New York base, which I easily won.

There was no way I was going to allow things to deteriorate back to the sorry state of employee affairs experienced for so many years, and I was determined to do whatever possible to prevent that from happening, especially after witnessing all the good that could be accomplished when everyone worked together. I was to assume office on March 1, 1986, a little over two months hence. Would a new accord be reached by then? The amendable date of the current agreement was February 26, 1986 and during thorny negotiations, talks normally extended well beyond that date, sometimes for years. *Why was Schulte so concerned at this early point in time?*

The terms of the Federal Railway Labor Act (RLA) govern negotiations in the airline industry. If no agreement was reached by February 26, negotiations would normally continue indefinitely, while the pilots kept working under the old work rules and pay rates until one of two things happened: an agreement was reached or the federal mediator from the United States National Mediation Board (NMB) assigned to the negotiations ultimately released the parties into what is known as the thirty-day cooling off period. If new contract terms had not been agreed to after those thirty days, the pilots would be free to strike and management could impose their latest offer.

Once the negotiations appeared to be at a standstill, talks normally continued for a lengthy period under the auspices of the federal mediator in an effort to avoid a crippling strike, the latter viewed as a failure.

"I'll fill you in," Schulte sighed, and he began reciting a litany of ongoing problems. "Our contractual requests are quite small, but management's

demands are anything but. They're trying to take away virtually everything
of value and are setting up a poisonous environment, making it difficult to
reach *any* agreement. It makes absolutely no sense," Schulte quickly added,
shaking his head. "For example, a number of times and in numerous crucial contractual areas, we've conceded to management's every demand, but
to no avail. We've even agreed to no raises for the life of the contract—"

"You did what?" I interrupted.

"Let me finish," Schulte insisted, his gray eyes flashing. "Every time we
accept an item on their laundry list, they pull it back off the table and raise
the ante until they know that we can't possibly agree. It's to the point that
even if we were able to get their proposals through the MEC, we'd be
lynched by the line pilots."

I felt like getting up and leaving, but only my morbid curiosity, gut
instincts, and fear of what he still had to impart kept me seated. Schulte
seemed to sense this and hesitated. *Would he now try to sugarcoat everything?*

"It's as though a crisis is being purposely created," he continued, no
doubt trying to ignore the intensity I was wearing like a loud, brightly colored South Beach T-shirt, "and I don't know how long I can hold off what
is probably rapidly approaching."

"What do you mean by rapidly approaching?"

He waved his hand and evaded the question. Making eye contact he
added, "I need your help. That's the reason for this get-together. If management wants a strike, we'll give 'em one. I want the vast majority of the
Eastern pilots showing they're ready to hit the bricks. If we can accomplish
that, I'm certain they'll back off and we'll reach an agreement that's acceptable to everyone. This is where your services will be needed."

This statement raised a red flag concerning the speed of the negotiations. *What might be the true role of the supposedly neutral NMB mediator?*
I knew that former NASA astronaut and current Eastern chief, Frank Borman, had friends in very high places in Ronald Reagan's Administration,
including the President himself. This meant the NMB's role might be anything but what is was supposed to be—impartial. Its then-head, the late
Walter Wallace, was a Reagan appointee. Schulte's use of the dreaded *"S"*

word "strike" was also of great concern because we were still over two months from the date the contract even became open to change. How could he be talking strike at this early stage *if* negotiations followed the routine pattern? Maybe he knew more but wasn't letting on. Schulte must have sensed my foreboding because he immediately stopped speaking and signaled the waitress.

We ordered dinner and a bottle of wine. I didn't know what else to speak about, as we never enjoyed the type of rapport where we discussed our kids, wives, or hobbies. And I didn't want the waitress to overhear what was being discussed because when it came to Eastern, Miami was indeed a small world; it housed Eastern's headquarters and lots of people worked for the airline. The overpowering silence only added to the stress floating in the air like the garlic odor. The waitress took our dinner orders and Schulte resumed, describing the specific negotiating troubles in greater detail.

"I believe Frank Borman is orchestrating this entire thing," he said.

When his name surfaced, my thoughts were redirected. The diminutive Borman appeared in many Eastern television commercials touting the airline and its service, and as result, the mention of his name would conjure up an image of Eastern. But very few outsiders knew what it was like to work under him. The programs he instituted and the methods used to launch them produced serious employee problems.

* * *

Eddie Rickenbacker was the first well-known and a sometimes controversial Eastern President, a tough, but fair boss. Although Captain Eddie, as he was commonly known, could be viewed as abrasive and contentious outside the airline, this was not usually the case within. He was a topnotch World War I flying ace whose brash but blunt way of conducting business commanded the loyalty of most employees, especially the pilots. He had taken Eastern from a tiny mail carrier and built it up into one of the largest airlines in the world, always mindful of his obligations to the employees. Rickenbacker, who was also a Medal of Honor recipient, instituted the first airline employee stock purchase plan and wrote a paper entitled "My Constitution," outlining twelve personal and business principles that guided him and from which he never wavered. Rickenbacker set his annual wages at $50,000 in 1938 and that never changed for twenty-five years.

After Rickenbacker, following a series of more businesslike bosses, Borman, or "The Colonel," as he liked to be called, was the next highly visible Eastern head. A 1950 West Point graduate, he subsequently commanded the 1968 *Apollo 8* lunar mission. As millions of viewers sat glued to their TV sets watching this historic event, they were treated to sights and sounds of Borman reading from the Bible while orbiting the lunar landscape below. The televised piety transformed him into an instant hero in the eyes of many Americans and bestowed him with a traditionalist, God-fearing image.

In 1969, then-Eastern President Floyd Hall hired the forty-one-year-old Borman as a technical consultant and public relations persona, a part-time position that paid him a flat consulting annual fee of five thousand dollars, plus expenses. Newspapers reported he was also offered a top-level job working for the Nixon White House in some undefined political capacity. Although Borman accepted the Eastern position, the Nixon offer gave him entry into the closed inner sanctum of the White House, where he subsequently was a caller on a number of occasions during the Nixon presidency and again during the Reagan and Bush years. Borman was also appointed as a Presidential "special ambassador," visiting various heads of state as an official representative of the U.S. government. On these occasions, he was granted the use of *Air Force Two*, basking in the glow of worldwide media attention and travelling throughout Europe and the Far East, unsuccessfully seeking the release of United States prisoners of war that were held in North Vietnam. He also publicly, verbally, and visibly backed Ronald Reagan's sacking of the air traffic controllers in the media, many of whom were military veterans, whose firing, in my opinion, carried the very real risk of negatively affecting airliner safety. Borman also served on committees to elect George H. W. Bush and other Republicans. By 1970, Borman had assumed the position of Eastern's vice-president of Flight Operations—the pilots' boss—at an annual salary of sixty thousand dollars. In May of 1975 he was elected President and Chief Operating Officer. Later that year he was named Chief Executive Officer, and in 1976,

he also became Chairman of the Board. One of Borman's major impediments was that he lacked the essential business expertise needed to run a
large, complex airline, as his only experience was confined to the political
world and the tightly controlled military and NASA programs. Eastern
employees soon discovered what his lack of business acumen and latent
anti-union mindset meant, perhaps best exemplified by the fact that, prior
to Borman's tenure, Eastern was known as The Pilots Airline. That was why
I wanted to work there. But by the time Borman was done, it was the airline whose pilots were departing in droves.

As an executive who worked closely with him for years, Mort Ehrlich
was familiar with what Borman truly represented, having labored directly
under him as Eastern's Director of Marketing. He later told me that Borman was always most concerned about how he was viewed by the general
public and would devote much of his energy to making certain he
was seen in the most favorable media light. (You will read more of Mr.
Ehrlich's important revelations later in this book via a personal interview
I conducted.)

Working as a pilot throughout Borman's tenure, I had previously witnessed abrupt turnarounds by a number of ALPA union representatives.
After being elected, some turned their backs on the very people who had
entrusted their careers to them and instead did Borman's bidding. What
made them reverse their loyalty? After being elected to ALPA office for the
first time in 1978, it didn't take long before I discovered Borman had a specific *modus operandi*, one that I personally experienced. His initial step was
an attempt to go around the Representative he viewed as errant and deal
directly with the pilots they represented through one of his oft-held pilot
base meetings. In this, his forum, someone in the audience would mention
the representative and solicit Borman's opinion. Once that subject was
broached, Borman used his clout to portray that person in a bad light. Like
the general populace, many pilots held Borman in awe. If a pilot union official, an equal, was vilified by Borman it usually signaled trouble as his criticisms were malicious and often accomplished under the façade of cutting
humor. As a result, some ALPA reps caved in to his demands and avoided
another confrontation. But if this approach didn't work, Borman went fur-

ther to bring the stubborn representative around to seeing things his way by initiating personal contact. His method took a variety of approaches, ranging from a friendly phone chat or an invitation to attend a private dinner to discuss pilot-related issues, as seen through Borman's eyes.

For a number of years I had performed my flying job and stayed out of the limelight. This also meant I had endured Borman's frequent employee letters that only fostered insecurity and were always signed "God Bless You," along with continual monetary and contractual demands as his panacea to profitability. With a young and growing family, the numerous Borman-demanded givebacks equaled months of difficulty providing my family with a decent standard of living. Mine wasn't turning out to be the expected life of an airline pilot. In 1978, I attempted to change this by running for union office. A fellow Eastern pilot who shared my perspective, Charles H. "Skip" Copeland, also ran. The ruggedly handsome "Silver Fox," as Copeland was dubbed for his full mane of gray hair, possessed enormous insight. Tall, with penetrating cobalt eyes, Copeland also had an uncanny ability to accurately analyze just about any situation in a short period, another vital asset. The icing on the cake was that we immediately clicked, listening to and respecting each other's opinions. We handily won election to the Master Executive Council from Eastern's large New York base and set out to rebuild the pilot contract.

An important first step toward this goal would be through the round of contract negotiations about to commence. By 1978 airline deregulation was looming and the Eastern pilots' earnings were rapidly eroding further due to runaway inflation. The airline was in good financial health, but with inflation running well over twelve percent annually, Borman, of course, was predicting more doom and gloom. There was a small window of opportunity to recover some contractual items that had been given away earlier, so our top priority became their restoration.

The MEC had elected a four-member negotiating committee empowered to do the bargaining for a new contract after the MEC set wide-ranging goals. Any contractual modifications would then be ratified or disapproved by a majority of the MEC, as at the time we had no pilot membership balloting. In private conversations with members of the negotiating team we made it clear our position was unequivocal; after many years of givebacks, the time was ripe to restore the Eastern pilots to a fair position within the airline industry. In exchange, we pledged our total support, keeping the weaker members of the MEC in line.

Many months of haggling followed until well beyond the amendable date. The negotiating committee ultimately informed the MEC their latest proposals were reasonable, but management refused to come to an acceptable agreement. Although there was apprehension on the part of some, including now–MEC Chairman Schulte, we fulfilled our part of the agreement, keeping support for the committee high. Borman discovered that Copeland and I were the driving force, and in his now-frequent New York pilot base meetings never missed an opportunity to take a personal shot. We had determined beforehand that the majority of New York–based pilots felt as we did, however, and through an effective communications effort, we kept them fully abreast of proceedings.

One morning my private telephone number rang. Surprisingly, Borman greeted me on the other end. I didn't know how he got that number, but he said he wanted to discuss a letter critical of him that had been posted throughout the New York base on the locked ALPA bulletin boards. Borman said he was embarrassed because the letter ridiculed some items from his career at NASA that he claimed were false. I quickly agreed to remove it, but to my surprise he continued, stating he was aware that Copeland and I were behind the contract demands and went on to tell me that we needed to be patient. But I knew we couldn't wait much longer as the pilots had gone for years without a raise or any promotional opportunities.

I just listened, but before I could say anything, he quickly added, "I want to let you know there's a place in the executive ranks of the airline for an assertive individual like you."

Was Borman trying to entice me with a management job offer to alter my position? I simply responded that it wasn't proper for us to have a private discussion regarding contract negotiations. He politely thanked me and hung up. Maybe he got the earlier givebacks by making similar offers to others, as a number of former union reps had taken managerial positions after their terms of office ended. I finally concluded Borman must have felt that he had his back to the wall, hence the call. Or maybe his concern stemmed from what pilots pay increases would do to his emerging anti-union image? I phoned Copeland, told him what transpired and we came to the consensus that we had the upper hand. Several phone calls convinced enough MEC members of the need for a special meeting to discuss what we described as an impending negotiating impasse. After some initial haggling, we pushed through a unanimous resolution that stated our negotiating committee had three days to get a finalized contract or we would take a strike vote. Not surprisingly, two days later we had the contract. Borman never called again, but that one encounter provided precious insight into how he operated.

As Schulte continued spouting vitriolic words about Borman, I recalled another of Borman's divisive boondoggles, the Variable Earnings Program. One of his claims for the need for this was that the airline's long-term, excessive debt dragged down earnings. To accomplish the dual goals of debt reduction and consistent profitability, Borman implemented a negotiated wage giveback program, the VEP. Under its terms, Eastern withheld three and a half percent of all employees' wages, which theoretically were to be used to reach a predetermined annual profit. But Borman conveniently omitted telling employees that the Boeing 757 purchase he just made greatly *increased* Eastern's debt load, one of the very reasons why the VEP was instituted. Only after the 757 financing terms were publicly disclosed did workers realize they'd been duped. Because the labor contracts had been signed, employees were saddled with the program, but had no say about how their money was spent. Consequently, for the first time, worker dissatisfaction with the Colonel was reported in the media as employees were burdened with long-term contracts that included the VEP.

In subsequent contract negotiations Borman utilized repeated threats to attempt to force a continuation of the VEP, which by that time many employees more commonly dubbed the "Variable Extortion Plan." He went so far as to direct VEP money to be withheld from workers' checks after its contractual expiration date. The International Association of Machinists (IAM), however, went to court and forced the withholdings to cease. The court ruling ended the VEP withholdings, but Borman's attacks continued. Next came public threats of bankruptcy and employees were forced to view a Borman-narrated videotape, where they were told Eastern might file for Chapter Eleven bankruptcy—as Frank Lorenzo had done at Continental Airlines—unilaterally voiding all labor contracts. For three long years employees worked under this continual duress.

The Eastern Board of Directors was now mostly Borman appointees, and while each time Borman openly threatened bankruptcy thousands of passengers booked on other airlines, nothing was done to stop this behavior. Although at the time no one in management would openly acknowledge this was the cause of many problems within the pilot ranks, my thoughts turned to the Flight 980 crash and the subsequent close calls in South America. From what I surmised, flight safety wasn't viewed as a benefit to corporate earnings. Eastern's flight safety-related problems were subsequently demonstrated by the then-unprecedented $9.6 million fine the Federal Aviation Administration levied on the airline for its faulty maintenance practices—required airplane repair work which was never accomplished but signed off as though it had been. At the time, this was the largest FAA fine ever levied against a major airline. After it was announced Borman feigned shock and stated he would fight the penalty all the way to the Supreme Court. In response, the FAA stated it would then enforce the full amount of the fine, which totaled over $70 million. The $9.6 million figure had been a compromise.

Gazing across the table at Schulte and the obvious stress he was under made me consider how the approaching pressure would affect the Eastern pilots. Many years of living under Borman's repeated threats *must* have taken a toll. These concerns that were finally brought into the light of day, when soon after the Texas Air purchase of Eastern, ALPA took an unprecedented step by hiring Dr. Linda Little of Virginia Polytechnic Institute to look into the Eastern pilots' psychological problems and how they might be affecting their job performance, flight safety and personal lives. A twenty-four hour counseling hotline was established, and so many pilots and spouses called that counselors had trouble keeping up. Dr. Little also surveyed comparatively sized pilot groups, and compared the Eastern pilots with their counterparts at two other airlines that at the time had good employee-management relationships. The Eastern pilots failed miserably in every category.*

The Eastern pilots didn't arrive at this juncture overnight and this survey had very negative flight safety implications. But no one from any federal oversight agency showed the slightest interest.

---

*Virginia Tech, under contract with ALPA, used two written pilot surveys to attempt to discover why there were so many problems at Eastern, and to see if these problems were commonplace throughout the industry. Comparative written surveys were sent to pilots from Eastern and from USAir and Piedmont (the combined US Air/Piedmont/PSA airline was known subsequently as US Airways, and had problems of its own).

I won't quote the entire survey, only the most pertinent parts:

- Responding to the question, "Feeling hopeless about the future," a full 25.2% of the Eastern pilots said they felt this way. This compared to only 1.5% of the USAir pilots.

- "Decreased attention" was experienced by 20.4% of the Eastern pilots versus 3.7% of the USAir pilots.

- "Accident proneness" was reported by 4.2% of the Eastern pilots compared to only .4% of the USAir pilots.

- "Feeling like a pressure cooker about to explode," was experienced by 8.4% of the Eastern pilots compared to 1.3% at USAir.

- "General dissatisfaction" was experienced by 40.8% of the Eastern pilots compared to only 5% at USAir.

- This survey went on to measure the stress being experienced on a scale of four, five or six levels. On "Pilots indicating high stress on 6 or more stress measures," 14% of the Eastern pilots fell into this category compared to none for USAir.

- By June 30, 1989, there had been a total of 1,667 calls to the hotline. Of these, 161 were defined as "crisis" calls, in need of immediate attention and support.

CHAPTER TWO

As Schulte sat there talking the tough-guy strike lingo, my thoughts returned to the previously described contract negotiations. Back then, Schulte fervently took the position that we should capitulate. He was eventually persuaded to take the hard line by the majority opinion, but was clearly fearful over having to stand up and fight. Had he undergone a transformation, or was he privy to other information that he wasn't sharing? I suspected it was the latter, which was seemingly confirmed when he finally stated that it appeared as though management wanted to accelerate the negotiating process and force a quick confrontation. He claimed to be clueless why this was happening. One thing was apparent to me: he was in way over his head.

The waitress brought our meals and nothing further was spoken during dinner. As we finished, Schulte got around to discussing the particulars of my involvement. He wanted me to set up a communications network, with emphasis on the written word, preparing the pilots for a strike vote, emphasizing this be accomplished as quickly as possible. This further confirmed that he knew more about the timeline than he was letting on. I couldn't help comparing the John Wayne–type seated across the table to the wimp who had earlier pleaded surrender. I wondered how he could have been so emotional then and remain so outwardly unruffled now, because if the situation he described was correct, my gut instinct was the shit was going to hit the fan, and very soon.

Schulte next began blabbing about the International Association of Machinists union, the IAM. I didn't want to hear about them and told him so. Yet he continued rehashing the past, when the airline was brought to the brink of a strike over the IAM contract negotiations. Maybe his mind was stuck in a time warp, because back then Borman's hype to the press and other employee groups prior to that strike deadline was that Eastern would fly through it. But airline insiders and some in the media wondered how any planes could be in the air when all the mechanics would be out and needed repairs couldn't be accomplished. Borman had caved at the eleventh hour and signed a contract containing raises for the IAM, but by then Eastern had lost tens of thousands of potential customers and many millions of dollars in revenue. Borman's public proclamations also frightened the pilots and flight attendants into giving monetary concessions. It turned out the IAM pay increases were paid for with that money, which created massive in-house discord. One employee group became pitted against another, which created internal strife that continued well beyond the signing. This tactic might bring any corporation down, but could be particularly damaging to a service business like an airline that required the cooperation of a wide array of workers.

Even though that dispute settled down, the IAM head, the late Charlie Bryan, remained concerned about the low morale of the now-divided workforce. He was also troubled because Eastern wasn't expanding, recognizing that under airline deregulation a carrier's size would be the decisive factor; the larger the better, as was subsequently proven correct. So, Bryan offered Borman a productivity carrot, a way to expand and bring all Eastern's workers together and simultaneously give Eastern the ability to grow without having to hire any additional IAM workers, thus lowering overall labor costs as a percentage of operating expenses. For example, workers who had serviced ten aircraft would now do twelve, as well as allow the cross utilization of the IAM-represented workers in various jobs. To accomplish this he tied these productivity givebacks to a guarantee that Borman would grow the airline. This would be accomplished in a simple manner by pegging the work-rule concessions to the number of block hours flown.

After some haggling management agreed, but they claimed the productivity givebacks alone weren't enough; monetary concessions were also needed. Ultimately, in exchange for *voluntary* pay concessions from IAM workers, Bryan proposed providing not just the IAM personnel, but all Eastern employees with a large number of shares of Eastern's common stock. Along with this went a special, newly issued preferred stock. The common stock amounted to partial employee ownership. Eastern's employees soon became major stockholders and by the beginning of 1985 workers were purported to have owned an estimated total of twenty-eight to thirty-two percent of Eastern's common stock. Copeland subsequently discovered, however, that although the employees were led to believe by management that they held approximately thirty percent of the common stock, the Eastern Board of Directors had quietly passed a resolution allowing for the issuance of millions of additional common shares. If dispensed, these unissued but authorized shares would severely dilute employees' holdings.

This IAM-sponsored accord, which was negotiated with the assistance of William Usery, the former Secretary of Labor under President Ford, also stipulated that each group of workers was entitled to be represented on the Eastern Board of Directors, with the number of Board members determined by the dollar amount of common shares each group collectively owned. Because of their higher monetary concessions, the pilots placed two non-pilot, business types on the Board. At the time it was felt by a majority of the MEC that these individuals' backgrounds made them better suited for such a position than a pilot. I had doubts about this reasoning. The IAM and Transport Workers Union installed the leaders of their respective unions, Charlie Bryan and Bob Callahan, which I believed was a better choice as both of these individuals had more allegiance to their workers and the airline.

Another significant portion of this pact called for the creation of the Employee Involvement program, the committee on which I was the sole pilot member. This was an unprecedented arrangement that would give personnel from every part of Eastern's workforce a collective voice on how the airline was run. It would allow them to interface with management in a non-adversarial manner and introduce innovative ideas into the workplace, which many did. This unique arrangement was publicly touted as a totally new relationship at Eastern and the media carried many positive stories on it, as it was the first of its kind for a large United States corporation. It was followed closely by people in government and the business community.

Schulte snapped me back to the present when he asked, "Are you privy to any internal, non-public data due to your committee position showing why we went from best ever profits to record losses, virtually overnight, during the latter part of '85? I ask because these are what's purportedly causing the problems in our contract discussions. Every time we bring up just about anything, the people on the other side of the table just shake their heads and say they can't afford anything."

I replied, "Other than knowing when the record earnings turned into huge losses, approximately July of this year, although I made inquiries, no one, including the top-level management member, professed to know the reason." Schulte just shook his head, so I continued. "As the profits rolled in during the first half of '85, workers developed selective amnesia, over-looking the horrible experiences of the past. The committee was presented with lots of well thought out ideas that collectively saved the airline many millions." I knew that others gave of themselves in countless ways that were difficult to quantify, but which added plenty of bucks to the bottom-line profits, and the airline's fortunes soared. To underscore just how well this program worked, I changed seats and showed Schulte some papers I had brought along that were distributed at the meetings. I had taken them with me in the event he brought this up. Pointing to them I told him, "These show that in 1983 Eastern experienced net losses of $184 million. The Employee Involvement program was instituted halfway through 1984, and the losses fell to $38 million. Its effects and other cost savings, as well as the contractually mandated expansion were evident for the first seven months of 1985, when the airline showed an operating profit of almost $300 million and an all-time record net profit of $168 million. After this, there was a huge sigh of relief and workers got on with living normal lives." I didn't say anything to him, but this was also the case on a personal level. "I also believed that the internal conflicts were over, never to return. Except for the Flight 980 crash, everything was quiet."

"What crash?"

"The 727 that went down in South America on the first of the year, the one that was never properly investigated."

"Oh, yeah, I forgot all about it."

"You and everyone else," I muttered. Putting that aside, I took out another sheet of paper. "From these on-time figures, you can see that for the first half of '85 the airline was running smoothly and on time. But now, those stats also went down the shitter along with the profits."

It was Schulte's turn to frown.

"We were promised that this new, employee-friendly corporate philosophy was going to be carried over into innovative, non-adversarial contract negotiations. What the hell happened?" I said.

"It was supposed to. But it reverted back to the same shit, only worse, when the airline started losing millions. That's all I know."

"You sure? You holdin' anything back?" I probed, looking into Schulte's pale eyes, trying to break through his emotionless veil. The eyes said he was withholding something important that he wouldn't share. He just shook his head for the thousandth time. I returned to my seat, taking my papers with me. "Were these conniving bastards just setting us up for more contract concessions?" I asked. "That makes no sense because everything went smoothly and everyone benefited: the bottom line, management, shareholders, workers, *everyone*." I paused. "What are our people on Eastern's Board telling you?"

"Not much," he answered. "I asked, but they claim ignorance."

"Then, what the hell good are they?" I wanted to pursue this subject further, but what he had already put on my plate was enough. "I've recently had the impression that our nightmare is about to pick up where it left off." I felt the dull throb of a headache beginning in the front of my skull. It had been quite a while since I'd experienced this one-time-common malady. "What the hell is top management *really* up to? From what you've just related, it's clear their actions in the labor relations arena make no sense and don't reflect any new concepts, just more of the old bullshit that we thought was behind us, for good."

Remember, we're talking here about the 1980s, a time when Bolshevism and unionism were the prime demons. Reagan went after the Russians and destroyed the air traffic controllers union simultaneously. Frank Lorenzo did the equivalent to the unions at Continental. So what would another busted pilot union mean to someone like Borman? I finally asked the million-dollar question. "All right, let's get down to specifics," I said. *"Exactly* what do you want from me?"

Schulte repeated that he wanted me to take on the task of educating the pilots and preparing them for the strike vote and strike, the latter only if necessary. He next dropped the bombshell I had sensed might be coming. "It will probably be only a very short time before the National Mediation Board releases us into the thirty-day cooling-off period and establishes a strike deadline."

"What makes you believe that? When? How can that be?"

Ignoring my questions, he replied, "When that happens we'll have only a brief window to bring the pilots to the realization they were duped and it's just more of the same old management crap." A somber Schulte continued. "We—no, make that *you*—need to convince them everything they cherish in their jobs and perhaps in their lives is in danger. Maybe you can give them a cram course in labor relations, and show 'em why they have to be willing to put it all on the line and vote to strike. If we can get an eighty percent positive strike vote, we'll win. Faced with so many pilots willing to hit the bricks, Borman and his cronies will come to their senses, back off their unreasonable demands and negotiate fairly. They won't let the pilots shut down the airline. Of that I'm certain," Schulte confidently assured me. My gut feeling wasn't convinced of that and it must have shown on my face, so he continued. "You'll have to turn the Eastern pilots into junkyard dogs, ready to kill by withholding their services. That's what I want from you. Give this your best shot."

Would he be a junkyard dog when that time came, or was he play-acting? One thing was clear. His portrayal of management's negotiating tactics was far different from anything ever witnessed in the past, even during the worst of times, and this concerned me greatly. These tactics were a new approach, the demands were way too large, and the methods just didn't fit. They were more akin to Frank Lorenzo's. Was someone else, a new person or faction behind the scenes, calling the shots? Was more at stake than a simple contract dispute? What could that be? All these thoughts flashed through my mind faster than the 727 jet I piloted. I was troubled but said nothing more to Schulte about my gut feeling because

I needed time to sort things out, try to rationalize why this was happening. One thing was clear. Accepting this undertaking would require my daily presence in Miami. Management's negotiators were headquartered there and the ALPA bargaining unit was just a short distance away in Coral Gables, and the contract talks would take place at those locations. In Miami, I could receive daily updates and keeping myself informed would be a vital component, because during negotiations the situation could quickly change. I needed to be fully briefed on the most intimate details of the negotiations from changes in bargaining positions down to the names and facial expressions of the people across the table. I would also need about two weeks to first examine the situation and speak with the ALPA negotiators. Only then could I even attempt to formulate an overall strategy. I informed Schulte of these requirements, and he assured me that if I took the job, I would have unfettered access to the negotiators as well as all the requested information.

Christmas of 1985 was rapidly approaching and I had enough seniority to spend a quiet and peaceful holiday at home with my family—or so I thought. "I've also got to hash this out with my wife, see if she objects," I told Schulte. But my initial feelings and presentiment said I was going to accept this challenge because it could very well be a race to the death, one I couldn't decline. I felt like Peter Graves on the show *Mission Impossible.* *"If you accept the assignment, it will be your job to . . ."* But this wasn't acting. It was for real. And with so much at stake I prayed what I would be attempting to accomplish wouldn't be impossible.

Schulte interrupted my thoughts. "The entire strategy on how to get the crucial strike votes will be your call, with every ALPA resource at your personal and immediate disposal. But please, also remember because of what I told you about the National Mediation Board, time, or the lack thereof, is going to be the critical element. If you decide to do this you'll need to move swiftly."

"Why would the NMB want to expedite anything?" I uttered. "Normally, they try to slow everything down to avoid a strike. They must realize with the pilots' backs to the wall, a strike is a real option."

"I don't know what the fuck is with them," Schulte reiterated, not looking me in the eye. "With a bit of luck, a high strike vote will be all that's needed and not an actual strike." The last portion of his statement bothered me greatly.

I recall again thinking that unlike *Mission Impossible,* when Schulte was done speaking there was no tape to self-destruct. Only the harsh reality remained. No matter how hard I tried, I just could not shake off the foreboding that something sinister was taking place. Winning would represent a real challenge, whatever the true definition of "winning" might be. I had never before attempted anything of this magnitude.

* * *

It was getting late, so Schulte paid the tab and dropped me off back at the hotel. It was a warm and comfortable evening, something I normally longed for because it was a welcome escape from the frigid New York winter landscape. But there were no warm feelings that night. "It looks like this might be for all the marbles," he offered as I exited the car, a smile on his face, making me wonder if *he* really believed all he had just told me. If true, the last thing he should do is smile. He quickly added, "We'll make certain this will also be Borman's final hurrah, 'cause we'll kick his—"

"Do you have any idea why this is taking place?" I interrupted, not wanting to hear more bravado. "And why now?"

"I don't have those answers," he replied, the smile gone. "I'm fairly certain it has to be tied into the fact they're losing so much money, so quickly."

"That's exactly what I mean," I reiterated, trying not to lose patience. "As part of the agreement to place people on the Board of Directors, ours were supposed to have unfettered access to *all* of the required insider information and be able to obtain answers like these. Are they just sitting there with their thumbs up their asses, or out drinking with the boys and buying the bullshit they put out?" Schulte just shook his head side to side. It was clear that I was getting nowhere. "What about the ALPA economic analysis department? That's their job. Do they have any clues as to why the huge losses? There haven't been any dramatic fuel price increases or massive fare wars." I wondered if this situation was created intentionally, knowing the answer to that question was key. But Schulte obviously either didn't know or wouldn't tell me. "You need to get some truthful answers, right away, because this will be an important piece of the puzzle."

"One thing I do know," Schulte interrupted. "That little backstabber Borman has got to go. He led us down this primrose path and when this is over, I want him the fuck out," he hollered. "I'm going to task another pilot with the chore to make sure that happens. But look," he said with a wave of his hand, "we can talk more about all this after you decide whether to take the job. And, please let me know as quickly as possible because if you won't do it, I'll have to try to find someone else."

I nodded my head, but didn't shake his hand. He put the car in gear and sped off. I needed some downtime, alone, to think this through, to try to make sense of it.

I couldn't sleep that night, insomnia that wasn't caused by the lousy food. And even with the room air conditioner turned up full blast I was sweating, and angry. First, I watched the car headlights flickering across the ceiling, then, I got up and paced. I finally dressed and walked around outside for a while, savoring the warm air. I'm a logical person, but top management's actions were illogical and that created a dilemma. I could sort out most situations, but they had to have some semblance of reason. But when events and actions defied logic, I became derailed because I couldn't follow a commonsense path to the reasoning behind them. I returned to the room, lying there, once again looking at the ceiling, speculating on what might really be afoot.

My thoughts next shifted to my young family, who along with the hundreds of thousands of other innocent Eastern workers and their families, at that very moment, were sleeping peacefully with absolutely no idea of the tempest they were about to be thrust into and the effects it would have on their lives. I contemplated how in the airline business everything is determined by job seniority; for pilots it was cockpit position, earnings, number of days off, time away from home, etc. It was difficult to move to another carrier because a pilot, if he or she wasn't considered to be too old, would have to begin anew at the bottom of the stack, including pay. Seniority wasn't portable. At that moment I concluded that I had to engage in this struggle. No matter how hard I tried, I couldn't shake off thoughts of how many people were about to have their lives irrevocably altered or completely shattered, unless I not only fought this battle, but prevailed. From Schulte's description, I believed there would only be one winner. No ties would be allowed.

I finally gave up trying to sleep and took the first morning return flight to New York. After discussing the seriousness of the situation with my wife and what I believed would be at stake, she reluctantly agreed that I should take the assignment. But she was not a happy camper, knowing I would be away for an extended period starting right after Christmas. That also bothered me, because I didn't want to find myself working for the pilots and simultaneously working to keep my marriage from going down the tubes—what Borman claimed would happen to the airline. I immediately notified Schulte of my decision.

* * *

I attempted to put on a happy face over Christmas but that was difficult. From my almost-daily conversations with Schulte, I learned the negotiating atmosphere had deteriorated even further. I also couldn't spend any more time reviewing the Flight 980 crash material because every waking moment was spent studying the items that Schulte had shipped via FedEx. Reading this data, I simultaneously mulled over various strategies. I removed myself from the flight schedule and took ALPA leave for two months. Unlike the Rolling Stones, time was *not* on my side.

Using all available ALPA resources, I delved into a thorough analysis of Eastern's latest fiscal "crisis." That was no easy chore because the finances of a company like Eastern are, by design, very complex. The first conclusion I reached was that the public explanation given by management for the current economic plight—some nebulous fare wars with low-cost competitors—was false. My research showed Eastern was the instigator of the ones that were underway. This made me wonder if the losses were self-inflicted. If so, then the looming, still-unanswered question remained—why would a huge money-losing situation be intentionally created? Was that legal? Was it done to simply gain a bargaining advantage over the unions? This didn't make sense because the airline had been thriving financially with the unions' cooperation. Borman had been publicly taking the credit, going so far as to tout this via televised advertisements in which he appeared with large numbers of smiling employees standing behind him. Why change a successful formula when everyone was winning? Not being able to identify the true motive and management's negotiating tactics left me at a disadvantage, as I didn't want the accuracy of any of my correspondence called into question. My information had to be truthful, credible and hard hitting. I eventually wrapped my arms around a strategy that I believed would carry the message, without identifying exactly why the airline was losing mega-bucks. But I became more certain than ever that a dreadful nightmare was about to commence.

CHAPTER THREE

The Railway Labor Act (RLA) is the federal law that governs the conduct and tempo of labor contract negotiations within the airline industry. This includes broad regulatory powers given to the aforementioned federal agency, the National Mediation Board (NMB), which is supposed to be an autonomous and neutral agency comprised of three members nominated by the President of the United States. Each serves a three-year term with the approval of Congress. A member's appointment or reappointment is solely at the President's discretion.

The 1978 federal deregulation of the United States airlines made workers a convenient target for some airline managements in this labor-intensive industry. The airlines pay pretty much the same for everything needed to run their business, apart from labor costs. As a result, following the enactment of airline deregulation, it became the norm not to have a new contract by the date the old one became amendable. Actually, to have one was pretty much the exception. Deregulation also meant the process leading up to a new working agreement became much more arduous and drawn out, especially when both sides start out far apart, or there are exceptional, one-sided demands. In this case, management's demands placed these negotiations in the "extremely difficult" category. Under comparable circumstances, other airline contract bargaining periods extend far beyond the amendable date. That was the reason why Schulte's warning about the speed of the negotiations troubled me. During negotiations, if either party is of the opinion no agreement can possibly be reached, they may petition the NMB to have a federal mediator assigned to assist in attempting to reach an accord. This mediator is normally not brought in until it's crystal clear that the parties remain far apart, and to reach this juncture typically takes many months or even years of bargaining.

Once a mediator is assigned, he or she is normally required to first meticulously study the particular situation to get a complete grasp of the issues and the ramifications to both sides. Only after this arduous task is completed would the mediator enter into negotiations. This is particularly true for complex pilot contracts as there are many sections besides pay, which can also affect air safety. Once the mediator fully understands a particular contract, there would normally be some friendly arm-twisting to move both parties into giving and taking, with the goal being to reach a mutually acceptable compromise so that a confrontation, a strike, can be avoided.

Ordinarily, only after an extended period, if a mediator eventually determines negotiations are hopelessly deadlocked, the three members of the NMB would convene and after hearing from the mediator, *might* declare that an impasse has been reached. At that point each party has two choices. The principle of binding arbitration can be employed—but only if both parties agree—with the federal mediator assuming the role of contract negotiator for both sides. Whatever resolution the arbitrator reaches is final and binding on everyone. The other option is for the two parties to continue nonstop negotiations during the thirty-day cooling-off period with assistance and support from the mediator in an effort to avoid a strike.

Even though the brief talks had thus far been one-sided, Schulte informed me prior to Christmas that he still believed an agreement might be reached. Was that wishful thinking? Perhaps. I was very surprised when, shortly after Christmas, he disclosed that there had actually only been two negotiating sessions and that management had raised the ante to the point their proposed changes were so draconian that the union couldn't agree. After only those two bargaining sessions, management stated they felt the discussions were deadlocked and petitioned the NMB to assign a mediator. In light of historical negotiating patterns and the history of the NMB, he told me that he believed this request would be denied. But inexplicably, it was immediately granted. Only much later, I discovered that Borman had personally intervened and pleaded for this in a face-to-face meeting with then-NMB Chairman, Walter Wallace. While attending and taking notes at a subsequent MEC meeting held on January 8th when Wallace addressed them, I was still unaware of Borman's personal visit. Speaking of the pilot negotiations at that meeting, Wallace made odd, one-sided comments for a purportedly unbiased person. His statements included things like: "The survival of an airline (Eastern) is at stake." "A special effort is needed." "Time is running out, meaning accelerated negotiations." "The NMB timeframe has February 26th in it." "Fairness has nothing to do with this, as the circumstances are so unusual they call for special handling." "There will be no due process, as what's at stake is the unthinkable." He also declared, "I'm on the management side when not in government," going on to state that he was previously the vice president of a major paper company. So much for the neutral stance promised in the NMB's charter.

It became abundantly clear to me from these one-sided remarks that the only remaining step was for an impasse to be declared, commencing the start of the thirty-day cooling off period. Unfortunately, I only learned of Borman's personal visit with Wallace many months later, after the airline had been handed over to the Texas Air Corporation. The distinguished-looking Wallace and I were seated together at an ALPA-sponsored dinner and were discussing Eastern's labor problems when he informed me of Borman's visit. Considering the neutral role the National Mediation Board is supposed to assume in contract negotiations, I asked Wallace why he had taken Borman at his word about the alleged grave condition of the airline and acceded to his plea for an expedited process. The following response is taken directly from my notes, which were subsequently transferred to my personal computer, as were all of my notes, when those came on the market.

"Well, put yourself in my position," he replied. "A former astronaut and perceived American icon comes to my office and implores me to help. He claimed an early and speedy resolution to the pilot contract was needed; that without the contract resolved in the airline's favor, Eastern would be bankrupt and for all purposes out of business in a matter of months. He also showed me the projected loss figures."

My discussion with Wallace took place months later, when the Eastern employees were embroiled in a host of labor disputes with Texas Air, but before the IAM strike began. He looked me directly in the eye and stated, "Eastern is an old American institution and I didn't want the responsibility for its bankruptcy on my hands, meaning the pilots had to make some extreme sacrifices. I honestly felt that a bankruptcy filing and all its inherent problems would far outweigh any troubles caused by speeding up the negotiating process in the company's favor. Borman was very convincing."

When I pressed him, Wallace ultimately admitted he had made a grave error in accepting Borman's statements without determining exactly why the airline's losses were so high. Borman obviously relied solely upon his stature and reputation to persuade him. For Borman's plan to work it was crucial that Wallace not look beyond the obvious and delve further into the cause of the airline's financial situation. Borman's luck held. Wallace simply took him at his word and did as requested.

During our conversation, Wallace also indicated he had received marching orders from above, which in this case could only mean the President of the United States. When Borman made his request of Wallace, there was no public hint yet of Lorenzo's Texas Air Corporation's interest in Eastern. From all outward appearances it was simply a contract dispute between Eastern management and the pilots. Although he never acknowledged it outright, the sense I got was that Wallace woefully regretted what he had done. But this offers no solace because, thanks to Wallace, the scheme was now like a brakeless freight train running full speed down the tracks to its final confrontation.

CHAPTER FOUR

Believing I had to hurry due to the obvious NMB deadline meant putting all else aside and spending every waking hour coming up with a strategy to ensure the Eastern pilots would be willing to stand up and fight when the time came. The biggest hurdle I would have to overcome would be the apathy created by the harmony of the recent past. By early 1985, most pilots' lives had returned to a semblance of normality and the majority believed a bright future lie ahead, meaning they must be convinced this latest threat was genuine. This would not be easy to accomplish. A few Master Executive Council Members grasped that something was amiss and began spreading the word among their constituents. Due to the crew-room banter, where pilots meet before, during and after their trips, word began filtering out that management was not to be trusted—again. But things were in a mixed-up state because some MEC members naïvely believed nothing was wrong, as management continued to outwardly profess they wanted to work together to reach a new accord.

Compounding matters further, the National ALPA Officers also refused to accept that there were major problems, which only caused additional confusion. In this one respect, Schulte was a hundred percent correct. My education process would be vital. It needed to be fast, hard hitting, believable and effective, and would require every ALPA resource. *Everything* else had to be relegated to the back burner.

My very first order of business was to go through ALPA's and the Company's contract bargaining positions line by line. I saw that when initial proposals were first exchanged, ALPA had asked for a very small wage increase and minor work-rule changes. But the company's opener was proposing to gut virtually every section of the contract, items that had taken almost fifty years of hard bargaining to achieve. It began with a twenty-percent pay cut and went downhill from there. Vacations would be reduced by a third. Major work-rule changes were proposed, which meant working more days for a lot less money with many demotions from captain back to copilot, meaning for those affected pilots the pay reductions would be draconian. There were sizeable decreases in retirement-funding contributions. There was the start of a "B" wage scale, meaning even lower pay rates for all newly hired pilots. When totaled up, the price was an approximate thirty-five to forty percent reduction in pilot wages and benefits. A light bulb went off in my head and I realized that these demands gave me exactly what I needed; the ammunition to rouse the pilots to support a strike vote. As I had read them, they had riled me, so hopefully, if presented properly every pilot should feel the same. I concluded that the focal point of my strategy would be the proposed contract changes, along with the management that had proffered them.

The Eastern pilot contract was a lengthy, book-sized document containing numerous sections that collectively affected nearly every aspect of a pilot's life. Most parts were linked to the hours worked per day and month, as well as time away from home and the rest time between trips. These were called duty rigs. The remainder involved pay and retirement.

For my brainchild to succeed I had to first dissect the contract line by line and section by section. Through a series of letters, I would then compare what we presently had to what we would have if we complied with management's demands—not in contractual language, but in plain, everyday examples of the lifestyle changes their proposals represented. Based upon my wife's reaction, I decided to compose the letters so pilots' spouses would also know the consequences management's demands would have on family life. If anything would rouse the pilots' ire enough to strike, it should be these items taken collectively, with their wives and husbands standing right behind them, pushing them to vote to walk out the door.

I was able to complete some of the groundwork at home, but the remainder required my presence in the Miami ALPA office. I packed my bags, kissed my wife and kids goodbye and departed right after Christmas. After checking into the Miami Airport Marriott for an extended stay, I

kept in constant touch with the ALPA negotiators in order to remain up
to speed. I also needed to try to anticipate when the assigned NMB mediator, Bob Brown, would release the parties into the thirty-day cooling-off
period. February 26th was the date the contract was amendable to change,
so I subtracted thirty days and this became my target date.

The timing was almost as important as the mailings; not too early and
not too late. In 1986 there were no emails or Internet, so all the correspondence would be done via first-class mail. The letters had to be hard-hitting,
and on an ever-increasing frequency, so there would be no opportunity for
the other side to respond, attempting to twist what was stated.

As I pored over management's proposals in order to spell out exactly
what their effects would be, I realized this was an enormous undertaking
that would consume a huge amount of time. Besides the basic contract,
there were also a large number of contractual side letters of agreement—
in total over five hundred contract pages. Extra attention was needed not
to misinterpret or misrepresent anything, or management no doubt would
immediately point out any inaccuracies to try to destroy the credibility of
everything. As I began the letter writing, the dual chores of first defining
the changes and then composing the letters was far more time consuming
and complex than I had envisioned, and my personal schedule went by the
wayside. To make matters worse, the timetable was set by the NMB and
entirely out of my control.

From the daily briefings it became clear negotiations were quickly
going nowhere and this piled on even more pressure. After two weeks of
eighteen-hour workdays I needed a short respite, so I returned home for a
weekend. When I attempted to secure a seat on a return flight, I discovered that all seats were booked. This meant I would have to utilize the jump
seat, an extra seat in the cockpit. The captain of this jumbo jet was a check
pilot, meaning also a member of management. Shortly after takeoff, the
cockpit conversation turned to the contract negotiations.

Approximately an hour into the flight and after much discussion, I
asked the crew, if the talks broke down completely, would they be willing
to strike? The copilot and the flight engineer indicated they might, but
the captain was adamant, saying that he would not, under any circum-

stances. "Eastern's been good to me for my entire twenty-five years. I think the least we can do is to give them a little in return during hard times."

I suggested that, from what I had heard, management was insisting on more than just a little, that their demands would gut the entire contract. But his response remained the same. This captain's comments, unbeknownst to him, helped me later.

Back in Miami, I continued poring over the documents, including any changes in negotiating positions, while simultaneously writing the letters for mailing at the appropriate time. I was still working eighteen-hour days. But then, while at the union office I spotted a fairly thick envelope addressed to Schulte from a Tampa-based pilot named Dale Brown, a former ALPA MEC member. It had been opened and the contents were strewn about the secretary's desk. After skimming a few paragraphs, I couldn't believe what it contained. Brown had somehow obtained a copy of management's original contract proposal and had compiled a lengthy document informing Schulte why the MEC should reject it, including a section-by-section breakdown of the many of the proposed changes. After reading it, I realized that much of the needed work was in front of me, with a few mistakes, albeit important ones. After correcting those, it was relatively simple to go through Dale Brown's comparisons and put the spin I intended to place on it. He had saved me many grueling hours of hard work.

Under the pretext of huge monetary losses as its justification, management's outlandish demands were increased even further, most of which the ALPA negotiating committee ultimately rejected. With a mediator already assigned, I was certain that an impasse would be declared thirty days prior to the contract amendable date. Sure enough, on January 28th, NMB mediator Brown officially stated an impasse had been reached. He proposed binding arbitration, which ALPA readily accepted but which management rejected, outright. Had management's *only* goal been to consummate a favorable contract, company executives would indisputably have agreed to binding arbitration, because the final working agreement would be one imposed by the NMB. This meant, as later confirmed by Wallace, the airline's alleged poor financial condition, as described to Wallace by Borman, would be taken into full account and the contract would have been an extremely beneficial one for management. Borman knew this. As far as I was concerned, their rejection of this offer was additional proof that something else was afoot that I wasn't aware of. Whatever the true motivation might be made no difference, however, because the thirty day cooling-off period was now underway, with the pilot strike deadline set for February 26, 1986.

My job now became one of writing style and timing. My authorship of the strike correspondence was a closely guarded secret, with only Schulte's signature as MEC leader affixed, so it would appear as though he had written each. I prepared and kept the letters safely hidden away to be signed by Schulte and sent at the appropriate time. The strike ballot would be issued approximately two weeks before the strike deadline, so February 12th became my target finishing date. Although Schulte was unaware of my overall game plan, since each letter would bear his signature, we had agreed his approval was necessary prior to each mailing. We had also agreed that if he wanted to make any changes, we would discuss them beforehand as he didn't know what I had subsequently planned for later in the overall scheme of things.

I received his approval for each letter just prior to mailing, pointing out one contractual section at a time how management's demands would negatively affect every facet of the pilots' and the pilots' families' lives. These letters were mailed from the main Washington, DC, ALPA office with ever-increasing frequency, always referencing the impending strike ballot. My strategy was to pick up the tempo and tone of the letters, so when the strike authorization ballot finally arrived pilots should be angry enough to vote to strike. I also planned a final, lengthy mail-out to be sent just a day before the strike ballot with a short recap of all management's major demands, stating that a positive strike vote was the *only* way to bring them to their senses. I finally informed Schulte of this and kept my fingers crossed that the tactic would work. It *had* to.

With the strike-ballot deadline looming, management's negotiating posture evolved into three seemingly simplistic choices, which in reality were anything but. These stated alternatives were to either "fix it," "sell it," or "tank it."

"Fix it" meant that employees, beginning with the pilots, had to kick in enough monetary and work-rule changes to keep the airline and, through inference, the current management team intact. The pay cuts remained an astronomical twenty percent, plus additional, huge work-rule concessions. The total amount of worker concessions was valued at approximately $300 to 350 million annually.

"Sell it" meant exactly that, but with one oft-stated uncertainty. Borman would *attempt* to find a buyer, but he also let it be known this was unlikely. He felt that if another company or individual indicated a willingness to purchase Eastern, chances were good that the acquisition would be financed with borrowed dollars. Borman maintained that the added debt would be a staggering burden that no entity could bear. This also carried with it the threat that due to its precarious fiscal situation, no one would want to purchase Eastern.

This led to the avowed third choice, to "tank it," meaning the airline would be placed into bankruptcy proceedings. Here, another caveat was attached: Eastern would probably never emerge from Chapter Eleven, reorganization bankruptcy. Instead, it was more likely to be placed into Chapter Seven bankruptcy proceedings—liquidation. This would mean "the end" of Eastern Airlines and every worker's career.

So besides being publicly humiliated and blamed for the purported sorry fiscal state of the airline, Eastern's workers were faced with three dreadful choices.

Within this setting, time was fast approaching for the pilots' strike vote. My Schulte-signed letters were dispatched in rapid succession, one after another. From my limited feedback it seemed as though the letters and other simultaneous strike preparations were beginning to achieve results. Unlike the prior year, when pilots' pent-up *positive* feelings had been unleashed, this time all of their *negative* emotions resurfaced.

Along with the letters, Family Awareness group meetings that included spouses and satellite teleconferences from Miami were conducted in all pilot bases. During these teleconferences Schulte gave rousing, tough-guy, person-in-charge-like speeches to everyone who flocked to these well-attended gatherings, hopefully further stimulating the pilots

into voting to strike. I felt these three prongs of attack—letters, Family
Awareness group meetings and teleconferences—would deliver the
desired result as all were on the same page, with the same singular goal. I
sensed pilots' moods were rapidly changing and many now wanted to
strike. Almost to a person they also wanted new management. I had this
confirmed when I returned to Miami after a weekend at home to have a
tooth repaired. Although this flight wasn't full, this time I wanted to sit
on the cockpit jump seat to gauge the crew's feedback. As luck would have
it the captain was the same one who had previously stated he would not
strike. The cockpit discussion revolved entirely around the impending
strike vote and I queried each pilot on his stance concerning the possibility of a walkout. The copilot and flight engineer said they would vote to
authorize a strike and walk out, if needed. The big surprise was the captain, however, who said, "I never thought I'd be willing to hit the bricks,
but the company contract proposals are so onerous I have no other choice."
The strategy was definitely working.

At this juncture, however, a number of strange incidents occurred. Even
though he was supposed to be involved with a host of important items
including radio and television interviews, Schulte mysteriously disappeared
for a four-day hiatus without leaving a telephone contact. As a result, I
couldn't reach him to get the needed approval for the letters, which were
vital due to the impending strike ballot. A number had to be postponed
because of his inexplicable absence. Then, immediately after returning from
his mysterious sojourn, out of the blue he requested that I delete from the
letters that top management must be replaced.

I wanted to know where he'd been for four days, suspecting he might
have covertly met with Borman and come to some furtive cloak-and-dag-
ger agreement. He refused to answer, contending that he "just needed a few
days off." I argued that that if suddenly we didn't insist on new top management, it would cost a tremendous amount in terms of credibility and,
more importantly, strike support. After a lengthy discussion he reluctantly
agreed, but I could see he was uncomfortable. I also didn't believe his explanation of where he'd been and pressed the issue, but to no avail.

At this point, yet another odd episode took place. During late 1985 and early January 1986, a Miami-based pilot, Jerry Loeb, was the Chairman of the MEC's Legislative Affairs Committee. A good-natured, affable, gray-haired pilot from California, Loeb had held this position for a number of years. I had stumbled upon Loeb at the MEC office and he disclosed that Schulte had asked him to get some powerful Washington politicians to lean on the NMB to slow down the negotiating process. He was unsuccessful in this endeavor, but Schulte had approached him with another, more challenging request.

Loeb informed me that in December of 1985, around the same time that he had initially spoken with me, Schulte had also met secretly with Loeb and requested him to provide a method to replace top management. Although part of my correspondence was to drum up support within the pilot ranks for a management change, it would be Loeb's specific task to implement it, either through members of the Eastern Board of Directors or the Washington politicians that Borman liked to hobnob with. As Loeb began articulating the particulars of his involvement, I became concerned because the MEC office was a small, single-story building and, with the exception of Schulte's workplace, afforded virtually no privacy, especially for the length of time that I suspected Loeb needed to speak.

I suggested we instead have dinner together, and it was here where Loeb outlined the specifics of his involvement. "Schulte said he wanted Borman out and asked if I could come up with a blueprint. I said I would, although I thought perhaps management's depictions of the airline's financial troubles were accurate. I scrutinized the situation, along with all the available data and also spoke discreetly with some upper management executives and members of the Eastern Board. But nothing came to light that would explain the huge losses. I came to believe the airline's financial situation was being fabricated to get at the union contracts, although I didn't know how or why. So, I presented Schulte with a confidential strategy to oust Borman. Although there were a number of different methods, I felt the simplest and easiest way would be to make it appear as though it would be a voluntary departure, sparing any embarrassment. Borman would be offered a high-ranking government post and would voluntarily leave." Loeb went on to explain that he felt he could make this happen by utilizing his

Washington connections, especially since Borman had been politically involved with U.S. presidents and was highly visible.

I interrupted. "If it appears like the unions are forcing him out he won't leave. His ego's too large."

"That won't be a problem," Loeb answered. "All the public statements would declare Borman would be leaving Eastern to serve his country like he did in the service, at NASA and for a couple of presidents. I believe the current path management is on could lead to the destruction of the airline," he continued. "It's already created a great deal of employee rancor and sympathetic politicians wouldn't want to see the airline fail, especially if something as simple as placing Borman in a high-level government post could prevent it." Loeb continued, explaining that prior to implementing this strategy, he had written a lengthy report for Schulte's eyes only, outlining different methods to achieve top management's removal—both voluntary and forced, the latter in case the voluntary plan didn't work.

This paper was entitled "EAL Management: A Tactical Plan for Incumbent Management Removal and Installation of New Management." He completed it on December 26th and forwarded it to Schulte marked CONFIDENTIAL and RESTRICTED. He told me, "This nineteen-page document contained my ideas, all of which were a direct result of Schulte's request. It was broken down into ten major categories, such as political, financial, labor, etc. Although we agreed that Borman should be offered the government position, the report was written in such a way that Schulte could examine every other option in the event he had to pursue another course of action."

I was unaware of this undertaking and hadn't seen the report, but it aroused my interest. I was engrossed as he continued. "With Schulte's approval I went forward and set up a number of meetings with high-ranking appointed and elected Washington officials." Loeb put a frosty look on his face. "But I ran into an unanticipated snag when Schulte inexplicably began to distance himself from me. I was unable to reach him to confirm his attendance at these important appointments. Nothing could be accomplished without his presence because he's the pilots' duly elected leader and legal spokesperson. By January 10th, three meetings had been arranged, but were cancelled at the last moment because Schulte never responded to my calls to confirm his presence. By rebuffing several powerful United States Senators whose assistance I had solicited, he created doubt about whether or not ALPA *really* wanted this. I had explained to the Senators' aides that the union considered this to be of such importance that immediate action was required. But they wanted this confirmed by Schulte himself, something he never did. Schulte next claimed that he couldn't attend yet another meeting with Senator Warren Rudman scheduled for January 20th, so I rescheduled that meeting for the 21st. This was the fourth time it had been rescheduled because of him. Then, he cancelled it on January 20th. I rescheduled it for the 24th and even though I left numerous messages for him, detailing the time, place and agenda, I got no response. As a result, this meeting was also called off." Loeb shook his head and went on. "There was another repeat of this scenario on January 26th. We both knew time was running out, yet Schulte still wouldn't return my calls." He hesitated. "I was so frustrated with what was happening that I fired off a mailgram to him on January 28th urging his immediate involvement or the airline might well suffer the consequences of a devastating strike."

Loeb was agitated at what Schulte had done. "Next, an unexpected response came in a mailgram dated January 29th, not from Schulte, but from Don Davidson, the MEC's Boston captain representative. Davidson urged me to take *his* personal advice—cease and desist at once from any further activities until or unless I receive direct orders from the MEC. I became confused because as requested by the MEC Chairman, who is the leader of the MEC, I'm working on achieving top management's removal in the least damaging way possible. Yet suddenly, I'm being ignored by Schulte and attacked by an outspoken MEC member for carrying out Schulte's orders. On top of this, some MEC members led by Davidson have begun vicious personal attacks on me based upon innuendo and hearsay." He asked, "What the hell is going on? What am I supposed to do next? You know why this is happening?"

"I don't know," I replied. "But I can tell you that I overheard discussions at the MEC office and whenever your name was brought up, Davidson would describe you with terms like a 'loaded cannon' or you were 'crazy.' These were all within earshot of Schulte, but he never uttered a word in your defense."

It became apparent that Loeb believed he was doing Schulte's bidding and would be insulated from attack by MEC members, but apparently that wasn't the case.

"What should I do?" he asked.

"I had surmised there might be some type of personal problems between you and Davidson. Are there?"

"I hardly even know the guy!"

"Then if I were you, I would be *very* careful and not have any dealings with him. In my opinion he's not a nice person," I offered. I silently wondered why Davidson singled him out. Maybe something different was going on behind the scenes. Conspiracies are only supposed to happen in modern fiction. But this could very well be for real and I became concerned. I was also working for Schulte and didn't want to wake up one morning and find a blade sticking in my back. "Did anything else happen between you and Schulte?" I asked.

He related a now-familiar story. After returning from his inexplicable four-day break, Schulte had implored him to back off Borman's removal. Loeb had argued against that, as he believed resolution of the airline's problems required new top management. Just as he had done with me, Schulte had reluctantly agreed to continue. "You noticed any recent changes in Schulte?" Loeb asked.

He was startled when I told him of Schulte's attempt to have me also remove all references concerning the replacement of top management and how I too had disagreed.

Although there were a number of other pilots working on different aspects of the strike preparation effort, I wondered why Loeb was targeted by Davidson. For the present, that question would remain unanswered. But I later discovered the reason. We parted company, vowing to keep the lines of communication open.

* * *

As the looming strike-ballot deadline approached, another unexpected event occurred that further heightened my concerns. I normally worked in the Miami office Monday through Saturday. However, during the week of February 7th, I developed a problem with the same tooth that again required immediate attention. My dentist could only see me Friday, so I left the office on Thursday night, after informing Schulte of the reason. I was patched up in no time and spent an uneventful Saturday at home.

Upon my return to Miami on Saturday evening, however, Schulte was again nowhere to be found. Another letter was ready to go, and I attempted to contact him to get his approval, but to no avail. Schulte finally returned my phone call on the following Tuesday afternoon. *Where had he been?* As we discussed the latest letter over the telephone he dropped another bombshell. He stated, "I sent out the entire package."

"What package?" I said. He responded that he had sent the original pages Dale Brown had prepared in a single mailing to all pilots. But it was still too far from the strike-ballot deadline. I told him, "We had an agreement that nothing was supposed to change until we discussed it ahead of time. I told you that I was also planning a total re-capsulation, but only after I corrected Brown's errors, and then I would mail it just before the strike ballot. There's over a week 'til the ballot mailing, more than ample time for management to point out the obvious errors. That could destroy the credibility of *everything*," I heatedly replied.

Schulte's response made no sense whatsoever. He said that management had moved off some of their hard-line positions in negotiations and because of that our strategy was no longer valid as it didn't reflect management's most recent positions. I was steaming because he had screwed up everything. I repeated something he already knew—although management might appear to change their contractual demands as of that moment, they could alter them again, tomorrow. At the end of the cooling-off period it was only their latest contract proposal that would be imposed on the pilots. And we both knew it would be very close to their original position, gutting the contract. In fact, Schulte and I had discussed this very item a number of times. Furthermore, from the feedback I was receiving, I knew the original plan was going so well there was no reason to change it.

Next, Schulte stated he had attempted to contact me throughout the weekend to discuss this, but couldn't reach me. Before I could respond to that misrepresentation, he added that although I might be correct in my assessment, it was too late. The entire package had already been mailed out from ALPA's main office.

"You said the strategy on getting the strike vote would be mine," I told him, my voice rising. "Plus, I was home all weekend, so don't bullshit me. You never tried to call. Furthermore, you can take this job and shove it. I'm outta here. But rest assured that I'll make certain *every* pilot knows what you did."

"Stay in Miami. I'll be there tomorrow," he replied.

"You'd better hope I'm *not* here when you arrive, because if I am it won't be pleasant," I hissed. "And where the hell were *you* until today? I did attempt to reach you everywhere, all weekend long, but all I got was your answering machine. And the hotel said you weren't there either." He never responded and only kept urging me to stay.

"I'm no fool," I told him. I slammed the phone down and began cleaning out my belongings. But a moment later one of the secretaries hesitantly poked her head in the office. Schulte was on the phone and wanted to speak. "He told me to tell you it's vitally urgent," she added.

When I picked up the phone all he said was, "I stopped it."

"Stopped what?" I said.

"I stopped the package from being mailed," he said, adding that as soon as our conversation ended he immediately called the Washington office and discovered the package had been printed and stamped, but not yet mailed. "Will you stay in Miami?"

I was silent while contemplating what he said, wondering if it was true.

"Will you? Please?" he begged.

I sighed and finally told him I would, provided he didn't pull any more stunts like that. He once more promised to consult with me if he thought there was a need for any changes. After hanging up, I sat there contemplating this latest incident and decided that there was no way I could trust him. I felt that the only reason for my treatment versus Loeb's was because I was about to assume MEC office on March 1st. I made a personal vow to keep a very close eye on him. It was obvious that he was struggling with something.

With the strike-ballot deadline fast approaching, the pilots were bombarded with written material, Family Awareness meetings, phone calls and teleconferences, the latter run by a now-deceased pilot, Pat Broderick. The pilots were definitely pumped and there was almost a festive attitude, believing that the problems of the past would soon be banished. The final *coup d'état,* the corrected package containing all the summarized material, went out on schedule the day prior to the issuance of the strike ballots. This gave the pilots a full day to assimilate the contents before casting a vote. All the hype was over. It was now like Super Bowl Sunday, with everything on the line.

I breathed a sigh of relief when the secret ballots were tallied and 96.35% of the Eastern pilots voted to strike, a then-record high percentage voting in favor of a strike against *any* major airline. I had done my job and hoped that this would be the end of the battle. Little did I know what was yet to come.

* * *

Even though I was finished, I would remain in Miami "to continue to assist in the strike effort." But the genuine reason was my distrust of Schulte. Thanks to my letters, virtually every Eastern pilot viewed Schulte as a feisty, macho-man, labor leader. He seemed to revel in his new tough-guy role. Maybe he'd even start going to the gym.

But I knew better. As Copeland aptly put it later, "There really was no 'tough guy' Schulte. He was the embodiment of you and everyone else that ran the communications effort."

I couldn't have put it better myself.

PART II

THE MEETINGS

CHAPTER FIVE

It was now the afternoon of February 23, 1986, a bit more than two months after I received that fateful December telephone call from Schulte. What he had originally depicted as a relatively straightforward contractual dispute had turned out to be anything but, as the huge favorable strike ballot did not produce the desired results Schulte had predicted. Management was still taking a very hard line in negotiations. Next came another startling development that concerned me greatly—Borman found a buyer for Eastern.

* * *

Pounding my fist into my hand, I nervously paced the living room area of the room in the Miami Suites hotel, located on the eastern boundary of Miami International Airport. Other than the roar of the departing jets, I could hear only indecipherable whispers, but knew that New York ALPA union leader Skip Copeland was speaking with the head of the IAM, Charlie Bryan. Having worked with Copeland for a number of years, I knew that if anyone could resolve this latest crisis, it was he. Like me he had grown up on the hard New York streets and wasn't afraid to fight, yet also knew when to admit defeat.

Frank Borman's name had been spoken countless times during the preceding days and nights when Copeland and I had brainstormed on what to do about Frank Lorenzo's Texas Air Corporation's bombshell offer to purchase Eastern. The time was here. It was the ninth inning of the World Series and we had concluded that all of Borman's demands had to be met to keep the airline out of Lorenzo's anxiously outstretched hands.

Although after the successful pilot strike vote Borman's official line had

47

changed to state that only two of the three unions that represented Eastern's workers had to concede to his demands for a twenty percent pay
reduction and additional work-rule givebacks, we concluded that this was
just a red herring to get at what he perceived as his true nemesis, Bryan.

The Eastern flight attendants union, the Transport Workers Union
(TWU), was already working under an imposed contract, meaning for all
practical purposes they had already given, although not yet officially. This
meant that Copeland, the only pilot representative that Bryan trusted,
would have to convince him that he also must throw in the towel. That's
what this phone call was all about. *What if Bryan won't give?* I pondered,
anxiously pacing back and forth. And if Bryan refused, would the pilot
concessions we were about to offer be sufficient to stop the Texas Air transaction, a deal we unquestionably knew would lead to Eastern's certain
destruction?

I stepped outside the air-conditioned room and into the late-day balmy
stillness. I could now see some of the Miami sights along with the familiar airport sounds, wondering how much longer I would be hearing them
if the Texas Air deal went through. I considered going to the lobby to grab
some iced tea, but after what seemed like a lifetime, Skip finally emerged
and grumbled a barely audible, "Charlie's in."

I snapped out of my dark reverie and breathed an audible sigh of relief,
while muttering, "From your lips to God's ears," in this case meaning Borman. "You'd better call him—*now*," I insisted.

My last statement wasn't necessary as Copeland was already dialing
Borman's private office number that he had been given during some prior
supposed crisis. The phone must have been picked up immediately because
I heard him say, "George Jehn and I would like to meet with you as soon
as possible." There was a short pause until he stated, "We'll see you in a few
minutes," and hung up. Back then there was no security as there is today. I
knew the local roads and quickly drove my rental car onto the airport
perimeter road to Building 16, avoiding all the bumper-to-bumper local
traffic. This way it would be only a five-or ten-minute ride from the hotel
to the *Taj Mahal*, the moniker for the looming, gleaming white cement
façade structure housing Eastern's top executives, located on the corner

of Le Jeune Road and Northwest 36th Street, Eastern's head office. We didn't speak during the drive because the time for talking was over. We knew what was needed and would get it done.

We stopped at the guard shack, where Copeland and I passed our Eastern ID's to the uniformed guard and informed him we were here to see Borman. While he made a quick call to confirm that, I glanced about at the ramp. The scene ran the full gamut. There was a large hangar where a three-engine Eastern Boeing 727 Whisper Jet was receiving some type of major overhaul, with a large number of men in overalls scampering about. Off to the right sat our destination where various executives dressed in three-piece suits entered and exited. Other workers, in both white and blue collars, scurried about performing various tasks. I was thinking that what happened during our impending meeting would have an effect on each, yet they had no way of knowing. I pondered this as the guard raised the gate and nonchalantly waved us through.

I could feel my heart pounding and nervous sweat forming under the armpits of my shirt as we exited the car. Yet at the same time I was also excited, certain the proposal we were about to make would stop the Texas Air transaction and save *our* airline. This emotion conflicted with the knowledge that we were capitulating to Borman's demands. But this had to be done.

As we entered the building with the gleaming marble floor, surprisingly there were no guards to direct us. The usual din and conversation was also missing, in its place only nerve-racking silence. Everyone was by now aware of Lorenzo's offer. The men in suits or sports coats and women in dresses or skirts seemed to sense that something dreadful might happen, and soon, though none probably knew exactly what that might be. We walked to the elevator, and Skip pressed the button for the ninth and top floor: Borman's office.

With a pit-of-the-stomach lurch we were off. Other than Skip, anxiety was my only companion. Upon exiting the elevator we quickly proceeded directly to Borman's place of work. There was no secretary. Instead, a haggard-looking Borman greeted us and motioned us to follow him into his private domain where all the secret deals were cooked. We had yet another one to offer that we believed he couldn't possibly turn down.

It was just the three of us, along with a southerly view overlooking Miami International Airport. As we shook hands I took note of his wet and clammy palms. Why should our presence make him so nervous? But it was his appearance that was the real shocker. He looked worn-down and old, nothing at all like the self-assured, poised former astronaut seen strutting around Eastern's jets on the TV commercials, with hordes of smiling employees behind him. His cheap-looking suit was badly wrinkled and fit poorly over his short frame, giving him the appearance of a square box or even a Neanderthal. He was hunched over like a person twice his age with a lined and worn face, seemingly carrying some heavyweight burden that bowed his shoulders. Was it pressure? Guilt? Staring at the figure standing in front of me, I recalled one of Copeland's favorite lines for those who held Borman in awe. "Strip away the façade and he's no different than you, me and everyone else. He gets up in the morning and puts his pants on one leg at a time."

But there was no room in my heart for pity. I could care less what he'd chosen to do to himself; rather, my concern lay with what he was contemplating doing to the tens of thousands of loyal Eastern workers and the daily nightmare they had endured for the past few months because of him. With Lorenzo at the door, I believed at Borman's invitation, now it was even worse. Many workers had blindly followed this guy and continually given in to his demands, and he was prepared to kick them off the cliff—unless he got his way again. I forced these thoughts aside as they weren't in keeping with why we'd come. We were here to talk peace and eat humble pie. In fact, we would put even more on the table than what was demanded.

He motioned for us to sit. As we took our seats across from his desk, assorted feelings on what we were about to offer raced through my mind with strobe-like staccato. This was only the second time I'd been in his office and I'd forgotten how austere it was. The last time was many years prior when I'd gone to interview him for an ALPA magazine article I was writing. That was during the mid-seventies, and I was surprised by its simplicity; just a plain desk and a few family portraits. And it was still the same, definitely not what was expected for the head of an airline as large as Eastern. I came away the first time with only a gut feeling that he was no flower child at heart. Now, the decor evoked how well the surroundings fit his public persona, nothing extravagant or flamboyant, just one of the regular guys. But I didn't believe that latter description for one second because of his many powerful friends in Washington government circles and now-overt anti-union mentality.

As we sat down Borman excused himself. *Where was he going? What was he doing?* Others had mentioned that he had a private toilet in his office. Did we make him *that* nervous? Or maybe there was a hidden tape recording device?

He returned a moment later, looking as though he was ready to cut and run if we indicated any hostility. But we had come in peace. He finally asked, in a fairly affable tone that was so low I had to lean forward to hear, "What can I do for you?"

We had agreed that Copeland would do most of the speaking, as he was the senior member of our two-man team, and as a current MEC member could deliver the needed votes.

Copeland began by stating, "We're aware of the Texas Air offer," and I nodded my head in agreement, at the same time wondering how long ago this Texas Air scheme was hatched. Did Borman bring it to Lorenzo? Or was it the other way around? Deals like this one aren't concocted overnight or on a whim, *or* just to get to a union. "That means the time for quibbling or not believing is over," Copeland continued, interrupting my thoughts. "I've seen a hard copy of the agreement and what we are about to offer is done in the belief the Texas Air proposition is legitimate." Copeland had obtained a bona-fide copy from a management source, so we knew it was authentic. He looked Borman in the eyes and continued. "I'm offering *everything* you demanded from the pilots. In return, all we ask is that Eastern not be turned over to—"

Borman interrupted with a scowl on his now-reddened face. "What about Charlie? He won't give a nickel," he hissed.

Copeland again raised his hand. "Please. Let me finish. In exchange for *only* your promise not to sell, I can guarantee a twenty-percent pay reduction from the pilots and all organized labor groups, *including* the

IAM, plus the requested work-rule changes from the pilots. As far as I can tell from the figures you put out, a twenty-percent pay cut isn't really needed. Your own numbers indicate fifteen percent would suffice. Nevertheless, we'll guarantee the full twenty percent. Later, but only if *you* want to, you can say that you had originally needed twenty percent but determined all that was needed was fifteen. But I want to emphasize that is solely *your* prerogative. This deal is not contingent upon that. This guarantees you more than $350 million in cash annually for a minimum of five years, almost two *billion* bucks. Plus, the work-rule changes will add on a lot more." Copeland and I were staring intently at Borman, but there was no outward reaction, so he continued, "In addition, we'll also do our best to raise your stature amongst the Eastern employees. The past months have been difficult ones and many place the blame squarely on you for what's gone on."

Borman tilted his head to the side and was listening intently. I sensed it was my turn to speak, so I broke in. "I've written all the pilot strike ballot–related correspondence. Now I'll turn my pen on Lorenzo and depict you as the hero who intervened at the eleventh hour and rescued the airline from his clutches. If you want, you can be the head of Eastern for life."

Copeland nodded his head in agreement and spoke once again. "We, George, will inform the pilots that you were the one who convinced the Board of Directors *not* to sell and were solely responsible for saving the airline."

Borman's face got even more crimson as he again growled, "Yeah, but what about Charlie? Winpisinger said that he can't control Bryan. So how can you?"

Perhaps William Winpisinger, the President of the larger international unit of the IAM, might not be able to "control" Charlie Bryan, but Copeland and Bryan had something that went much deeper and was of much greater value: friendship, mutual trust and respect. The *only* pilot Bryan trusted was Copeland, as many other pilot representatives had attempted to blame Bryan for the airline's ills, but never Copeland.

I later discovered that when Copeland called Bryan they had analyzed the situation together. Copeland had then informed him exactly what we were intending to do and had requested his full participation. Bryan had agreed to do whatever was necessary to keep Eastern out of Lorenzo's clutches, including giving up an additional fifteen percent IAM pay on top of the five percent his members had already just voluntarily given. (In order to demonstrate the IAM's commitment to the airline and the employee ownership program, in October of 1985, just four months prior, the IAM membership with Bryan's backing, had approved a five-percent voluntary wage reduction to unambiguously demonstrate that they would do whatever was needed to insure Eastern's long-term success.) Bryan had explained to Copeland that he couldn't make a public offer at this time because any statements like that could be interpreted in the legal arena as meaning he had "opened" his contract. Although the IAM contract wasn't open, under the Railway Labor Act, the mere mention of such an offer might be construed as making it immediately amendable to change. This could place the IAM in an extremely vulnerable position, possibly with no contract in place if Lorenzo wound up owning Eastern despite our offer. That's the reason Bryan had to use Copeland as the middleman.

Copeland reconfirmed, "Bryan's in. You have my word. If you agree, within a moment you'll have verification from Charlie himself, with absolutely no strings attached," he told an obviously shocked Borman. Copeland reached into his pocket, pulled out a white piece of hotel notepad and held it up. "You can call Charlie at this number and he'll confirm everything I've just told you. But it has to be after you've verbally accepted this proposal. He knows, just like we and you do, what will happen if Lorenzo gets control of Eastern. He'll destroy it bit by bit. However, he also doesn't want to be in a position that notwithstanding our offer, if Lorenzo becomes the new owner, his membership doesn't have the protection of a current, valid contract."

Copeland further pledged that if Borman accepted this proposal, there would never be any mention of this private meeting anywhere, anytime, to anyone, sparing all parties from accusations of private deal-making. Copeland also had a more personal motive for doing this. In the past, he had publicly criticized other MEC members for dealing directly with Borman. In this particular case, however, we felt the gravity of the situation demanded immediate action. This was coupled with the fact that only Copeland could bring in the IAM. The hardest part was now over. *If* the bottom line in this entire mess was *really* the bottom line, we had just delivered the way out. Borman had won.

But, to my chagrin, Borman just sat there, seemingly lifeless. How could he even ponder this? I thought about leaving, allowing him to make a few private phone calls, including the one to Bryan that would seal the deal. But, as we waited, he didn't ask us to leave or move to pick up the phone. My mouth was getting dry and the unnerving sweaty feeling was returning. *Why was this taking so long? He couldn't possibly turn down an offer that gave him even more than he demanded; a deal worth almost $2 billion and Bryan's head on a platter. He had won not only the lottery, but the grand prize. Why would he even hesitate?*

Instead of looking flushed with victory, however, his reptilian look conveyed something else, with eyes continually darting from Copeland to me and back, never stopping long enough to look either of us directly in the eye. To me, they expressed cunning rather than intelligence, like he was wondering which card to play next. I was perplexed.

After a moment that seemed like an hour, he finally responded in a low tone, again almost a whisper. The level was so low I had wished I had a knob to turn the volume up a notch or two. I was now fairly certain this was no victory lap on his part. Leaning closer I heard him utter that we had made an excellent offer and, "I appreciate what it represents from both the pilots and your personal perspectives." There was no gloating and the tenor got higher, seemingly indicating he *might* want the deal. And, for a fleeting moment I naïvely believed he might. "But I can't agree," he blurted out, his eyes again darting around the room. He conveyed the impression of fright, taking on a deer-in-the-headlights look. To me, it was as though he might be taking orders from someone higher up that he *had* to obey. His facial expression clearly conveyed that he was withholding something important, a vital piece of this puzzle that was making less and less sense. "We'll just have to pray for the best," he finally murmured.

I couldn't believe this and glanced at Copeland, wondering if I looked as befuddled as he. His eyes were still fixed on Borman with a glacier stare that could have frozen over the entire city of Miami on the most sultry summer day. I was going to ask Borman if he realized that he had just sealed Eastern's fate. But he already knew that. I felt like a heavyweight fighter after getting pounded for fifteen rounds. I had nothing more to say, as it was clear that any attempts to change his mind would be futile as there was nothing more to offer. We had placed everything on the table, including Bryan's capitulation. The silence of the room was deafening. We simply stood, and as we turned to leave, he again offered his hand, but we ignored it.

Unless we came up with an immediate strategy, Eastern was in a deadly spiral, about to be purposely thrown into a tailspin from which it couldn't recover. The airline would no doubt crash, taking countless thousands of lives along with it. His rejection of our offer meant its certain, ultimate destruction, and he knew that. What he had just done was comparable to allowing a terminal disease to take its unrelenting, ultimately fatal course, even though a cure existed. So many workers had blindly followed Borman, entrusting their hopes, futures and their lives and those of their family members to him, and he'd just betrayed them all.

Copeland and I got back into the elevator and the door silently rolled closed with a deathlike quiet, hopefully not also closing the book on Eastern. My knees felt like putty, but the burning question foremost in my mind during the painfully slow elevator hell-like descent was, *Why? Why had he rejected our offer?* Borman was someone whose image was singularly most important to him and we had just made a proposal that would not only preserve, but enhance it. He was definitely *not* the Miami Better Business Bureau's poster boy. I knew that when otherwise rational people do irrational things that make no sense, something much larger must be at stake. Something was definitely fucked up with this entire situation. Right then and there I made a personal vow to find out what that was, no matter how long it took me or wherever my quest for the truth might lead.

But at the moment, Copeland and I had a much more immediate crisis to face: how to prevent Eastern from being handed over to Lorenzo. *Everything* else had to be placed on the back burner.

CHAPTER SIX

"It's gone, George," was all Copeland managed to utter in his gravelly voice as we slowly descended on what had been an elevator of hope on the way up, but was now one of dark despair. He didn't need to say that because I also knew that despite all the hype and deceptions, Eastern had already been handed over to Lorenzo. It was a done deal, with all the hoopla surrounding the Eastern Board of Directors approval just a perfunctory sideshow. At that moment I believed that the entire world had gone crazy. My head pounded and gut churned as I pleaded, "Why? Why did he do it?" I knew that Copeland couldn't answer. He simply shrugged his shoulders and uttered, "We'll have to wait until another time to get that answer."

I attempted to fight my emotions, but that was difficult. I tried to think, to rationalize. But reasoning wasn't working because this was utter madness. I exhorted Copeland to come up with another plan, and quickly. At all costs, we needed to stop what only we now knew was headed our way, faster than a Boeing 727 cruising at Mach .84.

We had to lay hands on a strategy before the MEC meeting that was about to commence at the airport Ramada Inn. The MEC was comprised of three elected representatives from each of the nine Eastern crew bases, a total of twenty-seven pilots, plus three officers elected by them. Schulte had called them into this emergency session that would run concurrent with the Eastern Board of Directors meeting. I still hadn't decided the true reason he had convened them, because the pilot contract still had several days to run before it was even open to amendment. If the MEC members were out flying their trips or at home, none of management's demands could be considered. Did someone get to Schulte so he would summon them to this meeting? Would he urge them to concede? That wouldn't surprise me. But like my many other suspicions, this one would also have to be placed on the back burner because these twenty-seven elected representatives would be meeting to decide the pilots'—indeed all Eastern employees'—futures.

We stood outside pondering what next to do next beside the large fountain with a statue of Captain Eddie Rickenbacker looking down on us. The fireball was setting in the west and everything was tranquil. This was normally my favorite time, as I savored the sweet, lingering smells of the passing day, along with the seeming hushed silence of the coming twilight. But this time it was different. It represented the calm before the fast-approaching tempest. It would soon be dark and my soul felt even blacker than a moonless night. Unless we could come up with a way to halt it, in a few short hours a destructive tsunami would hit, which would irrevocably alter the lives and destinies of hundreds of thousands of people. I turned to Copeland and spoke words that surprised even me as the magnitude of what Borman had done hit home. "That guy over there," I muttered, pointing to the statue, "will be only one of the many thousands who'll be grieving by this time tomorrow unless we can come up with a way to put the brakes on this madness."

As we stood there, Borman exited the building and walked toward his car. As best as I recall, it was some type of Chevy, maybe a Blazer, with blackened windows that only let in a hint of light, a plain-wrapped vehicle that no doubt helped him fuel his public persona of being just an honest businessman, one of the regular guys, which I now believed he was anything but. He saw us and as he walked past shaking his head, muttered that whatever happened next was "in God's hands." He didn't utter another word as we turned away.

As he drove off, I recalled the excitement among the Eastern workers when he had first come onto the scene. Everyone's expectations were so high. But now I wondered how these same people would judge him. The destruction of Eastern would be his legacy, forever. He would certainly try, but how could he ever justify refusing our offer that would have allowed Eastern to flourish and kept its colorful fifty-year-plus history flying high? Borman's actions were especially difficult to fathom because he also knew a Texas Air buyout would ultimately mean the end of the airline. Knowing him, if the Texas Air deal went through that somehow, in some manner, he would attempt to shift the blame for Eastern's demise to someone else, something he was quite adept at doing.

But for now, Copeland was in a quandary, created by his solemn promise not to inform anyone but me about Bryan's willingness to concede if our offer was rejected. Only Copeland and I now knew that even if all three major unions acquiesced, the airline would still be handed over to the Texas Air Corporation, the holding company Lorenzo used to accomplish his dirty work in the airline industry. We played our ace card and had been rejected. Now, if the MEC caved in they would be facing the worst possible situation, in that any pilot concessions meant far less money and more days worked—for Texas Air. The pilots would be paying for a large chunk of the Lorenzo buyout and become the instruments of their own demise. But if Copeland relayed the information about Borman's refusal to the MEC, he would be betraying Bryan's trust and perhaps forfeiting the IAM's contractual protection. Therefore, the paramount question became what else could we possibly do to stop the takeover?

I drove at a snail's pace to the Airport Ramada where the Schulte-called MEC meeting was to commence, gripping the steering wheel of my rental car so hard that I thought my knuckles would break. The Ramada was a cement-and-stucco structure that at the time was just east of Miami airport, off Le Jeune Road. Copeland sat eerily silent, seemingly comatose. Knowing him, he was deep in thought and I could almost smell his gray matter burning as he tried to comprehend what to do.

I parked at the Ramada so we only had to walk a few feet in the heat that now felt like blast furnace and into the conditioned air. Upon entering, I immediately recognized many elected representatives and other ALPA committee people, whose facial expressions betrayed their angst. Most were simply airline pilots, unpretentious men who could fly their jets safely through just about any conditions, but many of whom, most likely including Schulte, were thrust into a state of affairs that Skip and I suspected was way over their heads. Based upon events I had witnessed since becoming involved, I believed that a select few, like Davidson, were putting themselves, their wants, or whatever their *true* motivation might be above the best interests of the pilots who had entrusted them with their collective careers and lives.

Copeland and I went directly into the small hotel restaurant to attempt to sort things out. I ordered a Coke and managed a slight smile when Copeland opted for a mug of hot coffee. "You better call Bryan and tell him what happened," I suggested. Copeland nodded his head as we sat down at a round table and went over the few arrows we had left in our quiver, ultimately deciding that since we still had time until the contract became open to change, if the MEC didn't give in to any management demands that night, *perhaps* Lorenzo would walk away from the deal with a pilot strike looming? Or, if we could buy that vital day or two, we could possibly meet with some members of the Eastern Board of Directors and after checking with Bryan inform them of our offer? Even though most were Borman clones, maybe they would force him to accept it? So, the ultimate strategy for that night's meeting would be for Copeland to attempt to stop the MEC from taking any action.

We were joined briefly by the late Paul Page, the insightful captain representative from the Miami base. Page and Copeland were good friends, and his vote from that large Eastern pilot domicile would be crucial. Without telling him of Bryan's offer, he concurred with our premise: Lorenzo might not want to take over with a huge percentage of the Eastern pilots ready to go on strike and agreed to help stop the MEC from taking any action. In addition to the MEC members, some of the Washington-based national ALPA leaders, along with a bevy of lawyers involved in related legal matters, were present. Page informed us that one of the MEC officers had called the MEC together late that afternoon, hurriedly briefed them and repeated the line that if two of the three unions didn't agree to the pay cuts and work-rule changes, the Eastern Board would be meeting to consider selling the airline to Texas Air. Under no circumstances could Copeland let the other MEC members take the *perceived* easy way out by ratifying a contract in the false belief that it would stop the sale.

Along with Page, our plan had to be laid out ahead of time with other key MEC members whose votes would be needed. Copeland subsequently met privately with a number. But could he *really* count on them? It was late afternoon on February 23rd, meaning time still remained in the current pilot contract and some other things might occur during the intervening period to alter the course of events. For example, Borman might inadvertently spill his guts and report our offer to someone on the Eastern Board. We also still held out hope that given sufficient time to mull everything over, perhaps he might scuttle the Texas Air deal? Maybe he wanted to be the hero after all. In addition, Bryan could decide to go public with his offer, putting on even more pressure. Despite their tough-guy façade, Texas Air might not want to acquire and attempt to run an airline that for all practical purposes would be shut down by a pilot strike in just a few days. We also needed additional time to confer privately with our legal advisors about the possible ramifications of Borman's refusal of our offer. This would be covered by lawyer/client privilege, and perhaps the lawyers would confirm that we could pursue a stockholder derivative legal action that would reveal that the company had been needlessly sold that a better offer had been made and rejected to the detriment of shareholders. This lawsuit could then seek to overturn the deal on those grounds.

I left Copeland in the restaurant and drove to my room at the Marriott to freshen up for what portended to be a very long night. I needed time to think, so after showering I dressed and stepped out of the room into the warm evening air to mull over the whole ball of wax. I recalled that when management placed their opening contract position on the table, it represented a radical departure from any previous ones. So much so that I had spoken about this with ALPA veteran attorney and personal friend, the late John Loomos, who had been involved in over twenty years of Eastern pilot contract negotiations. He had cautioned me, "George, something is seriously amiss. I've never seen an opening position like the one they presented. They've created a poisonous atmosphere that will be difficult or impossible to reverse." John had gone so far as to attempt to sound the alarm with the MEC, but was ignored by most. I now realized that difference from the norm was no doubt due to Texas Air's intervention. They were calling the shots. The contents and tone of the contract opener and subsequent tactics fit their exact negotiating strategy. As I stood there looking out over the now-darkened parking lot, I heard the phone ring. It was Copeland and he informed me he believed he'd convinced a slim majority of the MEC to hold off taking any action.

The ALPA Master Executive Council meeting was about to convene. It would start at nine o'clock on Sunday evening, February 23, 1986. The weather in Miami might be warm, but I was pretty certain things would reach the boiling point during this assembly. This was no social gathering and would undoubtedly run into severe turbulence that would dwarf any encountered in the sky. What ultimately happened would determine the future of Eastern Airlines—that is, if our airline had a future.

CHAPTER SEVEN

Schulte called the MEC meeting to order in a large Ramada Hotel conference room. It was a windowless box with thirty seats arranged around rectangular-shaped, Formica-topped tables, with the large empty space in the middle, reminding me of the Roman Coliseum. Would some reps be cast to the lions? This was the pre-cell-phone era, so it had been decided that the details of the Eastern Board meeting would be relayed to Schulte over the public telephone or in person by Bob White. White was a New York–based pilot and a MEC committee person whom I did not trust. He, Davidson and another pilot, Jim Duffes, were members of Schulte's Contingency Planning Committee that was formed in order "to cover all the possibilities in the looming crisis." Davidson was the Chairman, and Schulte had selected White because he claimed to have experience as a bankruptcy referee in the State of Texas. (I doubted this was true, as White was not an attorney and to the best of my knowledge had no legal experience.)

This committee was charged with studying the consequences of an Eastern Chapter Eleven bankruptcy filing should management go that route. My concerns stemmed from the fact that White and Davidson were frequently locked up alone behind closed doors at the ALPA office discussing who-knows-what or surreptitiously meeting with top executives. I believed this committee had overstepped its bounds and had changed their allegiance, now working for management. My suspicions were heightened further after learning from a management source that White had met a number of times in private, one-on-one meetings during the unfolding crisis with Eastern President Joe Leonard. When I specifically inquired of White the reason for these meetings, he was stunned that I was aware of them. He finally stammered something about an undefined maintenance problem he had encountered while flying, but I didn't buy his story.

During his first brief report to the MEC, White stated that Texas Air had formally announced the conditions of their purchase offer to the Eastern Board, but he returned to the board meeting before stating what those terms were.

In addition to White, Mike Connery, an attorney for a large New York law firm that had been retained as outside legal advisor by ALPA National, also attended the Eastern Board meeting.

Since this would no doubt be a crucial gathering, I took detailed notes throughout. Even before the opening gavel came down, I could sense so much hostility in the room that you could almost cut it with a knife. Before commencing their debate, MEC members heard from a variety of individuals who were involved in an array of issues during the strike preparations. Some of these people, only days or even hours prior, were adamant that the pilots should not give in to *any* management demands. However, from the dialogue, it became evident some were now wavering. What had Schulte told them?

Schulte quickly related some events he was involved with during the past few days. He stated that he received a call from Borman, who informed him that the Eastern Board of Directors had passed a resolution directing Borman to seek a purchaser for the airline. Borman maintained that Lorenzo was the only one he could find, and *apparently* omitted telling Schulte that Eastern had paid Lorenzo a $20 million, nonrefundable "inducement fee" merely to tender his offer. I say apparently because although he was no doubt aware of it, Schulte never mentioned this fee. This considerable sum came from Eastern's coffers and Lorenzo would get this money whether or not the deal was consummated. This very important detail was only uncovered later. How many other parties might have shown similar interest if offered a comparable amount?

Schulte apprised the MEC that the *only* alternative to the Lorenzo purchase would be a new pilot contract that included all the draconian concessions, that without these the company would be sold. He stated Borman had personally informed him that Texas Air would purchase Eastern whether or not the pilots went on strike, and without the sale to Texas Air or a new pilot contract, Eastern would declare bankruptcy on Wednesday, February 26th, the date when the pilots were free to strike. Borman implored him to use his influence to have the proposed pilot contract ratified, stating it would be the only way to avert the Texas Air transaction. Schulte didn't elaborate further on any other items that might have been discussed, but finished by strongly suggesting the MEC ratify the proposed contract. He claimed that he was making this recommendation even though the contract "wasn't a good one," which was a gross understatement. I felt the *real* Schulte was now emerging.

Tom Boggs, one of the two non-pilots the MEC placed on the Eastern Board of Directors, spoke next and discussed in greater detail some of the terms of the Texas Air offer. He stated Merrill Lynch had determined the price would be in the range of 5 to 13 dollars per Eastern common share and that Lorenzo could get fifty-one percent of the shares "almost overnight" by purchasing the authorized, but never issued shares, the very same ones that Copeland had expressed concern about. Boggs related that either Lorenzo or Borman could walk away from the deal if there were antitrust problems raised by federal government agencies, or if Eastern declared bankruptcy. He also parroted the now-standard line that if two of the three unions agreed to new concessionary contracts, there would be no sale. He further stated when he departed the meeting the Eastern Board of Directors was divided. A vote had not yet been taken on the buyout and a midnight deadline had been established. Boggs felt that if the pilot contract wasn't in place by that time, the sale would go forward, and added that a ratified pilot contract would prevent the sale and urged speedy ratification. Boggs returned to the Board of Directors meeting at 10:00 p.m.

ALPA National President Henry Duffy next addressed the MEC. Duffy, a Delta Airlines pilot, stated the MEC had to weigh the good, preventing the sale, against the bad that was contained in the proposed contract. He agreed that the deal currently on the table was not a good one and stated that ALPA National didn't want to get to the strike deadline without a contract and with Texas Air as the new owner. Duffy was obviously in way over his head and ready to surrender. He no doubt believed that if the contract was rejected there would be a protracted pilot strike, like the one ALPA experienced at Continental Airlines when Lorenzo was in charge there and Duffy was at the ALPA helm. That battle had been bitter, expensive and politically damaging to Duffy, because he got his ass kicked and ALPA was decertified as the pilots' bargaining unit. He also urged ratification, if for no other reason than to keep Lorenzo out. Duffy also disclosed that, based upon information he had, Lorenzo would be putting up very little cash for the purchase. He stated the proposed concessions from the pilots would provide more money for the airline than Lorenzo's offer, thus insuring the survival of an intact Eastern. Duffy was advocating an *apparent* easy way out: The MEC simply had to capitulate to management's demands and the immediate problem with Lorenzo would disappear. Not surprisingly, Duffy failed to consider the worst-case scenario; the pilots would give in, but still be stuck with Lorenzo. Copeland publicly questioned Duffy about this possibility and he responded that he had Borman's "solemn word" that this would not occur. As Duffy once again urgently pleaded for ratification, Copeland and I looked glumly at each other.

I later discovered that Duffy had met secretly, one on one with Borman on at least two prior occasions and assured him "the pilots would stand by the airline," presumably meaning they would not go on strike. I'm sure he conveyed this to Schulte.

White returned and again took the floor, this time claiming a new working agreement had been reached with the Transport Workers Union representing the flight attendants. He stated they had agreed to all the needed concessions and that only the pilots' agreement was now needed to avert the sale. He departed without taking any questions from MEC Members. These presentations collectively carried a lot of weight and conveyed the impression that the lack of a pilot contract was now the sole obstacle preventing the buyout.

Thus far, *every* speaker had recommended approval of the contract. Copeland was batting zero, and from their comments, some MEC members who were committed to Copeland, including another representative from the New York base, Gary Brodt, were wavering.

I was squirming in my seat when Copeland glanced over his shoulder at me. His blazing cobalt eyes clearly conveyed what he was thinking. *Should I tell them of our meeting with Borman?* I said nothing, my silence letting him know this would be his decision and whatever he decided was okay with me. But always true to his word, he never brought up our meeting or Bryan's offer.

After numerous trips between the head of the table and the lobby telephone to receive updates, Schulte again took the floor, reiterating that the contract proposal was not a good one. "There should be no question about that," he declared, breathlessly stating, "But you *must* pass it. The flight attendants have already given, so it's out turn to step up to the plate." He added that he would personally take all the criticism from the pilot group that was certain to follow. My notes here contained the remark, "MEC members are under tremendous pressure."

Comments from individual Negotiating Committee members, the pilots who had bargained virtually every day for the union, came next. Chairman Bill Lankford stated that, as was the norm, this time there would be no official recommendation from the committee either for or against the contract. He further added that although the majority of the committee felt this way, the proposed contract was so bad that if passed by the MEC, he personally would not be a party to nor affix his signature to it. Lankford was the first to speak against ratification and his words carried considerable weight and gave the MEC pause. Questions to Lankford that followed finally gave Copeland some much-needed breathing room. During this question-and-answer session, other Negotiating Committee members were queried about their positions. They were not as forceful as Lankford and most indicated that they weren't certain which direction the MEC should take, making me again wonder if Copeland's support would survive.

Next, Don Davidson introduced a formal resolution to accept and ratify the new contract. Debate on this resolution would follow.

But there still was a potential legal hurdle in the way. In the past, the Eastern MEC had ratified a number of concessionary contracts, followed by much protest and disapproval from the pilots. Because of this there was now a section in the ALPA/MEC Policy Manual that included the following:

"Any agreement that substantially changed the Eastern pilots' pay or work rules, after MEC acceptance, will be subject to membership ratification."

This statement meant precisely what was stated. The individual pilots would get to vote on this contract, a process that could take anywhere from three to six weeks. This rule was contained in the MEC Policy Manual. Policy was determined by the MEC and, as a result, Davidson stated that this section could be changed at any time by a simple majority vote. Copeland promptly countered that any modification without prior notification of the proposed change required a two-thirds vote, which was correct according to Robert's Rules of Order, which govern business conducted by the MEC. Of course, Schulte ruled that Davidson's interpretation was correct. His pronouncement meant that only a simple majority vote of the MEC was required to uphold his ruling and a majority did so. As a result, if the vote for the proposed contract passed, individual pilots would not get a vote.

This was followed by a lengthy and passionate debate over Davidson's resolution, and things got so heated that I felt as though I was at an Ali/Frazier rematch. First came formal discussion, then arguments began on the sidelines. This was followed by invitations to "discuss it in the hallway." At least two fistfights broke out, and I personally broke up one. At another point, Schulte was sitting dewy-eyed, all alone in a corner. I went to him and asked what was wrong.

"All the pressure's really getting to me," he sniveled.

"You need a good night's sleep. Why don't you adjourn the meeting until tomorrow and sleep on all this?" I suggested, knowing if he did there would be no way the MEC could approve the contract that night. He only glared back at me through bloodshot eyes.

After a lengthy discussion period, a vote on the Davidson ratification resolution was taken. Copeland's support held and a slim majority defeated it. We breathed a sigh of relief.

The MEC was next informed that the Eastern Board, without further explanation, had inexplicably extended the voting deadline on the Texas Air offer past midnight, awaiting "final" word on an agreement from the pilots. A recess was quickly called and passionate lobbying efforts began both in and outside the meeting room.

When the meeting reconvened, at approximately 1:30 a.m. on the morning of February 24th, there was a motion passed to reconsider the failed resolution. Bill Robinson, the copilot representative from the Boston base had voted on the prevailing side and therefore could make the reconsideration motion. He later told me, "In looking back, I realize I was duped by Davidson. He continually hounded, browbeat and threatened me, said that if I didn't make the motion to reconsider, he would tell the Boston pilots that *I* was the person solely responsible for whatever happened next. Simply put, I caved in. That was the biggest mistake I've ever made, and I'll have to live with what I did for the rest of my life."

Unfortunately, it was but several months later Robinson's life was cut short when he was killed in a private plane crash.

There was a tremendous amount of pressure put on Copeland's supporters during the recess and when the meeting was reconvened he felt that he might no longer have the required votes. "I'll filibuster the goddamn thing to death even if I have to stay up all night and day until the 26th," he whispered to me in a voice now even more raspy from constantly talking. This meant he would use a variety of parliamentary maneuvers and keep speaking to prevent anyone from "moving the question," which would require a two-thirds vote before another vote could be taken. He knew he had at least the one-third number of votes required to block that. By 2:45 a.m. there had been numerous, but unsuccessful attempts to limit debate and halt the Copeland filibuster. He was speaking continually and some of the representatives were starting to yawn and doze off. I believed he might be successful when Schulte was once again summoned to the phone. The lethargic representatives were abruptly revived when at exactly 2:57 a.m. Schulte ran back into the room and, from the rear with bated breath and looking like Chicken Little who believed the sky was actually falling, screamed out at the top of his lungs, "Pass it *now* or it's sold!"

The MEC Vice Chairman, Larry Wells, was holding the gavel when the entire room erupted into total confusion and in the ensuing uproar a vote was abruptly taken without any further debate, with the proposed contract passed by a vote of nineteen in favor to eight opposed. Copeland attempted to get the floor to demand how a vote could be taken without first having the two-thirds required to "move the question." When that plea was ignored, he repeatedly insisted on a roll-call vote, meaning that each MEC member would cast one vote for each pilot he represented, which would have doomed the motion. But he was again snubbed. Schulte and Wells later claimed that his demands weren't heard.

There was initially glee among some who believed the vote had prevented the sale, with a number smiling broadly. But the joy was short-lived as a few moments later it was officially conveyed to Schulte that Eastern had been sold, allegedly formally handed over to Lorenzo at 2:38 a.m., nineteen minutes before the MEC vote was taken. No explanation was ever given by Schulte as to why he supposedly wasn't aware of that crucial Eastern Board decision, even though he was repeatedly asked. Or did he know? He later maintained that he had screamed out, "Pass it now because it's sold," but that was fictitious bullshit. Had he shouted that, there would have been much further discussion and debate, and the outcome could very well have been different, as the reason to ratify or not ratify the contract proposal would have been totally different. Copeland and I suspected that someone had informed Schulte the airline had already been surrendered to Texas Air, but that he didn't have the *cajones* to face Lorenzo without a pilot contract in place, no matter what the price turned out to be, with his urgent plea a ruse. However, as a result, the MEC had given away twenty percent of the Eastern pilots' pay, an amount totaling well over $120 million annually in 1986 dollars, plus numerous other benefits and working conditions, for absolutely nothing!

Oh, wait. Please allow me to correct that last statement. In doing this, the MEC had paid for a large chunk of Lorenzo's buyout, dooming Eastern and ensuring the pilots' demise in the process. Chicken Little had indeed invited the fox into the henhouse. As it dawned on the MEC members what had actually transpired, they filed out of the room the atmosphere was funereal.

Copeland and I remained for fifteen minutes or so, quietly discussing what we might do next, indeed what we *could* do, finally deciding that for now there was nothing. I wanted to go out for drinks, but Copeland didn't drink and I didn't want to go alone. Maybe I'd call my wife. But I dismissed that as well, as all that would accomplish would be to upset her in the middle of the night. Instead, I returned to my room and again showered, trying to wash away the filth that was heaped on the pilots. I did get the smell of the meeting room off, but not out of me. I now fully understood what people mean when they say their heads are "swimming." At that moment I had so many things running through mine that I felt as though I was sinking into the deep end of the pool. I eventually collapsed into a fitful slumber.

CHAPTER EIGHT

The MEC meeting reconvened at ten-thirty that morning. Right out of the box, Davidson attempted to alter events of the early morning by suggesting that the minutes reflect unanimous acceptance of the contract, in his words, "For the sake of unity within the pilot group." At first I believed he had to be joking, but Davidson was serious and what he meant was showing a different vote than was actually taken. In many cases the mists of time do enough to distort the truth, so this ploy was immediately stopped dead in its tracks by a number of MEC members who threatened to take legal action if any changes were made to reflect anything other than the actual vote.

Mike Connery next disclosed some *very* important particulars of the Eastern Board meeting and the terms of the Texas Air buyout; items that inexplicably were never mentioned that fateful morning by White, any of the MEC leadership or Henry Duffy.

In attempting to keep the airline from being sold to Texas Air, Charlie Bryan, who was present as an Eastern Board Member, threw a "Hail Mary" pass with an additional fifteen-percent wage-reduction offer, with the *only* caveat being that Borman had to agree to resign—not immediately, but at an unspecified future date. This IAM wage reduction would amount to over $300 million during the remaining life of their current contract and these monetary concessions represented more than all the money Texas Air had put up. But a majority of the Board rejected Bryan's offer, stating that they would not acquiesce to the request that Borman step aside. The rejection of Bryan's offer was certainly strange as the Eastern Board accepted the Texas Air agreement, allegedly with the same stipulation. The

Texas Air deal only put Eastern further into a financial hole and Borman allegedly would be leaving sooner.

Connery's report was also at odds with assertions made by other individuals during the course of the previous evening and early morning. He stated the Eastern Board believed from the start that the pilots and flight attendants would concede, meaning the IAM was the target from the outset. So much for the "two out of three" bullshit that employees were constantly bombarded with. Connery also affirmed that Borman admitted that the story about only the pilots and flight attendants having to give concessions was a ruse; that he had concocted that lie. Connery offered no justification or rationalization as to why the Eastern Board had ignored Bryan's offer with its superior monetary value.

Borman later bellyached that Bryan was willing to give "only" fifteen percent and not the twenty that he was demanding. This was supposedly another of the Eastern Board's excuses for turning down Bryan's offer, conveniently "not recalling" that the IAM had just recently voluntarily contributed five percent. More importantly, had the MEC been informed of Bryan's offer prior to the vote being taken, Copeland would then have apprised the MEC of our meeting with Borman and *exactly* what had transpired. But once again, neither Schulte nor Duffy ever relayed this important information. Not surprisingly, after Lorenzo took over Eastern, management went to Court and unsuccessfully argued that in making his offer, Bryan indeed had "opened" his contract.

* * *

Connery also revealed to the MEC for the first time that Eastern's original investment banker for the Texas Air deal wasn't Merrill Lynch, but Solomon Brothers. But they withdrew, refusing to endorse the sale due to their concern that the pilots' strike would disrupt Eastern's critical cash flow. It was also later discovered that Solomon Brothers had refused to render a "fairness opinion" on the Texas Air stock price offer, making the Eastern Board Members individually liable should the sale go through to the detriment of stockholders. But the Eastern Board ignored this advice and instead threw out Solomon Brothers and replaced them with Merrill

Lynch. The Board members were well aware of their personal monetary threat because in exchange for going through with the deal, Texas Air put up liability insurance protection for *each* individual Board member of $35 million apiece! The implications of this were tremendous. It meant that *if* the pilots had gone on strike causing financial problems for the airline, the Eastern Board might have been forced to reverse its decision to sell or suffer potential severe personal monetary liability. This liability would have far exceeded Texas Air's $35 million insurance, as Eastern had annual revenues in excess of $4.5 billion. He also made it known to the MEC for the first time that a pilot strike would have stopped the Lorenzo deal. This was crucial information. Copeland had made that very argument. Indeed, that was a cornerstone of his strategy. Connery's statements made it clear that a pilot strike would definitely have killed the sale or overturned the transaction if the Board had already approved it. However, a new pilot contract was now in place, so nothing further could be done. I wondered why the MEC and/or ALPA National leadership withheld all this crucial information and came to believe that fear of facing Lorenzo without a contract in place was the reason.

*   *   *

But Connery still wasn't finished communicating other important, but previously undisclosed, specifics. Texas Air was putting up a total of $256 million. Incredibly, Eastern was financing the remainder of its own purchase with borrowed money. This cost amounted to $339 million and would be added to the airline's existing debt load that, according to Borman, was supposedly dragging the airline down. But oddly, neither the Eastern Board nor the various government agencies that subsequently rubber-stamped the deal objected. None of the principals were ever forced to explain to anyone how a buyout that added $339 million to the airline's debt load would resolve *any* of Eastern's purported problems. Likewise, it was never explained why the MEC members weren't informed of the particulars before casting a vote. Connery also disclosed that Lorenzo and Texas Air were also granted a "signing bonus" of $34 million. Of that amount, $20 million, the previously mentioned "inducement fee," was irrevocable. Had all this information been previously forthcoming, the final MEC members' votes would no doubt have been different.

But a way to possibly kill the deal remained. According to the ALPA Constitution, any contract must be signed by the ALPA President, meaning Duffy. He was in the room and Copeland immediately asked if, in light of this newly revealed material, he would refuse to sign it? In response, Duffy sighed, "I've already signed it. Right after the MEC ratified it." This further confirmed in my mind that the singular fear of Lorenzo was the impetus, as Duffy was no doubt aware of the particulars all along.

I now knew something was seriously off beam with this entire deal, as it made absolutely no sense from *any* perspective, except Texas Air's.

* * *

Connery departed and Schulte notified the MEC that Borman wanted to address them after lunch. Copeland turned and asked me, "You wanna hear what he has to say?"

I didn't know whether to laugh or gag. "Listen to him? I never want to see his face again," I replied. So Copeland, another friend and rep from the New York base, Al Gallo, and I went to the Marriott hotel for an extended lunch; long enough to insure that Borman was gone when we returned. As the minutes that felt more like hours passed my attention wasn't focused on the food in front of me, but on the sellout. And that's what it was, a sellout. Borman had betrayed every loyal Eastern employee.

I'm certain Borman was pleased that we didn't attend his little post-sale get-together. I received a blow-by-blow description of what transpired, however, from another representative. A teary-eyed Borman stated that he and the Board of Directors believed all along that the pilots would concede, and the sole reason that Eastern was handed to Texas Air had been Bryan's refusal to go along. This amounted to the classic "blame everyone but me" Borman.

Borman also stated that the Eastern Board had considered Bryan's pay-reduction offer during its midnight deliberations and rejected it because of the proviso that he had to leave. In my opinion, this was simply more BS. He then contradicted himself, telling the MEC in a sniveling, purported farewell that he was leaving Eastern, as soon as he had the time "to return to my office and clean out my desk—that is, if the new, heartless management will even allow me that luxury."

After hearing this I wondered if Borman took the time to remove the bulletproof vest that his top-management minion, then Eastern President Joe Leonard, claimed Borman donned daily during the height of this latest "crisis." That was probably why he looked so boxy when Copeland and I met with him. He was no doubt wearing it under his cheap suit.

Alas, Borman also conveniently omitted mentioning his *million dollar* golden parachute or his new paid position on the Texas Air Board of Directors, the latter contradicting his statement to his own Board members that, "He could never work for Lorenzo." Subsequent official statements stated that Texas Air, as part of his "retirement package," was providing Borman with the million dollars. More likely, it was compensation for him delivering Eastern to them.

When we returned from lunch, Duffy was addressing the MEC, mentioning that he had dined with Lorenzo earlier and that Lorenzo had solemnly promised to "mend his ways." I almost fell down laughing when I heard this naïve crap. As previously mentioned, with Duffy at the helm, ALPA had waged a personal, nasty name-calling campaign against Lorenzo during the Continental pilots' strike. I couldn't see Lorenzo simply shaking hands and putting all of that behind him. I wasn't impressed with Duffy's handling of anything during his tenure as president. Furthermore, as a Delta pilot I mistrusted him having *anything* to do with Eastern, knowing that if Eastern failed, Delta, as its chief competitor would be the main beneficiary. Ultimately, this assessment was proven correct.

Absolutely nothing positive had been gained by Eastern in the buyout. Texas Air, however, reaped untold benefits. A short time later, the Eastern computerized reservations system known as System One, with a price tag placed anywhere from $250 million to close to $1 billion, was "sold" to Texas Air for notes that came due in 2012 totaling $100 million and Eastern was immediately charged to use it. Texas Air also charged Eastern a $15-million-per-year management fee. Eastern formerly purchased its own fuel, but was now forced to buy it through Texas Air and pay Texas Air

$13 million annually for that "privilege." In October of 1988 Texas Air announced the sale of the relatively small but highly profitable portion of the company, the Eastern Shuttle, to Donald Trump for $365 million in cash, more money than Texas Air had put up for the entire airline! The Ionosphere Clubs, valuable real estate holdings and aircraft with the most favorable financing terms, were either transferred to Continental or sold outright for cash, as were Eastern's Latin American routes and Miami hub, later. The latter two were sold to American Airlines for almost half a billion dollars. On top of all that, Eastern loaned Texas Air $200 million at very low interest rates. Eastern then turned around and borrowed $220 million at much higher rates. So much for Eastern "being worthless" as Borman had claimed.

With previous cuts in the block hours of flying in place, which I will discuss in depth later in the book, and the transfer and/or sale of assets, Texas Air milked Eastern dry, like a cash cow. All these actions purposely created huge monetary losses, setting up and seemingly justifying the "final showdown" that would come when the IAM contract was open for negotiations. The enormous deficits would become the ostensible justification for the onerous demands that would no doubt be made by management to the IAM—ultimatums that no union could agree to, and the subsequent sale of even more of Eastern's crucial resources. Texas Air's final contract proposal to the IAM was basically their opening proposal, the one they first placed in the table, almost identical to what they had done with the pilots. The final backbreaker was the change they wanted to make to the mechanics' scope clause. Management's proposal would allow Eastern to outsource engine and other mechanical work anywhere, anytime they wanted, costing thousands of jobs. Additionally, there were pay reductions in the neighborhood of thirty to forty percent, along with severe cuts in vacation time and sick leave. All of this was done by design. What better way to ultimately destroy what was left of the airline than to blame it on a supposedly greedy union?

All of the foregoing was easy for Texas Air to accomplish since they now owned the airline. They transformed Eastern, first by creating separate, incorporated mini subsidiaries. Then they either shifted them to Texas

Air or sold them outright, transferring the cash to Continental, a process known as up-streaming. In this case, it amounted more to manna, meaning cash, from heaven. In an arrangement that made absolutely no business or economic sense from Eastern's standpoint, Texas Air got a company with approximately $3 billion in tangible assets and almost $5 billion annual revenue for 256 million borrowed dollars, of course minus the money that the pilots and flight attendants had "contributed." To neither Copeland's nor my surprise, the day of the Texas Air sale marked the beginning of the end for Eastern Airlines.

But alas, Borman still wasn't done. He had another unfinished agenda to complete and needed a bit more time than the amount he had stated was required to return to his office to clean out his desk; a number of important loose ends remained to be cleaned up, concerns that at the time no one suspected were connected to the sale.

* * *

Even though many questions remained about the transaction, the new management immediately assumed an authoritarian role in Eastern's day-to-day operations, and the Employee Involvement Committee was quickly relegated to the trash can. At the few subsequent meetings that were actually held before the committee was completely disbanded, I could almost taste the acrimony in the air that now flowed from the management appointees toward their former union "colleagues," particularly those from the IAM. We were told that items routinely handled by the Committee were now proprietary information and every request was routinely denied.

As Texas Air was busy laying the groundwork to do their dirty business, I returned to studying the Eastern Flight 980 crash.

I also vowed to try to simultaneously uncover the *true* reasons for the "garage sale" of Eastern. I decided to work backward from Borman's refusal of our offer and look at major events to try to unearth why the airline was sold. Both tasks would be facilitated as I would now have access to enormous amounts of information courtesy of my third ALPA term of office, which began several days later, on March 1, 1986.

PART III

THE TIMELINE

CHAPTER NINE

As I delved into the details of the Flight 980 crash, a chill ran down the length of my spine and the tiny hairs on the nape of my neck bristled; I could almost feel the arctic-like surroundings on Bolivia's Mount Illimani where the Boeing 727 had gone down. My concern was fueled further because I was still having difficulty laying my hands on anything of substance from the NTSB, the official U.S. government agency that should have been in charge. I had once again pored over every single crash-related document secured from them, but they were all worthless. I found that bizarre since their duties and obligations officially state:

Background, Mission, and Mandate

The National Transportation Safety Board (NTSB) is an independent federal agency charged with determining the probable cause of transportation accidents and promoting transportation safety, and assisting victims of transportation accidents and their families. The NTSB investigates accidents, conducts safety studies, evaluates the effectiveness of other government agencies' programs for preventing transportation accidents, and reviews the appeals of enforcement actions involving aviation and mariner certificates issued by the Federal Aviation Administration (FAA) and the U.S. Coast Guard (USCG), as well as the appeals of civil penalty actions taken by the FAA.

To help prevent accidents, the NTSB develops safety recommendations based on our investigations and studies. These are issued to federal, state, and local government agencies and to industry and other organizations in a position to improve transportation safety. Recommendations are the focal point of the NTSB's efforts to improve the safety of the nation's transportation system.

NTSB Mission:

To promote transportation safety by

- Maintaining our congressionally mandated independence and objectivity;

- Conducting objective, precise accident investigations and safety studies;

- Performing fair and objective airman and mariner certification appeals; and

- Advocating and promoting safety recommendation. And to assist victims of transportation accidents and their families.

The NTSB had failed to do *any* of the above in this case, so I made an official request for all their Flight 980–related documents under the Freedom of Information Act (FOIA) on ALPA letterhead, explaining that I was a union representative for the pilots who manned this flight and the ones subsequently flying over the same route. I thought that perhaps they might respond, but my requests were again ignored. My only recourse was to file a lawsuit to attempt to get the requested information, a costly and time-consuming process. At the time I found it almost beyond belief that this U.S. government agency would withhold material related to flight safety, so my next step was a follow-up letter to the then NTSB Chairman, the late Jim Burnett. Once more I sent it on official ALPA stationery, again requesting the information for flight safety-related purposes. I waited over a month for a response but nothing came, so I resent the letter. Approximately three weeks later I received a reply from a Burnett underling, but still none of the requested data, in direct contradiction to their publicly stated mandate:

Since our inception, the NTSB has investigated more than 132,000 aviation accidents and thousands of surface transportation accidents. On call 24 hours a day, 365 days a year, NTSB investigators travel throughout the country and to every corner of the world to investigate significant accidents and develop factual records and safety recommendations with one aim—**to ensure that such accidents never happen again** [*Emphasis* *added*]. . . . Our most important stakeholder is the traveling public, and we are concerned with one principal objective, promoting transportation safety for the traveling public.

This certainly rang true if one looked at every prior airliner crash when they relentlessly scrutinized everything to come up with a probable cause, irrespective of where the culpability might lay. But here, their lack of proper investigation was tantamount to murder being committed with the police— in this case the NTSB—not only failing to investigate but not even wanting to show up at the scene of the crime! There was no inquiry of substance, no search for clues or other possible evidence, and even more damning—no *timely* attempt to retrieve the voice or flight data recorders or the bodies of the victims. Retrieval of the voice and flight data recorders, the Holy Grail of aircraft accident investigation, was crucial because the information contained on these virtually indestructible devices would have set the stage for an investigation and might even have disclosed the cause. Another immediate concern had been the number of subsequent close calls involving other Eastern South American flights that pilots had reported to ALPA and management. I wanted to make certain there wasn't a repeat of this tragedy. The NTSB had betrayed the very reason for its existence, and I wanted to know why.

I knew the ropes at ALPA and previously had some dealings with the air-safety staff people in the Washington, D.C., office. After making some inquiries, I discovered there were mounds of information available from ALPA that went far beyond the scant material that the NTSB had provided or would even admit existed. I spoke with one of the ALPA secretaries, and she obligingly copied and shipped me a huge box of material. With this info I hoped to uncover not only items that pointed to the likely cause, but also why the NTSB attempted to erect every possible roadblock. But the opposite happened: when I studied the ALPA material, the less I could comprehend the NTSB's actions—the same U.S. government agency that had never before refused to investigate a crash.

After reading the ALPA material, I realized that the NTSB *must* have many of the same lingering questions I did, since they were the experts.

Yet, their lack of interest in pursuing a thorough investigation led me to believe that perhaps the cause of the Flight 980 crash was something that no one wanted uncovered. But one *huge* question still hung in the air: why?

A number of items contained in the ALPA file were very revealing. Two were of great significance and were contained in copies of newspaper articles. The first was a report from United Press International (UPI) that peasants living in a small Andean town had heard a noise like a roar of thunder and pieces of the jet had fallen from the sky. An article from the January 3, 1985 *Miami Herald* contained the statement, *"Peasants living near the crash site told U.S. Embassy officials that they heard a 'huge roar of thunder' and that parts of the plane fell over the small town of Cohini, 36 miles south of La Paz, United Press International reported."*

This reporting clearly indicates the jet could have been sabotaged. Indeed, the *only* reason why there would be what was described as a "roar of thunder," with parts of the jet falling from the sky, was if it had been blown up in midair, like subsequently happened to Pan Am Flight 103 over Lockerbie, Scotland. Yet no one who witnessed this event was interviewed by NTSB personnel. From what I had read and knew, a potential terrorist act was never *officially* investigated or even entertained by any United States government investigative agencies—at least not publicly.

This was indeed interesting because there were reports also contained in Spanish-language South American newspapers that stated the Boeing 727 had been sabotaged by operatives of then-Paraguayan "President for Life," Alfredo Stroessner, or *El Excelentisimo,* as he liked to be called. Even though the terrorist possibility had been reported in the one American press article, the NTSB had never *publicly* mentioned this or even hinted this might be a possible reason. As a result, I began to suspect that something much larger might be at stake, especially since it was a well-known fact that Stroessner had made Paraguay a drug smuggler paradise and a comfortable home for many former Nazis.

The same January 3, 1985 *Miami Herald* story continued, *"U.S. Air Force Col. Donald Hargrove, who flew over the accident site twice on Wednesday, said Thursday that the crash might have triggered an avalanche that would make a search for survivors more difficult."*

This was yet another spin placed on what might have happened by a U.S. government official, confusing things even more, seemingly looking for an excuse—any pretext—not to conduct an investigation. There was no further identification of Colonel Hargrove, what his official capacity was, or why he had flown over the site. His name never resurfaced in any subsequent documents.

That same newspaper article continued. *"Eight experts from the National Transportation Safety Board and two from the Federal Aviation Administration arrived in Bolivia, trying to recover the plane's flight recorder and determine why the jet veered off course, into the mountain."*

Eight experts from the NTSB and two from the FAA *might* have flown to Bolivia, but their names were never revealed. Like Colonel Hargrove, they faded into oblivion with nothing further ever reported in any of the records whether or not an attempt was made to recover the voice or flight data recorder. But, in reading the wording carefully, they had already stated *". . . the jet veered off course, into the mountain."* This meant that without the benefit of *any* inquiry these ten individuals had already arrived at a hypothetical probable cause! Yet, if a huge roar of thunder was reported and pieces of the jet fell into Cohini, why didn't they check out the sabotage angle? Remember that all of this took place a mere two days after the crash.

The *Miami Herald* story went on to state, *"Among other questions the investigators planned to ask: Was the airport's instrument landing system working? Were the pilot's on-board navigational aids in order? Was the cockpit crew aware of the route's possible hazards?"* Yet here it was now over a year later, and it became crystal clear to me from the ALPA records that these important questions were never answered, much less asked.

The ALPA documents provided lots of information, and I intensely examined them. They contained a copy of the Eastern computerized flight plan, papers that confirmed that Eastern Flight 980 was a "stretched" Boeing 727-225B jet on a scheduled flight from Asuncion, Paraguay, to Miami, Florida, with a planned en-route stop in La Paz, Bolivia. These records showed that Flight 980 departed Asuncion for its scheduled two hour and eight minute flight to La Paz at 6:40 p.m. with nineteen passengers and ten crewmembers on board. The jet's route took it via the flight plan depicted on the Jeppesen navigational chart known as Upper Amber Airway 320 (UA320). Because of favorable tailwinds that day, the flight plan calculated a flying time of only one hour and forty minutes.

An airliner crash investigation must be a well-defined, step-by-step procedure that normally begins with the recovery and reading of both the cockpit voice and flight data recorders.* The data contained on these recorders becomes the foundation of the investigation. Allow me to provide a brief description of each device.

The cockpit voice recorder (CVR) is a recording device, back then a tape or digital recorder, which the Federal Aviation Regulations require to be installed in every transport category aircraft. At the time of the Flight 980 crash, it recorded all the voice conversations within the cockpit and over the aircraft's radios for the immediate preceding thirty minutes, with a constant erase feature beyond that.

The flight data recorder (FDR) records a number of various parameters of flight for the entire duration of the trip. For example, the flight data recorder would give the aircraft's headings and altitude, airspeed, rate of descent, angle of bank, the power output and internal temperatures of the aircraft engines, the position of the flaps at a given time, and the position of the landing gear. There can also be a host of other pertinent data recorded for posterity, depending on the type of recorder installed.

---

*Both of these important recorders are sealed in metal containers. At the time, there were three different models used by the various airlines. Eastern, with the exception of some 727 aircraft acquired from Pacific Southwest Airlines, utilized Fairchild recorders on their 727 aircraft. Both are virtually crash-proof, encased in fireproof titanium containers. Titanium is an extremely hard metal, and the recorders are located in the aft airstair area of the jet, the part of the aircraft most likely to remain intact in the event of a crash. A "water bath" protects both recorders from potentially destructive heat that can be caused by a fire. In the event of fire this water bath completely surrounds the recording device. There is also a pressure-relief valve installed to vent the steam should the water vaporize. To further assure the survivability for the all-important flight data recorder, its recording tape is constructed of fireproof material. Both of the cases containing the recorders are of a bright orange color for easy and immediate recognition at the crash site.

Scientists and engineers who are thoroughly familiar with the 727 systems and the airline's operations would read and then analyze the data contained on each recorder and would then be called upon to give their expert opinions based upon this information. This is a crucial first step in trying to piece together exactly what happened. This is very important in cases when no crewmember survives. All other pertinent background information on the aircraft, crew and weather is also compiled and studied in depth. This data is then used collectively to arrive at the "probable cause," or the officially designated reason for the crash. These investigations take a lot of effort by a wide array of experts, and the desire to find out exactly what happened is the one common objective that *should* be shared by all involved. Nothing can be left to speculation or chance because if implementing specific changes that come from discovering the probable cause, another disaster could be prevented. But in this case, we already had ten individuals state that the aircraft had *"veered off course, into the mountain"* before one shred of evidence indicated this. But even if this turned out to be the cause, the NTSB's specific job was to discover *why* this happened and correct any deficiencies. This team effort has always been the norm, based upon the assumption that everyone is driven by this singular motive. Moreover, many of those involved believe so much in what they are doing, if there is an attempt to undermine these efforts, they fail to notice. For example, much later I spoke with a former NTSB member and asked why, in his opinion, no substantive Flight 980 investigation took place. His response was, "It was the money."

I asked exactly what he meant by that.

"The [NTSB] Chairman didn't want to spend the money."

Although he might actually have believed that, I didn't buy this lame excuse. Never before had the NTSB failed to investigate a United States airliner crash for monetary reasons, especially when Americans had perished. Also, recall that this crash took place on January 1st, meaning there could be no budget constraints in place as the fiscal year for the NTSB runs from October to October, meaning this was barely two months into the 1985 fiscal year. Or, if for some mysterious and unprecedented reason monetary concerns did take center stage, at the very least the NTSB could have paid an experienced mountain climber, preferably an American, to recover the recorders. This would have been an insignificant expenditure.

As I read the large number of inconsistencies contained in the ALPA crash files emanating from different sources, I could see that they would confuse anyone interested in this crash. For example, the official news releases issued immediately following the crash stated that the Bolivians had invited Eastern and the NTSB to investigate, that an NTSB-led expedition to the crash site would take place "soon," yet without a date specified. Yet, at that exact same time, some ALPA aircraft accident investigators were claiming just the opposite, maintaining the NTSB seemingly didn't want to conduct *any* inquiry and that the Bolivians were impossible to work with and refused to accept American aid. These papers revealed that, interlaced with the NTSB's public statements, other sources at Eastern misled interested employees and a trusting public into believing that the cause of the crash might never be determined due to the inaccessibility of the site. This was reinforced by comments from an official Eastern spokesman, who made the following statement a mere five days after the crash:

"If there is any fuselage, it is buried in snow. The whole thing could be locked in a block of ice by now."

Buried in snow? Locked in a block of ice? In five days? This was not only a complete distortion, it was impossible! The seasons are reversed in South America, meaning it was summertime. So, even at nineteen-thousand feet, it would take months for the aircraft to become buried.

The more I studied the ALPA crash materials, the more apparent it became that equivocation existed from the outset. One possible motive for Eastern's reluctance to pursue an investigation might be that American staple, the dollar. If the reasons for the crash remained unknown or were deemed to be an "act of God," Eastern's insured monetary liability per deceased passenger would be the $75,000 limit set at the time by the Warsaw Convention and Montreal Protocols. These were treaties reached between the various countries on liability limits. However, if willful misconduct was proven to be the cause or even a contributing factor, the limit would not apply and the airline's and their insurance carriers' liabilities could extend into many millions of dollars per passenger.

Of course, Eastern management's public statements didn't suggest that the crash might be due to any type of willful misconduct, but their private assertions to employees suggested that Captain Larry Campbell was an incompetent pilot and had most likely caused the crash. For example, immediately following the crash, most pilots who had gone to the Eastern New York 727 simulator for their flight check heard instructors commenting about how Campbell's alleged poor piloting skills were no doubt the reason for the crash. *If* the statements spoken to employees were proven to be true, the airline could be sued for considerable amounts, making this a very thin line for management to attempt to walk.

A number of Eastern pilots, including me, wondered just what was going on, yet our questions were held at bay for an extended period of time by confusing NTSB actions. For instance, the NTSB initially stated that the agency *might* conduct its own investigation, but they weren't yet certain. Then, the timing of any possible NTSB-led trek was strung out just long enough—not so long that accusations of improper dillydallying or incompetence could surface, but long enough to preclude anyone else from taking action. There was definitely lots of doubletalk, exemplified by numerous newspaper articles in the days immediately following the crash that openly spoke about the amount of confusion and bureaucratic delays. These impediments bought *time*—the only insurance needed to make sure that any on-site investigation would never materialize or would fail if one was later conducted.

The following accounts were taken from the January 4, 1985 edition of the *Miami Herald:*

> *". . . the volunteer climbers decided to make the ground search after Bolivian and U.S. officials could not decide which country was in charge of the official rescue party . . .* [Note: No one ever reported the findings of these "volunteer" climbers, or even who sent them.]
>
> *". . . Eastern spokesman Parsons acknowledged that company officials in Miami did not 'have a real good handle' on the search-and-rescue operation. U.S. Embassy officials in La Paz who declined to be named also said that the ground effort was beset by bureaucratic delays. . ."*

Eastern management's ambiguous positions of informing the public the crash was an unfortunate accident, while simultaneously attempting to lead pilots into believing that Campbell was at fault, could only succeed as long as there was no official on-site investigation or retrieval of the flight and voice recorders leading to discovery of the true reason or reasons. When all pretenses of an investigation were finally abandoned, it was because the NTSB claimed they "couldn't get to the crash site."

The equivocation of this last statement is exposed when one looks at what was done by the NTSB in other airline crashes. The crash of a TWA Boeing 747, Flight 800, during the summer of 1996, is one example. That plane crashed into the Atlantic Ocean off Long Island, with sections of the fuselage buried in over a hundred and twenty feet of water. In that case, the NTSB, FAA and FBI spent over $20 million and many long months sending divers to comb the ocean bottom for hundreds of square miles in order to recover the flight and voice recorders, bodies, belongings and pieces of wreckage. The pieces of wreckage were collected and the aircraft was partially reconstructed in a hangar in Calverton, Long Island.

More significant to this case is that seventeen years after TWA Flight 800 went down, investigators who scrutinized it for the NTSB, ALPA and TWA came forward and claimed that the investigation was intentionally bungled to arrive at a false probable cause that was spoon-fed to a trusting American public. They alleged that critical evidence was tampered with and removed by federal government agencies for, at this point, reasons unknown. The NTSB, however, subsequently refused to reopen this case.

Although the veracity of the TWA Flight 800 accusations will never be known, in the Eastern Flight 980 case the same NTSB made the fabricated claim that the site was too remote to mount an investigation or even to recover the recorders. I discovered that the NTSB issued this statement even though they were fully aware that a number of expeditions had successfully reached the crash location.

It was apparent that this could have happened only if several parties, in concert, wanted to prevent the true cause of the crash from ever being uncovered. This was confirmed for me when a subsequent "probable cause" for the crash was ultimately revealed via a Bolivian crash report. Upon closer scrutiny, however, this Bolivian "report" and "investigation" were no more than inept comments based upon total conjecture. Yet this turned out to be the *only* official, government-issued report on this disaster. I will later quote parts of it. The frequent snowfalls at the crash site, particularly during the South American winter months, *would* eventually ensure the burial of the wreckage and recorders, which would make the recovery of anything of value virtually impossible. Therefore, the NTSB's illogical and unscientific behavior indicated something else had to be afoot. They seemed to be covering Eastern's tracks, so any attempt on my part to unearth the reasons for the crash would be not only to discover why the plane crashed, but also why the NTSB never conducted a timely investigation.

I immediately dismissed any NTSB motives concerning monetary liabilities against the carrier, as they had totally disregarded any such consideration in the past. So, was it also possible that another government agency, maybe the FAA, was somehow involved or responsible? If the navigation aids were inferior or inoperative, they would also be liable. If the crew was unaware of this, the blame would clearly fall on the FAA and the airline. But what I found confusing here was that, in the past, the NTSB had taken on the FAA and called them to task.

Although the NTSB had ignored all my requests for pertinent information, I nonetheless kept an open mind and began my examination with only one certainty: there was definitely a reason for the crash. This statement might sound obvious. But Eastern and the NTSB seemed to want to lead, or mislead, all interested parties to believe that the crash was a freak, once-in-a-lifetime mishap caused by Flight 980 circumnavigating a thunderstorm that had been reported on its route of flight, and that the aircraft had unknowingly flown directly into Mount Illimani. Although this was possible, without any supporting evidence, it begged the question of why they wanted to fabricate a cause without any supporting proof.

CHAPTER TEN

The sheer volume of ALPA material created further cynicism on my part, as I now had proof that the behavior of the American and Bolivian government accident investigative agencies was inexplicable and far different than any previously witnessed. Misleading information was circulated even though the NTSB knew almost immediately that the Bolivians weren't going to conduct an onsite investigation, and the NTSB only added to the confusion. They also issued contradictory statements, all of which had the singular result of buying time. Here are some specific examples:

This came from a story published in the January 4, 1985 edition of the *Miami Herald,* three days after the crash. Keep in mind that throughout this harrowing timeframe the NTSB spokespersons were publicly promising to undertake an immediate trek to the crash site and conduct a thorough, onsite inquiry. But this *Miami Herald* story told quite a different tale:

> . . . *Despite an outpouring of offers of help from mountain climbers who called the U.S. Embassy, both ground [search and rescue] efforts have been set back by organizational problems . . .*

When it became apparent that something was seriously amiss, a totally different spin was disseminated. The following came from another article in the same day's later edition of the *Miami Herald.*

> . . . *While both teams of mountain climbers were having problems on the ground, Embassy officials in La Paz and Eastern officials in Miami were busy tapping sources for a high-altitude helicopter to conduct a faster recovery operation. By day's end, Eastern's McGraw [Note: McGraw was Eastern's media spokesperson] announced they had found one.*

The January 5th *Herald's* headlines took on even more mysterious tones when that day's headline proclaimed, *"Confusion Hampers Efforts To Reach Crash Site,"* detailing some of the chaos caused by man-made problems that were purportedly preventing anyone from reaching the scene.

The following day, January 6th, a full five days after the crash, the *Miami Herald* bold headline stated, *"Plane Debris Found, But No Survivors,"* which misled a trusting public, and no doubt the reporter, into believing that an official search party had somehow reached the site, but unfortunately no one was alive. However, this was yet another fabrication since no official team was sent. All the deception is further shown in the following excerpt from the January 9, 1985 *Washington Post,* which placed yet another government spin on what was transpiring.

U.S. Says Search Suspended for Bolivian Crash Victims
LA PAZ, Bolivia—The U.S. Embassy says efforts to recover the bodies of the 29 people killed in the crash of an Eastern Airlines jet have been suspended to avoid endangering the lives of search crews. Press attaché Steve Seche said Monday that a U.S. Air Force helicopter would continue trying to reach the wreckage on Mount Illimani, the Associated Press reported, but the objective would be to retrieve the flight recorder from the Boeing 727 that crashed a week ago. Eight Americans were among the 29 people on board. Bernardo Guarachi, a Bolivian mountaineer who reached the crash site on Saturday after a three-day climb, told reporters he believed it would take four men six days to retrieve just one body. He said he recommended that recovery efforts by land be suspended until May, when there is less precipitation.

My subsequent probe showed all these spoon-fed stories were deliberately misleading and served only one purpose: to create further confusion and buy time. For example, there were ultimately two different stories circulated concerning the U.S. high altitude helicopter.

The first, which was told to me by one of the ALPA volunteers involved in the investigation, stated that neither the United States government nor Eastern ever publicly disclosed that the Bolivians, from the very outset, would not allow the use of the referred-to United States high altitude

Blackhawk helicopter that Eastern's spokesman McGraw stated was "found" on January 4th and was to be used in an attempt to recover the Flight 980 recorders. So how could a U.S. Air Force helicopter "continue trying to reach the wreckage," as was subsequently claimed by the U.S. embassy officials, when none was allowed into the country? Plus, there was never any explanation as to why the Bolivians refused to allow the helicopter in.

The second account surfaced only many years later, and claimed that the United States government did supply a Blackhawk helicopter that was purportedly going to drop an ALPA investigator at the site. However, according to this later story, the aircraft that brought the Blackhawk helicopter into Bolivia, an Air Force C-141, had to return to the U.S. "for another operation the next day." I doubt the veracity of the latter account because it would seem that recovering the recorders would have been a very high priority item. We'll just add this to the list of questionable U.S. government actions and numerous misrepresentations.

In addition, how could searchers' lives "be endangered" when no official search was underway? However, it was also later reported that a communications radio belonging to the enigmatic Guarachi-led group of mountain climbers, referenced in the *Washington Post* article, had inexplicably ceased working upon arrival at the crash site at approximately 2:30 p.m. on January 5th, only to mysteriously revive on its own several hours later.

Additionally, there were never any pictures shown or any official mention of what Guarachi found or recovered, or even the identities of the persons or agency that dispatched him, or who accompanied him. And if, as reported, Guarachi recommended that recovery efforts be called off until May, why did the NTSB then wait until October, after the harsh South American winter, before finally launching their belated, ill-fated attempt plagued by calculated blunders?

Nonetheless, to a layperson, when taken at face value, all these deceptive accounts would suggest that a valiant, but thus-far unsuccessful effort was being abandoned. Why would U.S. government and Eastern officials go out of their way to make it appear this was the case?

Consider this: Mount Everest has an altitude of over twenty-nine thousand feet, and to date approximately three-thousand climbers have successfully scaled that mountain. Yet Flight 980 came to rest a little over nineteen-thousand feet, but the U.S. government claimed that was too high to even recover the flight and voice recorders, "despite an outpouring of offers of help from mountain climbers who called the U.S. Embassy."

Since all these conflicting statements were either released by or had the official blessing of the United States embassy in La Paz, this meant that decisions were made at the highest government levels to falsify what was actually taking place. The question remained: Why?

The NTSB is the one agency that knows airplane crashes are never "unfortunate accidents." There is always a reason or reasons. Yet, with assistance from Eastern, it was now apparent that the top brass from the NTSB, and a number of other secretive United States government agencies, attempted to hoodwink a naïve and gullible public into believing that this crash was a mere fluke, with hints that it might have been caused by some otherwise-undefined pilot error.

This made me wonder if a U.S. government agency could be in a position of equal or greater responsibility than the airline. Was this a potentially serious political problem that top Eastern management was also linked to or involved with and likewise wanted covered up?

CHAPTER ELEVEN

If one uses the word "veteran" to describe a pilot, there is most likely a specific image conjured up in most peoples' minds, visualizing a self-assured, gray haired captain flying his aircraft through just about any conditions and delivering his passengers safely to their destination. Although the physical description might be appropriate, there is a great deal more to the meaning of the term. A pilot can only earn the status of a veteran when he or she has learned, either through actual hands-on experience or in-depth schooling, what to anticipate under a given set of circumstances. For example, a veteran would know, on a certain route approximately where to expect to turn the aircraft to stay on course or how to eyeball certain weather conditions and quickly determine whether it would be necessary to deviate left or right or change altitude. Therefore, the true veteran pilot is one who, through experience accumulated over the years, has become seasoned enough to know what to expect and how to respond to different situations.

But what happens to this same veteran pilot if you send him places he has never before flown, where the rules of the game are changed and he is transported back to the dark ages of aviation? Essentially, the veteran becomes a novice again. For most experienced pilots a few trips into this new environment might suffice to regain all that goes with the veteran title, while others might take a bit longer. The real danger is during the time period before the pilot reacquires the vital skills.

Eastern purchased the South American routes from a rapidly failing Braniff Airways, desperately in need of cash. The Braniff pilots were also represented by ALPA, and according to the union's merger policy, these pilots, many of whom had South American-specific route experience, should have transferred to Eastern. When Braniff acquired the routes from Pan American-Grace Airways, or PANAGRA as it was better known, those pilots transferred to Braniff. But neither top Eastern management nor the majority of Eastern ALPA MEC wanted them. Skip and I were MEC members at that time and, for two reasons, had vigorously argued to bring the South American-experienced Braniff pilots along with the routes. First, it was union policy and the morally correct thing to do. Second, they would bring the required knowhow, as flight safety was an important consideration. But greed became the overriding factor, as many on the MEC at the time viewed this acquisition, and all the promotional opportunities that would likely come with it, as a windfall for the Eastern pilots. As a result, our pleas fell upon deaf ears. ALPA National refused to force the issue, a true slap in the face to the many loyal ALPA Braniff pilots who should have been able to transfer with their seniority intact.

There are tremendous differences for a pilot when flying in South America. For example, there were language problems with controllers; outdated air traffic control procedures; poorly functioning navigation aids; and the lack of ground-based radar, to name but a few. Adding to these problems were the different Boeing 727 handling characteristics at high altitude airports like La Paz, along with unique procedures to be followed under both normal circumstances and in case of an emergency. When combined with South America's rugged topography, this spelled danger with a capital "D", as the flight safety margins were greatly reduced.

However, there were ways to eliminate, to a degree, many of these safety issues, even without the experienced Braniff pilots. The best way would be to give pilots a "hands-on" similar environment in a flight simulator in order to know what to expect. But even without this specialized training, there were other, much simpler steps that Eastern management could have taken. For example, each pilot could have been required to have a minimum number of South America cockpit jump seat observation hours before actually flying a trip, so they would have a chance to observe firsthand the differences they would be encountering. Another example: Eastern pilots were never informed that the aircraft were frequently overloaded, with no regard for flight safety limitations. But in spite of numerous requests, management refused to do anything because it all boiled down to dollars. As a result, veteran Eastern pilots like Larry Campbell became novices when flying their initial trips into South America.

The lack of any specialized training on Eastern's part got my attention. Prior to flying into South America, Eastern was required to submit their specific training requirements to FAA officials for their approval. At the time of the Flight 980 crash, Eastern's only "training" consisted of the requirement that the captain view audiovisual slides of the different airports prior to his initial flight into South America. For the La Paz airport there was the additional stipulation that, since the airport elevation was over ten-thousand feet altitude, the pilots had to don and use their oxygen masks for landing. In addition, a Check Pilot had to occupy the copilot's seat, but only for the captain's first landing, which occurred on the southbound portion of the trip. For the return Flight 980 trip, Check Pilot Captain Joseph Loseth was issued a first class seat back to Miami, meaning he was not in the cockpit. Why wasn't Loseth *required* by the airline or the FAA to be in the cockpit? That would have been a simple, no-cost requirement that would have greatly enhanced flight safety and could very well have interrupted the chain of events that culminated in this crash. Yet my inquiries into this item through the Employee Involvement Committee were stonewalled. Most Eastern pilots believed the South American "training" was useless and some had gone to the FAA and voiced their concern. But, prior to the crash, these valid fears were ignored and absolutely nothing changed.

*   *   *

I wanted to know what other airlines operating at the hazardous South American airports offered their pilots in the way of experience requirements and specialized training. Lufthansa, the German airline, has a large number of flights in and out of South America, so I wrote a letter to the Lufthansa Chief Pilot inquiring what, if any, schooling or special training requirements they had in place in South America in 1985. His immediate reply stated that Lufthansa also had audiovisual aids that all pilots flying there had to view. But in the case of La Paz, Lufthansa considered this airport so unique, so different, that they had a special group of pilots stationed in Lima, Peru who did all the flying into and out of that airport. This separate division included specialized training in the classroom, simulator and aircraft. Lufthansa also utilized a manual entitled, "Special Operation La Paz," which specifically briefed flight crews on the idiosyncrasies of that airport and its approaches. Lufthansa would not allow any other pilots fly that route, even if it meant cancelling flights. Yet the FAA sanctioned Eastern's inferior training and didn't insist on even the most meager requirement that each flight *must* have at least one pilot in the cockpit with prior South American experience. Nor did the FAA mandate using a more accurate means of navigation—Inertial Navigation System, better known as INS—on Eastern's South American flights, which at the time this was state of the art. These questions that screamed out for answers were never even addressed after the crash.

Before and after the Flight 980 crash, Richard Barbieri was Eastern's FAA Principal Operating Inspector, or POI. Each large airline has a POI who is supposedly the most knowledgeable FAA official regarding that particular airline's operations. This person is expected to oversee and ensure that the airline complies with the highest possible flight safety standards, a job that should be carried out with flight safety as the absolute top priority. I learned that despite the fact that a number of Eastern pilots had contacted and in some cases spoken with the FAA concerning safety deficiencies in Eastern's South American operations prior to the crash, these concerns had fallen upon deaf ears. One conceivable reason why the FAA failed to take action was because at the time, by law, the FAA had the dual responsibility for both promoting and overseeing civil aviation. This contradictory mandate was later changed, but not until after a later, 1996 ValuJet, [subsequently known as AirTran that ultimately merged with Southwest Airlines], crash outside Miami. As a result, in 1985, some FAA personnel might have viewed their primary role as insuring that the airline they oversaw remained prosperous. This also could explain Barbieri's inexplicable inaction before the crash; his concern for Eastern might have extended beyond air safety and into the economic arena. But the fact that the FAA allowed the continuation of the same substandard air safety requirements for some time after the crash was puzzling. Perhaps the FAA didn't want to change anything that could be taken as a tacit admission of guilt?

In the federal pecking order, the POI is not the final authority within the FAA. The POI's actions are subject to scrutiny by his superiors. If, as POI, Barbieri had approved substandard safety requirements before the crash, no one higher up at the agency would be aware of it until something happened to bring it to their attention. In this case, however, that should have been the Flight 980 crash. Following the crash, having gotten nowhere with Barbieri, some Eastern pilots went to his superiors, with the same result. Nothing was done.

One potential explanation for FAA inaction was that those up the chain of command were not willing to implicitly admit prior guilt and were trying to shield the agency from potential monetary liability. Any additional safety requirements placed on Eastern's South American operations immediately following the crash would have been tantamount to an admission that the prior safety standards were substandard. If the FAA shared in the culpability, it's also likely they would not push for a crash investigation, as they might very well be indicting themselves. As a result, Eastern was allowed to continue flying uninterrupted throughout South America without any immediate changes.

Just as was proven later, in the 1996 ValuJet Flight 592 crash and the Alaska Airlines Flight 261 disaster in 2000, many times the FAA falls short in meeting their airline oversight responsibilities. In the ValuJet crash, the FAA was cited in the subsequent NTSB investigation for not mandating smoke detection and fire suppression systems in cargo holds. In the Alaska Airlines disaster, the NTSB investigation following that crash uncovered widespread, significant aircraft maintenance deficiencies that the FAA should have uncovered earlier. Systematic problems were also identified by the NTSB in the FAA's oversight of maintenance programs at Alaska Airlines, including inadequate staffing and its approval process of maintenance interval extensions.

But in the Flight 980 case, because there was no timely or proper investigation, no conclusions concerning the FAA's oversight or lack thereof, were ever reached.

During the months following the Flight 980 crash, but before the Texas Air buyout, ALPA insisted upon and management finally instituted special South American training, including all the idiosyncrasies associated with it, along with minimum flight time requirements and simulator training for the pilot in command. However, almost immediately following Texas Air's takeover, that schooling was inexplicably terminated, with not a whimper of protest from the FAA.

Since the weather could also have been a contributing factor in the Flight 980 crash, I scrutinized Eastern's South American weather reporting and forecasting. At the time of the Flight 980 crash, the format and wording of the international weather reports was unlike that used in the States, creating some interpretation problems for Eastern flight crews. Once again, this difference could have been easily addressed through schooling.

Eastern's domestic operations also allowed the captain to get an up-to-the-minute weather briefing before departure over the telephone directly from the meteorologist on duty. But this service was not available in South America. Had up-to-date weather briefings been available to Flight 980, no doubt Campbell would have been warned from satellite pictures about the proximity of a large thunderstorm cell close to their route, and would have been cautioned not to attempt to circumnavigate it to the east, toward Mount Illimani.

The NTSB subsequently did become aware of Eastern's deficient South American weather reporting, and ultimately issued a report entitled *Meteorological Factual Report of the Accident Involving Eastern Airlines B727 near La Paz, Bolivia on January 1, 1985*, which stated, in part: "*...A reevaluation of Eastern Airlines Meteorological support for the South American operation is presently underway...*"

No further action was ever taken, other than a Texas Air decision to shut down Eastern's entire flight weather department, made approximately two years after the crash, and again, without any protest from the NTSB or FAA.

My crash scrutiny next zeroed in on other potential problems with the two separate and independent navigational devices used by Flight 980, the onboard OMEGA system and the La Paz VOR, the latter standing for Very High Frequency Omnidirectional Range.

OMEGA was a vastly inferior aircraft navigation system that Eastern utilized to save money. Eastern could have used dual, independently powered and operated Inertial Navigation Systems (INS). Most international airlines like Lufthansa did so, especially when their flights crossed over large expanses of water or other desolate areas where the navigational facilities are inferior or non-existent. But Eastern management chose not to.

Taken from the technology used in early models of intercontinental ballistic missile guidance systems, INS became available in the early 1970s for commercial use. It is a self-contained unit that works off a number of internal components, mostly gyros. Besides not relying on any outside radio signals, INS is very simple for pilots to operate. The pilot first enters the aircraft's position on the ground in latitude-longitude coordinates. From that point the INS takes over and flies the chosen route with either the pilot or the autopilot flying. From various inputs, the INS continually updates the aircraft's precise location, which is displayed in latitude and longitude coordinates.

Most airline flights do not fly directly from the departure point to the destination. Rather, they fly from one navigation fix, or waypoint, to another on various "airways of the sky," meaning a designated VOR radial or the intersection of two VOR radials, until arrival at the destination. Using these various fixes enables Air Traffic Control to constantly keep track of the aircraft's position even without ground radar, ensuring there is adequate separation between aircraft flying along the same or proximate routes.

Since INS is extremely accurate, it is better suited for this purpose, as these fixes are also displayed in latitude-longitude coordinates. Additionally, it gives the pilot other information such as the wind direction and velocity outside the plane and displays the aircraft's time to the next programmed waypoint and estimated time of arrival at the destination.

INS can also be programmed by the pilot to precisely deviate either left or right off course for a pre-selected distance, which was potentially very important in the Flight 980 case. The airways in South America are ten nautical miles wide, meaning a pilot would be able to select a course up to five miles either side off the centerline of the high altitude airway and still remain within its confines, assuring terrain clearance. If Flight 980 had been within the confines of the airway, it would not have impacted Mt. Illimani, if that was the reason for the crash. In less-developed nations like Bolivia, the maintenance of the ground-based VOR navigational facilities also often leaves much to be desired, another reason for utilizing INS.

At the time of the Flight 980 crash, Eastern's routes were confined mainly within the United States, which meant continual ground radar coverage in a tightly controlled air traffic environment. For years the airline flew to a very few remote areas. But with the sudden expansion into South America, the Eastern pilots' aviation clocks were suddenly rewound twenty years. Through the use of INS, management could have insured that this devolution would be safer, but didn't. A brief explanation of why management did not is—above and beyond the additional cost of INS sets versus OMEGA—at Eastern, like all other ALPA-represented airlines, additional hourly pay was negotiated into the pilot contract when INS was utilized. This would make up for the reductions in flight time pay caused by the shorter, more direct flight times. When INS was utilized, the Eastern contract called for three cockpit crew members to be paid additional hourly wages of $9.00, $7.00 and $6.10 respectively on top of their normal hourly rate, for a total of an additional $22.10 per hour. The Senior Flight Attendant also received an extra one-dollar-per-hour pay. The Eastern pilot contract specifically referenced INS, so the OMEGA system was chosen instead.

I couldn't understand why the FAA allowed Eastern to fly throughout South America without INS. The only requirement was for the ground-based VOR, which is like a wagon wheel with the VOR located at the center, and ADF, or Automatic Direction Finder. The VOR is a homing device that sends out a signal for each of the three-hundred and sixty compass degrees. The pilot would select which compass degree, or radial, to fly on in order to remain on the airway, and by keeping a needle centered on the instrument panel, it would show the aircraft was on course, with or without the autopilot engaged. A VOR intersection or "fix" would be where radials from two different VOR's intersect. ADF is a World War II vintage, low frequency unit navigation system, notorious for imprecision.

Rather than being viewed by the FAA as an essential flight safety tool, INS was instead relegated to contract negotiations between the pilots and management. The Eastern pilot contract did contain a stipulation that if OMEGA was utilized, the same additional INS hourly pay would apply, but only for flying done "outside of the North American Continental Area." Thus, the vastly inferior OMEGA system was used to save a grand total of $22.10 per hour, but only for the northernmost portion of the South American flights.

The Eastern pilots, however, weren't even well versed on OMEGA. The initial instructions in its use consisted of being handed a booklet, and being told to read and understand it. After some pilots raised hell, classroom OMEGA training was ultimately given approximately a year after its initial introduction. But by that time most pilots had learned to master it through trial and error.

Another major problem with OMEGA in South America was that there was no precise way to verify it for accuracy. Management had verbally agreed to install two OMEGA sets for crosscheck purposes on each of the three Boeing 727 aircraft utilized there, but this was never accomplished. Due to South American reliability problems with the ground-based VOR navigation facilities, however, pilots began to rely on OMEGA more and more as their primary or, in some cases, only means of navigating. This was an easy trap to fall into, because OMEGA gave the outward appearance of being precise, and like INS, is totally automatic, with much information available at the touch of a button. But unlike INS, OMEGA receives its input from outside sources, which were limited to a total of eight transmission sites located throughout the world. Accurate updates of exact position are susceptible to large errors due to time lag and adverse weather. With only one set on board Eastern's aircraft, in combination with what I later discovered were poorly maintained VOR facilities, there was no way for the pilot to verify whether or not the navigational information received in the cockpit was correct, including the all-important aircraft position.

The National Transportation Safety Board became aware of this problem following the flight 980 crash. Contained in the ALPA file was one NTSB report with the following statement:

. . . An Eastern Captain had previously written to management and stated that he had been very active in trying to get EAL to install another OMEGA navigation system in the "South American" B-727's.

Every other major air carrier flying in desolate places like South America using INS installs a minimum of two sets for comparison reliability and to have a back-up system in the event of a failure. Yet top Eastern management and the FAA ignored this very clear-cut safety item in favor of economic expediency.

I discussed this specific item on several occasions with now-deceased Captain Walt Brady, who was the straight-talking, no nonsense management pilot in charge of much of Eastern's South American flight operations. At the time, after requesting that our discussion be kept confidential, which I agreed to, he told me, "I forcefully argued that for safety reasons we needed dual INS sets installed on all of our South American aircraft. But the higher-ups vetoed the idea because of the additional cost. This was total bullshit because flight safety should have been the top priority and come before anything else. But the bean counters didn't want to hear it and the FAA never pushed the issue, so I couldn't force it."

After scrutinizing the ALPA documents, I also discussed a number of South American flight safety-related problems with Captain Don McClure, at the time the Eastern ALPA Air Safety Chairman who also wanted to upgrade the safety of Eastern's South American operation. He flew a trip identical to Flight 980's in September 1985, a little more than nine months after the crash, with a check pilot occupying the right seat for the entire duration.

McClure uncovered a number of critical flight safety deficiencies, which he documented. Of the many problems encountered, one was particularly ominous. McClure found that, in addition to other crucial navigational problems, the OMEGA continually steered the aircraft off course, approximately five miles to the east—in the direction of Mount Illimani.

The OMEGA's internal computer converts outside signals into latitude-longitude coordinates, so a pilot would normally first determine his exact position by cross referencing information from a VOR and then compare that to the OMEGA's latitude-longitude coordinates. In this case, the OMEGA-generated data indicated McClure's aircraft was right on course. He was not only cross-referencing his position with the La Paz VOR but, because the weather was clear, also with the physical terrain and other way-points on the en-route map. McClure could clearly see that his aircraft was not where it should have been. He continually checked, and finally narrowed the reason for the OMEGA error to incorrect latitude-longitude numbers. The numbers assigned to the airports and airway intersections on Eastern's Jeppesen maps and charts were incorrect. Thus, if a pilot believed he was in a certain position based upon the information presented on the OMEGA, he would still not be where the map indicated he was, even though he confirmed this by crosschecking the numbers. This could be fatal if it was dark or the pilot was flying in the clouds and unable to perform a visual check as McClure had done, which was most likely the situation with Flight 980.

When this problem was combined with another concerning the accuracy of the La Paz VOR at the time of the crash that I will describe, the net result was this left the Eastern pilots flying blindly with two signals from two different sources, both of which were dangerously flawed and inaccurate. The problems McClure revealed offered a plausible explanation of what *might* have caused the Flight 980 crash. Following his series of flights, McClure wrote the aforementioned report that contained all his observations and forwarded it to Eastern management. Here are relevant sections of that report. His flight took place on Upper Amber Airway 320 [UA 320] the same route Flight 980 flew. The entire report is appended.

While northwest bound on UA 320 OMEGA continually tracked to the right of course, this coincided with the off-set Southeast bound from night before. Over SUR Radio beacon VIR VOR radial read 143 DME (miles) not

147 as published on chart. Crossing AISRO intersection VOR 205 degree radial read 134 DME (miles) not 137 as charted. . . All the navigational facilities on this route are so weak and unreliable that there is no good way to cross check the OMEGA. . .

. . . The OMEGA tracks approximately 4 miles offset to the Northeast both Northwest and Southeast bound between La Paz and Asunción. This sort of inaccuracy is intolerable when flying over this terrain.

Now consider the following contradictory quote taken from yet another official NTSB Flight 980 report that I had again obtained from ALPA:

The Systems Group discussed the navigation equipment on board the 727-225 airplane, and also the navigation aids available along the route of flight. A copy of the computer generated flight plan, for use between Asuncion, Paraguay and La Paz, Bolivia was reviewed. The longitude and latitude coordinates listed for each waypoint on the flight plan were compared to the coordinates shown on the appropriate en route navigation charts. **All coordinates were in agreement.** *[Emphasis added].*

The coordinates might have been in agreement, but they were erroneous. After reading McClure's report, I scrutinized other charts utilized by different airlines flying into La Paz and found some startling discrepancies. Flight 980's flight plan had it cleared to the La Paz VOR and from there to the airport. I examined two different aviation charts and located two different sets of latitude-longitude numbers for the exact same La Paz VOR. The Eastern Jeppesen High Altitude Chart showed VOR latitude-longitude coordinates of South 1630.50/West 06813.90. But on another en-route aviation chart, the coordinates for the same VOR were South 1630.30/West 06813.54. Entering incorrect VOR coordinates meant Flight 980 could have been outside the safe confines of the airway, even though the crew believed they were on the airway centerline and could safely deviate around the bad weather reported over their route of flight.

The latitude-longitude numbers on the Jeppesen charts were provided by the Bolivian government, most likely the same one that, a year after the crash, produced an "accident report," which was anything but. By examining the same sets of different charts the NTSB could have uncovered the exact same latitude-longitude discrepancies I did, but apparently either did not or chose to ignore them. It was one of the FAA's jobs to ensure these coordinates were correct, but that was another responsibility they apparently ignored.

McClure also pointed out in his report that the DAKON intersection, which was also on Flight 980's route, was physically misplaced on the map. This intersection appeared as though it was positioned on a completely different radial from the La Paz VOR, a radial that took it directly over Mount Illimani.

Despite the gravity and immediacy of the situation, McClure's report was never acted upon. He informed me that not one person from Eastern, the FAA or the NTSB ever contacted him about his important findings and his report was nowhere to be found in the few NTSB papers that were sent to me.

But wait! Sometime after the Flight 980 crash, the latitude-longitude numbers on the Jeppesen navigational charts used by the Eastern crews were discreetly changed to reflect the accurate numbers. But McClure's information clearly shows that over nine months later, the OMEGA was still inaccurate.

Although the OMEGA should not have been used during descent below the minimum en-route altitude, many Eastern pilots did so anyway, but only if cross-checked for accuracy with a VOR. But this created yet another problem because, unknown to the Eastern pilots, there were also troubles with the La Paz VOR, meaning that neither navigation tool was precise. The La Paz VOR wasn't accurate because its installation and subsequent maintenance, as well as quality control, were poor or non-existent. And without precise VOR facilities, there was absolutely no method for the cockpit crew to reliably cross-check the precision of the OMEGA. Furthermore, the flight crew had no way of knowing that they were relying on incorrect information. When taken together, this created a potentially lethal combination and meant Flight 980 could have been

well outside the safe confines of the airway during their descent for landing at La Paz. When taken collectively, these problems meant this entire
situation was a disaster just waiting to happen.

But that still wasn't everything. Prior to the crash, there had been a fire
in the La Paz VOR that resulted in a large number of user complaints. Captain Bud Leppard, one of the ALPA accident investigators, related to me
that the Bolivians had "repaired" the navigation portion of the VOR, but
that they had used non-standard materials and never flight checked it after
turning it back on. Yet there is absolutely no mention of the fire, user complaints or the inferior Bolivian repairs in any NTSB reports.

The following is taken from that NTSB report on the Navigational
Aids at La Paz and surrounding area.

> The only known reported discrepancy with these navaids [VOR's and ADF's]
> involved the LPB [La Paz] VOR. The DME [distance measuring] function
> was notammed [notice given] out of service when the monitor system
> failed. The monitor was replaced in November 1984, but had not been
> rechecked and was still listed out of service. All other navaids were oper-
> ational with no known malfunctions or user complaints. However, the facil-
> ities do not have the same quality control exercised in the U.S. The La
> Paz VOR was installed in October, 1982, **but was never officially flight
> checked until after the accident . . . Following the accident** [Emphasis
> added] the FAA flight checked all terminal and en route navaids normally
> used by the flight, including ASU [Asuncion], LPB [La Paz], SRE [Sucre],
> and TCZ [Santa Cruz] VOR's. The results were satisfactory.

The La Paz VOR was finally flight checked for accuracy for the very
first time by the FAA three weeks *after* the crash. Of course it passed, but
according to Leppard, there was a representative of the VOR manufacturer
at the VOR site during the intervening time period, starting the day after
the crash, no doubt making any needed repairs.

Despite the foregoing, no corrective actions were ever undertaken by
Eastern following the crash and none were mandated by the FAA. The
FAA couldn't order any changes be made since they had allowed Eastern
to use the untested La Paz VOR as a primary means of navigation, in vio-

lation of their own rules. If they had done so, it would be yet another admission the agency condoned an unsafe operation.

Yet even with all these flight safety failures, Eastern could have, but did not, provide its crews with another fundamental, but important piloting tool that might have prevented the crash: en-route maps that clearly portrayed the location of the high terrain surrounding the airways. Lufthansa utilized these maps. A quick glance at them shows the pilot the exact location of the highest terrain along a specific route of flight. The ALPA Charting and Instrument Procedures Committee summed up the value of having such a map in several sentences. Pertaining to the Flight 980 crash, this report stated:

> . . . When you look at the Lufthansa charts you can see immediately what Captain Friend has been talking about. One asks, what if the Eastern Captain had charts like these? Would that have prevented the accident?

A quick glance at such a chart would have clearly shown the Flight 980 pilots that they should deviate around the storm in the opposite direction. This amounted to a lousy piece of paper. Where were the "guardians" of the flying public, the FAA? Through their silence and inaction, the FAA sanctioned all Eastern's rush-rush, cost-cutting efforts on its South American routes. Yet the NTSB didn't address any of these failures after the crash.

From what I uncovered, there was no doubt in my mind that this disaster might have been due to circumstances and problems over which the crew had no control or even knowledge. When I began my study, I originally believed that I might uncover some new information to narrow down the reasons for the Flight 980 crash. By taking the time to carefully review all the information in the ALPA file, I was able to follow a logical, step-by-step procedure. Even though I still hadn't discovered, with a hundred percent certainty, any singular item that caused the crash, I had exposed several possibilities. One thing my analysis did show was that critical information was available, yet was being withheld or ignored by the

NTSB, the same United States government agency that previously had a well-deserved reputation for never grasping at the obvious or rushing to a conclusion. Yet here, they were seemingly paralyzed, no doubt despite awareness of the same evidence I had gathered from the ALPA file. They were supposed to be the experts. But their feigned ignorance, denying my information requests, as well as leaving other areas uninvestigated, made me *very* suspicious. I could perhaps understand the reason for the cozy relationship between Eastern and the FAA; one guilty party covered for the other. But the lack of a proper investigation by the NTSB was an enigma. But then, during the Reagan administration, virtually every top appointed government job had political implications, which were placed ahead of anything else. The NTSB Chairman and Board members were political appointees filled by the president with congressional approval. The notion that higher political priorities could have prevented a proper investigation haunted me.

CHAPTER TWELVE

William Kelly was a director of the United States Peace Corps in Paraguay and one of the Flight 980 victims. On January 6th, his wife of sixteen years, Judith, received the "official" word that there were no survivors. First-time hints also began surfacing in the press, stating that victims' bodies might not be recovered and that an official investigation might never take place. An attractive and intense woman, Judith decided to undertake a trek to the crash site. She later told me, "I felt a strong need to reconnect with Bill. I believed that seeing where this happened would help make the whole nightmare more real and might also bring some closure. I could detect from the rapidly emerging doubletalk that there would not be any official investigation and this strengthened my resolve."

She undertook steps to insure she would succeed, first by reading a number of books on mountain climbing. Then, in February of 1985, she embarked upon an arduous three-month daily workout routine consisting of aerobics, nautilus machines and hiking. Her final training came in May 1985, when she participated in a grueling mountaineering course conducted on a frozen Alaskan glacier.

Prior to departing for Bolivia, she met with Jack Young, the NTSB Investigator-in-Charge of the Flight 980 crash. In her words, "Mr. Young explained to me what little he purported to know. Basically, he told me that I should forget about going, put all of this behind me and get on with my life. Perhaps you could say that to someone with a broken arm or leg, but not a broken heart. Because of their inaction, I felt that I had no choice but to go."

That one short meeting amounted to the full extent of the NTSB's "assistance." Judith departed alone for Bolivia on June 19, 1985. While in

La Paz, she gradually adapted her body to the high altitude, an important first step, while continuing her daily workout routine. She also met with Bernardo Guarachi, the guide she had hired—the mystery shrouded first person to be dispatched to the crash site. However, when Judith attempted to question him about this trek, his only cryptic response was, "I recovered nothing of value." She let that go, something she had to do because she needed his assistance. A few days later, she and Guarachi conducted a one-day practice climb to a 17,400 foot elevation. She handled this with no problems, so they next conducted a four-day climb of Huayna Potosi Mountain with a peak of 19,950 feet, higher than the crash site. This allowed him to judge how she handled an altitude and topography comparable to where the jet had come to rest. She again did well and, after a three-day break, Judith, Guarachi and his assistant departed for the Mt. Illimani ascent. They departed La Paz on July 2nd and reached the crash site on July 5th. On the climb, she continually pondered what they might find. *Would there be any bodies? Would she recognize any of Bill's personal effects?*

Upon arrival, they found wreckage strewn everywhere. Although it was freezing cold, it was also sunny. The snowfalls had just begun covering some crash components with a dusting. Judith found herself shivering, not from the cold, but from pondering what had taken place in this horrendous place. Despite standing in the midst of the plainly visible devastation, in her soft voice she read letters aloud to Bill that she had written, also reading others from friends and family. In her own words, "This small goodbye gesture and homage was very emotionally draining, but did give me a sense of closure, even though I still had no idea of what caused the crash. I hesitated, finally burying the letters in the snow. While doing this, Guarachi and his assistant photographed parts of the wreckage with my camera as they trekked around the mountainside and looked at the pieces of the carnage. It was clear that the crash represented something totally different to them than to me. I couldn't get Bill out of my mind. But they had never met him."

They completed the climb and descent in a total of five days. Upon her return to La Paz, now knowing exactly what the climb entailed and that many pieces of wreckage, including the tail section that she knew contained the flight and voice recorders, was still plainly visible and accessible, she spoke with Eastern Airlines South American personnel and United States Embassy officials, conveying her fervent hope that an expedition would be mounted.

But after the initial optimism came frustration, as it became evident that such an expedition was not going to happen. She still wanted trained investigators to conduct an on-site probe, as she believed that an investigation at the least could recover the flight and voice recorders. She was telling anyone who would listen from Eastern and the United States government, "I made it, a woman, on my own. Certainly the United States government and Eastern Airlines, with all your resources, can get up there and conduct a proper inquiry. I proved that it can be done." Whoever she spoke with seemed sympathetic, but there was never any follow-up. As a result, she flew home, clutching only still-painful memories.

Her first stop was Miami, where she headed unannounced to Eastern's corporate offices wanting to meet with Borman, hoping he would do something. "I wanted to meet with Frank Borman, implore him to have Eastern sponsor an expedition." Or perhaps after speaking with her, Borman could use his considerable clout with government officials to start an investigation. But Borman, who had previously expressed his "grave concern" for the families of the Flight 980 victims, never met with her. But after speaking with a person from Eastern's legal department, Judith ultimately left empty-handed, though still very determined despite these setbacks. If she could make it to the crash site, the NTSB clearly could. They had the authority. On the other hand, she had only the unrelenting desire to have many lingering questions answered. So she conducted yet another Washington meeting with the NTSB, but they wouldn't budge. She steadfastly refused to accept that. Her determination was fueled by the fact that there had been a number of successful excursions that she knew of. "Something brought that plane down. It didn't just drop out of the sky. I could deal with the true reason why it came down, whatever that might be. But never knowing? Well, that was different."

As a last-ditch effort, she tried to force the NTSB's hand by appearing on NBC's Today show, where she chronicled her experience for all of America. The tactic worked. The next day, ALPA accident investigators announced they would conduct an ascent to recover the recorders. But shortly thereafter, the NTSB announced it would lead an onsite investigation. There was one little known but key aspect, however, that went with the NTSB's participation: this would be their investigation and they would take complete control of every facet.

Unfortunately, this turned out to be a short-lived sigh of relief as the subsequent NTSB expedition turned out to be a catastrophe. That came through loud and clear from their after-action report. Their trek, which only came many months later, was handled so incompetently that, had they been investigating their own failure, it would have labeled as "Agency blunder, caused by failure to properly preflight." One failure was especially significant: They waited until October to send their expedition. Knowing full well that the seasons are reversed in South America meant they also had to know the wreckage would be covered with snow after the South American winter.

Judith wasn't the only American who lost a loved one in the crash. The other was the then-U.S. ambassador to Paraguay, the late Arthur Davis, whose wife, Miriam, was also killed. Following the crash, several South American newspapers reported that Flight 980 had been sabotaged for drug-related reasons, suggesting a tie-in between Gustavo Stroessner, the late son of Paraguayan President Alfredo Stroessner, and an attempt to assassinate Ambassador Davis. These newspaper stories stated that Davis was also originally booked on Flight 980 along with his wife, but had cancelled his reservation at the last minute. His wife, Miriam, however, was aboard. These accounts asserted that Davis had discovered Alfredo Stroessner was protecting his son and other narcotics traffickers and was in part utilizing United States foreign aid money for this purpose. A subsequent investigative story by Cox Newspapers alleged that Gustavo Stroessner collected huge payoffs from narcotics traffickers conducting business in Paraguay. It was reported that Davis had gone to the presidential palace to issue an ultimatum to Alfredo Stroessner: If his son did not immediately cease his actions, he would see to it that American ties and financial aid to Paraguay would be terminated. It was reported that Stroessner refused to meet with him and Davis was forced to deliver his message to an unidentified subordinate. It was further alleged that Stroessner used a loyalist who held dual Panama-Paraguay citizenship, to get needed information to sabotage Flight 980 in an attempt to kill Davis. This supporter, who had worked for Braniff before Eastern took over the routes, was alleged to have supplied to Stroessner the intelligence on which flight Davis was booked.

The possibility of sabotage had been downplayed and apparently never investigated by the NTSB, and wasn't even mentioned in any of their reports. Since the NTSB Chairman was appointed by the President, I wondered if the word "politics" now took on an added definition within the NTSB hierarchy, one that outweighed the value of human lives. Did their sacrosanct responsibility to protect lives play second fiddle to some other concern? Had this NTSB investigation first been stifled, then delayed and finally deliberately botched? With the total silence at the NTSB comparable to the absolute quiet that accompanies the many snowfalls in the bleak South American Andes Mountains, it appeared this might be so. Prior to these discoveries, I was as naïve and trusting as an innocent airline passenger. But all that quickly changed.

CHAPTER THIRTEEN

My naïveté regarding Flight 980 was caused by having witnessed the prompt and thorough NTSB investigations of other airline disasters when the only goal was to discover the cause or causes. A good example was the 1972 crash of Eastern Flight 401, a Lockheed L-1011 jumbo jet, into the Florida Everglades. All three cockpit crew members ultimately perished, along with a number of other crew members and passengers. That NTSB investigation came to the startling conclusion that a malfunctioning fifty-cent landing gear lightbulb had distracted the flight crew from their duties. During the late night landing in Miami, one of the pilots had disconnected the autopilot altitude-hold function by inadvertently banging his knee against the control column while attempting to figure out what was wrong with the landing gear. While the pilots were distracted in trying to resolve the gear problem, the jumbo jet began a slow, imperceptible descent and impacted the murky Florida Everglades. After the NTSB findings were issued, the FAA mandated the installation of an autopilot disconnect and altitude warning device to alert the crew, via a flashing red light located on the instrument panel, whenever the autopilot was disengaged, and another warning light whenever the aircraft deviated from its assigned altitude. Although the cost was significant, these became required equipment on all jetliners. This NTSB investigation and subsequent corrective actions are prime examples of how the system is supposed to work. But here, in spite of the NTSB's self-proclaimed inability to reach the Flight 980 crash site, three other groups were able to do so with relative ease.

From an investigative standpoint, due to its timeliness, Guarachi's first mystery-shrouded trek was the most important, yet there are no reports,

official or otherwise, published debriefings on any findings, or even who
sent him. This was unprecedented in the annals of airline crashes.

The first reported expedition was a private trek financed by Ramon
Valdes, a veteran Eastern Airlines pilot. Valdes, a tall, soft-spoken, independently wealthy Eastern pilot originally from Puerto Rico was hired by
Eastern in 1967. At the time of the crash, he was a 727 Second Officer
who was flying the South American trips.

Valdes' interest in the crash was twofold. Foremost was empathy for
the families of the flight attendants who were killed in the crash, as he had
flown with and knew them well. The second was most likely because Valdes
was supposed to fly that trip, but had bid off to be home with his family
over the New Year's holiday. Although he never admitted this, it was
undoubtedly upsetting to look at a crash and realize that, but for a twist
of fate, he could have been one of the victims.

I subsequently learned that Valdes was also deeply concerned about
lapses in South American flight safety. Following the Flight 980 crash he
initially believed management would take a hard look at the circumstances
surrounding the crash and institute vital safety-related changes that he
knew from firsthand experience were needed.

Valdes was also concerned with the NTSB's statements that seemed
to imply an investigation would take place. But when nothing happened,
he spoke with Eastern pilot flight management personnel, and as an experienced South American pilot, outlined the flight safety improvements he
believed were needed. After being assured his concerns would be promptly
addressed, he waited over a month, but nothing changed. Assuming that
perhaps he would be better off putting his suggestions in writing, he composed a letter and mailed copies to Borman, the late Captain Bob Shipner, at the time Eastern's system chief pilot, and Captain Frank Causey,
the Miami base chief pilot. Valdes believed that management would ultimately act and make the needed flight safety improvements. But no one
ever contacted him. In the interim, he continued to fly South American
trips, hoping nothing would occur on one of his flights or that he would
wake up one morning to discover yet another Eastern plane had gone
down.

Although no former Braniff pilots were brought over with the South American routes, the flight attendants were a different story. Many were foreign nationals from different South American countries where the job of flight attendant is a respected position and lifetime career. Apparently, Eastern management didn't want political problems with any South American governments, so unlike the pilots, who were American citizens, the flight attendants came to Eastern along with the routes. Many were considered older by American standards and had husbands or wives and children. Following the Flight 980 crash, members of the deceased flight attendants' families contacted Valdes and expressed disappointment that no investigation was underway. Like Judith Kelly, they were also concerned that no attempt was being made to even recover the flight data and voice recorders. As a result, some decided to attempt to reach the crash site themselves and try to discover what took the lives of their loved ones. Valdes had concerns about their safety, and had correctly interpreted the conflicting NTSB signals as an attempt to simply buy time and ultimately justify a decision to abandon any pretenses of an investigation. Because of familiarity with the weather and the unforgiving terrain, he knew the wreckage would eventually become covered with snow. Since the South American winter officially commences in June, timeliness would be a major factor in recovering bodies or finding the recorders. So when the Bolivian decision not to investigate was made public and the NTSB failed to comment, Valdes became skeptical.

"How can the richest, most powerful nation in the world state that they didn't have the resources or personnel to reach the crash site? Or the weather was too bad? Or they couldn't use the Blackhawk helicopter because the Bolivians wouldn't allow it? These lame excuses made no sense to me," Valdes told me after I learned of his expedition. "If they felt that way, why did they drag things out so long? Were they trying to hide something?"

Valdes knew that the flight and voice recorders might be scattered and difficult to locate. Nonetheless, he flew to Bolivia and, having the advantage of speaking the native tongue plus being familiar with the terrain from having flown over it, hired a mountain climbing team headed by Ronnie

Ibata, a native mountain climber and engineer. Ibata's team departed La Paz on March 15, 1985, two and a half months after the crash, and reached the crash site a mere two days later.

Although no members of this team were aircraft accident investigators, they hunted for the flight and voice recorders, which are brightly colored and emit a pinging sound for approximately a month, but reported to Valdes that they were unable to locate either. Following Valdes' instructions, they took a number of still photos that were later incorporated into a video. They also collected a few parts of wreckage and some personal belongings, and placed a small cross at the site. Valdes assumed, albeit incorrectly, that the NTSB would want the pieces of the wreckage in order to perform chemical tests to test for explosive residue, especially since some South American newspapers had reported the plane was sabotaged. But even though the NTSB learned of his expedition and findings, no one ever contacted him to request the fragments.

Ibata also reported that he was unable to find or identify any bodies or body parts, which was very strange. He also stated there was no evidence of fire. The latter didn't come as a surprise because there was insufficient oxygen at such a high altitude to support a fire. There was also a very strong smell of jet fuel everywhere. Most importantly, Ibata confirmed that the ascent was not difficult for trained individuals, provided all aspects were properly planned out, calling into question one of the NTSB's primary excuses for allegedly not being able to get to the site.

When word got out about this trek and who financed it, Valdes was summoned for a personal meeting with Borman and Eastern's Vice President of Legal Affairs, attorney Richard Magurno. Valdes was hoping that perhaps, after this discussion, Eastern would institute some of his suggested flight safety changes or sponsor an expedition. But he was disappointed, and he described the atmosphere in Borman's office as, "cordial and cool, at best." This surprised him because, for all Borman knew, the information he had might shed some light on what happened.

He briefed Borman and Magurno, emphasizing that Ibata felt it would be easy to dispatch a search team comprised of trained accident investigators. When asked why he had financed this venture, Valdes informed them there were two purposes. The first was he hoped to recover the recorders and the second was to photograph the carnage. Per his instructions to Ibata, Valdes made it clear that if an expeditious search for the recorders was unsuccessful, he didn't want to waste precious time and effort in a futile pursuit. Valdes thought it would be more important to take photos of as much of the wreckage as possible, hoping the trained eyes of the accident investigators from the NTSB could hone in on exactly where to look for the recorders. An expedition might then be mounted with that specific goal in mind. To hammer this point home further, Valdes repeated that Ibata believed that a search team comprised of professional aircraft accident investigators had better than a ninety-five percent chance of successfully recovering the recorders. But due to the changing weather, Valdes knew that each passing day diminished those favorable odds, so he put a question to Borman. "Can you put pressure on the Bolivians or the NTSB to conduct a full-scale probe?"

Borman didn't respond, so Valdes stated his concerns about the do-nothing approach of the Bolivian Ministry of Aeronautics, the NTSB and also Eastern. He also raised Eastern's lack of response over the flight safety items he had presented.

At this juncture, Valdes became wary because Borman and Magurno seemed more concerned about whether his climbers had recovered the flight data and voice recorders than anything else. Valdes purposely dodged any more questions concerning the recorders, but did raise another point, explaining that he had narrated a video created from the photos and wanted to set up a special "Flight 980 Fund" to provide money for the families of the deceased flight attendants. He knew that Eastern had sent only ten-thousand dollars to each family and that they were informed this was the final amount. Since there were nine children involved, this amounted to a drop in the bucket. He wanted to raise funds by showing the crash site video to Eastern employees and then solicit donations on a voluntary basis. This would be accomplished in a low profile, tasteful manner and wouldn't be construed in any way as being sanctioned by or connected to Eastern. All the money collected would then be placed into the special fund to be divided equally among the victims' children. Valdes had already

discussed establishing an account for this purpose with the head of the
Eastern Credit Union, Art Russo, who had enthusiastically endorsed the
idea. In response, Borman mentioned that might be a good thing, but
countered with a question. "If the family members were taken care of
financially, what would you do with your video?"

Valdes replied that, under those circumstances, there would be no reason to show it. Magurno requested a copy of the video for personal view-
ing and agreed to immediately return it when finished. Valdes supplied
him with a copy and went on to state that because there was no official
investigation, some of the relatives still wanted to climb to the crash site
to try to discover what happened. He suggested that someone should go
to South America to try to talk them out of it before they made this
attempt. Magurno replied that Eastern certainly didn't need any bad publicity, as would happen if additional people were killed or injured. Borman agreed and suggested Valdes should be the one to try to stop them.
Magurno also hinted that Eastern still might sponsor an expedition and
that perhaps Valdes could relate this to the relatives when he spoke with
them.

"As our discussion drew to a close," Valdes told me, "it was clear that
despite public statements to the contrary, there was no genuine compas-
sion on either man's part. They seemingly didn't want to discover what happened or enact any flight safety changes. They were trying to hoodwink
me into believing they wanted to see the truth uncovered, but I believed
this meeting was carefully orchestrated only to deceive. All they cared
about was how any publicity over the Flight 980 crash, or my fund, could
be kept to a minimum. I suspected that this was not for any altruistic reasons, but rather to keep anything having to do with the Flight 980 out of
the public limelight. I came away feeling like they were trying to paint me
as some kind of bad guy. I had believed, perhaps naïvely, they would want
to know what caused the crash, but they just waltzed me around. I had
no idea what they were up to, but one thing that was for certain, I didn't
trust either. I felt as though they were trying to hide something, but
didn't know what."

As requested, Valdes subsequently flew to South America and spoke with a number of family members, but didn't mention a word about any official expedition because he didn't want to raise false hopes. But he did explain the real risks and family members later decided not to make the attempt. He was truly shocked when shortly after his meeting Eastern increased each family's payment from $10,000 to $500,000. Valdes now had no reason to show his video. But the important flight safety-related items remained, for the time being, unaddressed.

Valdes subsequently learned that Magurno had copied his video and sent it to the NTSB, going so far as to suggest Valdes be prosecuted for interfering with an official government investigation—except no inquiry was underway. After hearing of the Magurno letter, Valdes wondered what was truly taking place. He came to the conclusion that it was beyond his capabilities to find out and hired a private investigator. But this effort was unproductive as Magurno determined someone was investigating him and that Valdes had hired the person. Valdes became a top management target, and although he had no way of knowing it, he wasn't alone in this regard.

After speaking with Valdes and other knowledgeable individuals, and after scrutinizing hundreds of pages of the ALPA crash documents and finalizing my timeline leading to the sale of Eastern to Texas Air, I came to a startling conclusion. The demise of the once-great Eastern Airlines, "the second largest airline in the free world," as their advertisement once proudly proclaimed, was directly related to what happened to Flight 980. The illicit dealings of powerful people had to be concealed at all costs, and the *only* way to safeguard them was to sacrifice the airline. It was but a relatively short time later when advertisements with catchy slogans like "Eastern, Number One to the Sun," were replaced by newspaper headlines that screamed out daily about its dismemberment and destruction. The "Wings of Man" were crashing, destroyed by the secretive actions of a number of people directly tied to the mysteries surrounding the crash of Flight 980.

Federal government oversight agencies also failed to do their jobs. Each separate entity, namely the FAA and the NTSB, as well as the most powerful people in the Executive Branch of the United States government, had motivation for wanting to make certain there was no Flight 980 trail that could lead to them. The truly sad part is that they were successful.

My quest for the truth about what happened to Flight 980 had turned into not only an account of an airliner crash, but also an exposé of raw and unbridled power, about how a system of checks and balances supposedly built to insure that no one got away with the type of transgressions that occurred with the Flight 980 crash, failed. But when unlawful undertakings engulf powerful, high-ranking individuals in government and industry, when they stand to lose everything they consider important, terrible things can and do happen.

CHAPTER FOURTEEN

The global International Civil Aviation Organization (ICAO) rules govern worldwide airline accident investigations. Although Flight 980 crashed outside the United States, the NTSB had the right to participate in or mount an investigation since a U.S. airliner had crashed and especially since there was no official inquiry of substance in the country where the crash occurred. Even though the formal NTSB line might have been that they didn't do anything because of difficulty getting to the site, or the Bolivians wouldn't let them, these feeble excuses did not hold up under further scrutiny. While ICAO Annex 13 are recommended practices, the NTSB had no reason to cower to any demands made by the Bolivians that they not investigate, particularly when there were so many potential extenuating circumstances, including suspected sabotage that cost American citizens' lives. These were manufactured reasons on the part of the NTSB hierarchy to conceal what was no doubt spoken behind closed doors. Furthermore, if as claimed, Bolivian opposition was the reason, then why was it okay to attempt to investigate ten months after the crash, but not immediately following it?

Gregory Feith was the NTSB investigator who headed the October 1985, NTSB expedition that was ultimately dispatched to the crash site as a result of the pressure applied by Judith Kelly's television appearance. Captain Mark Gerber, a now-retired captain with US Airways, and his brother, Allen, represented ALPA. The other participants were Al Errington and Jim Baker from Boeing, the plane's manufacturer. Royce Fitche went as a representative of the U.S. Embassy in La Paz. (As an aside, I found it particularly interesting that someone from the U.S. embassy would participate.) Bernardo Guarachi and Rene Quinsanilla were the guides.

Conspicuous by their absence was someone representing Eastern or the Bolivian government. Eastern's absence was especially puzzling, since any findings detrimental to the airline could put them at considerable monetary jeopardy.

The following comprises the core material found in Feith's official report submitted to the NTSB in November of 1985, a short time after the unsuccessful NTSB trek took place. The complete text of his report appears at the end of the book.

We began the climb on Tuesday, October 8, at 0800. The first leg of the climb was done on shale rock and snow that had a vertical slope of 10 to 35 degrees. We ascended 3300 feet to our first base camp located at the 17,800 foot level, arriving at approximately 1600. When we arrived at the camp, we were surprised to find none of our equipment that the Red Cross and porters had carried up the mountain for us. After some discussions between Royce Fitche and Renee Quinsanilla via two-way radio, we learned that the equipment had been moved up to our second base camp at 19,500 because it was thought by Renee that we were capable of a 5000-foot ascent the first day. During this portion of the climb, Jim Baker had developed a severe cough which was to be a result of the very dry air. Renee was requested by Royce to bring tents and cooking supplies down to our camp because we were not able to continue the ascent. After approximately 2 hours of waiting, several Red Cross people arrived with two tents but no stoves or fuel. Because of darkness, it was not possible to retrieve any further equipment and with the equipment we had available we were able to melt enough snow to make one pot of cold noodle soup that allowed each of us one cup. The two tents that had been brought down were two-man tents, there were seven men. Al Errington, Jim Baker, and Bernardo Guarachi agreed to bivouac which allowed myself, Allan and Mark Gerber, and Royce Fitche to share the tents. At about 0130, Jim woke us and told us that Al Errington had developed signs of pulmonary edema [editor's note: Pulmonary edema is fluid accumulation in the lungs] and that he was on oxygen. Jim said that he would monitor Al and if his condition became worse they would attempt to return to the low base camp that night. As it turned out, Al held his own through the night and at 0630 Jim and Al left the team and returned to the base camp.

The remaining team members, with the aid of several porters to carry our equipment, completed the second leg of the climb to our base camp at 19,500 feet. This portion was done on a snow slope that ranged from 25 degrees to 45 degrees. During this portion of the climb, we encountered only one problem. Royce had a crampon (spikes used for walking on ice) come off which caused him to lose his balance and fall over the side of the hill that we were climbing. We retrieved Royce, fixed his crampon and continued the climb, arriving at the base camp shortly after noon. The decision was made to remain at this base camp the remainder of Wednesday and Thursday so that the team could be well rested and fed before the final leg of the climb which would be the most difficult. In addition, we also used the extra day to allow some of our equipment that would be needed at the accident site to be brought up from the low base camp.

We began the final leg of the ascent on Friday morning at 0915. This part of the climb was done on a snow and ice slope ranging from 20 degrees to 60 degrees vertical. We encountered extremes in weather conditions, i.e., starting with a bright sunny day and warm surface temperatures, changing then to overcast, cold, blizzard conditions, then back to warm temperatures. The weather was constantly changing. We had two slight problems during this ascent, first, Royce fell into a crevasse while attempting to cross an ice bridge over it; second, I had a crampon come off while walking along an ice ledge which eventually collapsed due to the weight of me and my back pack. I had to leave my pack behind so as to complete that portion of the climb. We reached the accident site base camp at 1730, 8.5 hours after starting. During this portion of the climb, Mark Gerber began showing signs of pulmonary edema. His condition deteriorated during the evening and he was sick throughout the night. Saturday morning Mark's condition had deteriorated to the point that his balance and equilibrium was significantly effected [sic] and his thought process and speech was slow and inconsistent.

At approximately 0800, we began the process of locating and digging up wreckage in an effort to locate the cockpit voice recorder and flight data recorder. The aircraft wreckage was covered by snow ranging in depth from 5 to 12 feet. We used light weight aluminum grain shovels to move the snow.

The following portions of the aircraft were located and uncovered for examination:

1. An eight foot by five foot section of the left forward upper fuselage skin and window frame. The fuselage skin had a part of Eastern's logo painted on it. This part of the aircraft was buried to a depth of approximately five feet.

2. The vertical stabilizer with the upper and lower rudder, the "bullet" and a portion of the left horizontal stabilator was uncovered. A hole of approximately ten feet had been dug to reveal the lower portion of the vertical stabilizer. No. 2 engine compartment components were located as well as passenger cabin, galley and lavatory items. Various paperwork from the cockpit was also found in this hole. No evidence of the CVR or FDR was found.

3. Small incidental pieces of wreckage were found in a crevasse that runs through the wreckage path. I identified a deflated life vest, a part of a seat back, electrical wiring, and plastic pieces that looked like the overhead storage bin in the passenger cabin. I recovered a set of shoulder harness that was attached to a cockpit flight crew seat. The metal buckles had what appeared to be blood stains on them.

4. A section of the fuselage that I identified as the aft stair area where the FDR and CVR would be mounted. This section measured approximately four feet by five feet and was covered by approximately seven feet of snow. Again, no evidence of FDR or CVR.

5. In an area adjacent to the fuselage section described in No. 4, a portion of the fuselage was found that measured approximately ten feet long and five feet wide and covered by seven to eight feet of snow. A portion of this fuselage section was uncovered and several lizard skins that were being carried on the aircraft were found frozen to the metal. This section of fuselage appeared to be a portion of lower fuselage skin possibly near a cargo door.

6. There were numerous minute and indescribable pieces of aircraft wreckage uncovered, none of which could be readily identified or used to find the FDR or CVR.

   At 18:30, the digging efforts were terminated because of adverse weather and darkness. In addition, I discussed with Royce Fitche the health of the team members and because of my concern for Mark Gerber's, as well as Royce's poor physical condition, I decided to terminate the on-scene investigation and begin the descent as soon as possible.

Even though Feith's report was an official NTSB document, for reasons unknown, I was unable to secure it from the NTSB until approximately three months after it was written. But even at that late date, only a censored version was sent, possibly because it contained a number of criticisms of the agency, which he as the leader noted. For example, he cited having only three days notice before the departure date and a lack of money with which to purchase supplies.

Let's take a look at some of these questionable items.

Feith obtained a grand total of six hundred dollars from the NTSB. Six hundred bucks for a passenger jet crash investigation, with twenty-nine fatalities, from the wealthiest nation on the face of the earth! A properly planned and managed investigation of this magnitude would probably cost millions of dollars. But then, this investigation was not only never properly planned, but also unwanted from the NTSB's perspective. Feith claimed in his official report that it was because he was only given three days prior notice that the six-hundred dollars was the maximum under the NTSB's regulations for that short period of time. I believe that those at the head of the NTSB had purposely given him such short notice so they could scrimp on the money, assuring the expedition's failure. I do not believe, for one second, that the head of the NTSB, Jim Burnett, didn't know until three days prior when the expedition would be sent. Put another way, they created their own reason for severely limiting the amount of money and resources Feith was able to secure. Furthermore, the NTSB's decision to go was made in July, but wasn't undertaken until October. So how could there be such short notice with a timeframe that spanned over three months? Compare this six-hundred dollar figure to what the United States government spent on the aforementioned TWA Flight 800 crash investigation; over $20 million. And that was spent in the first four months alone!

Or consider the case of the Air France Flight 447, the Airbus 330 en route from Rio de Janeiro to Paris that crashed into the South Atlantic on June 1, 2009. The French government, Air France and Airbus, the plane's manufacturer, with assistance from the United States' Cape Cod–based Woods Hole Oceanographic Institution, spent almost two years and a combined total of over $25 million, with a commitment of another

$12 million, in an ultimately successful attempt just to recover the flight data and voice recorders. In that case, an unmanned submarine recovered the recorders from cavernous and rugged underwater mountains in depths of over twelve thousand feet.

An even more recent example involves the crash of Malaysian Airlines Flight 370, the Boeing 777 that crashed in March 2014, with only three American citizens on board. In that case, the United States government, along with the governments of China, Australia and Vietnam spent an estimated $44 million in the first month alone, searching for the flight data and voice recorders. If one included all of the countries involved, that figure would be much higher. That is the type of commitment the NTSB *should* have had in Eastern Flight 980 case.

But that wasn't all. Allen Gerber, one of the ALPA participants in the trek, informed me that in addition to utilizing their own gear, he and his brother, Mark, were both told they had to bring their own food for the climb! They were supposed to be reimbursed that cost, but never were.

There were additional serious problems with other resources. High up on Mount Illimani, vital equipment was left in the wrong locations. There was no water or enough tents to provide shelter for the entire investigative team.

I asked Judith Kelly to compare her preparation and training with Feith's description in his official report. After reading it, she told me, "I spent weeks training in preparation for my trek and enough time in La Paz for my body to get acclimated to the high altitude. But there was no mention of any prior training or high altitude acclimation for the participants for the NTSB's trip. It was so poorly planned and coordinated that it had to end in failure. This is so apparent that I still wonder if that was done purposely."

Although this NTSB expedition was the first time anyone representing a United States government agency had *officially* viewed the carnage, a confidential, transcribed debriefing I that obtained of this NTSB group's interview after it returned refers to other, unnamed individuals who had previously gone to the crash site. Once again, I secured this document from ALPA, and not one person from the NTSB even informed me of its existence. This paper indicates that someone from the United States State Department may have secretly visited the site prior to the Feith's NTSB expedition. Although no exact location of this meeting was provided in the report, I believe this debriefing took place at the United States embassy in La Paz and was held on October 15th. This would coincide with the time-frame shortly after the members of the NTSB's trek had returned. As best I could tell, there were twelve people present, plus the recording secretary. Greg Feith represented the NTSB, Al Errington and Jim Baker represented Boeing, Barry Trotter, Felix Forestieri, Augusto de la Torre and Rene Osorio represented Eastern. Mark and Allen Gerber and Eastern Captain Don McClure represented ALPA, while Steve Seche and Royce Fitche represented the United States State Department. The following comments from an unidentified speaker are contained on page 42 of this document.

> "The real planning season here is May through August. That's the uh, you can jump in before then, obviously people did. But you hit pretty deep snow. And when I climbed in April it was up to our knees a good portion of the way. This was very good snow. So that wasn't the problem."

According to the list of those present, all were either American citizens or Eastern Representatives. Interestingly, no one from the NTSB, Boeing, ALPA or Eastern was identified in any other accounts as ever having visited the site prior. But this statement confirms that *someone* from this group went there preceding the NTSB expedition. Who was that person or persons? Why did they go, and why was this mission secretive and any findings unreported? What was the specific objective? What, if anything, was uncovered? These are but a few of the questions that remain unanswered to this day.

I also discussed this with Judith Kelly, who was of the opinion that Fitche, the U.S. Consul General at La Paz, was the unidentified person. Fitche had admitted to her that he attempted to climb Illimani during the month of April, but claimed he was unable to reach the crash location. It was bizarre that Fitche would even attempt the climb, especially when the NTSB had claimed for months that any expedition, even a properly planned one, wasn't possible. Then, in the words, "... *it was up to our knees a good portion of the way.*" The use of the words "our knees" indicates there was more than one person. Just who the hell were these people?

Just like the expedition made by local guides that was given mere passing mention in the Bolivian report, this furtive trek also mysteriously vanished into oblivion, forever. But unlike the trek undertaken by Bolivian guides, at least one United States government official apparently embarked on this one. So, that raises yet other questions: Did anyone make it to the crash site? Did they find anything? The comment, *"This was very good snow,"* indicates that someone must have. Why was this secretive expedition also shrouded in mystery?

I conversed about the failed October NTSB expedition over the telephone separately with Mark and Allen Gerber, unbiased ALPA climb participants. My first conversation with these gentlemen took place shortly after their return, and again just before completing this book. Their most recent observations can be found in the epilogue.

In October of 1985, Mark Gerber was a Pacific Southwest Airlines pilot. When we initially spoke, he made it clear that he was a pilot and mountain climber, not a trained aircraft accident investigator. His area of expertise was mountain climbing and that was how and why he became involved. He learned of the planned trek after reading an article in *Aviation Week* magazine that stated an ALPA attempt to recover the recorders would be undertaken. Being an ALPA-represented pilot, after reading this, Gerber contacted the main Washington, D.C., ALPA office and informed them he and his brother were climbers. After a lengthy discussion on the many potential obstacles, the Gerber brothers volunteered their services. Mark also commented that, although he didn't know how or understand why, "heavy politics" came into play. He picked up this impression during discussions with the NTSB people and the other participants. The fact that this NTSB expedition hadn't been a voluntary one was yet another mystery to him. He related, "We held one meeting at the NTSB office in Washington and during this meeting it was made abundantly clear that they didn't want to do anything, but were forced to do something by Judith Kelly's television appearance." He also couldn't comprehend why they had conducted the expedition, in his words, "on the cheap." As experienced climbers, the Gerber brothers knew the best way to lower the risk of high altitude edema was to spend a minimum of two weeks at the La Paz high altitudes, which range from 9,840 to 13,450 feet above sea level, getting their bodies adjusted. Judith Kelly had done this. This acclimation decreases the severity of the symptoms should a climber nonetheless contract pulmonary edema. However, they were given less than a week to complete the entire climb and descent, even though in Mark's words, "the risks were greatly increased and that with that short time period someone would be injured." This is even more perplexing considering that time was obviously not a critical factor after waiting over ten months to embark on the expedition. What would an additional week to insure everyone's safety have meant? Mark Gerber told me, "Here it was ten months later, and once I saw the amount of hard-packed snow atop the wreckage, I strongly suspected we would never find the recorders. If the investigation had taken place sooner, before the snowfalls, it would have been relatively easy to get to them."

Gerber questioned Feith about the time aspect, but Feith stated that he had no input whatsoever over the date, and that his superiors never informed him why they waited so long, even though he had asked. I believe that Greg Feith had no knowledge of what was taking place during the secret closed-door meetings held at the NTSB's headquarters, then located on Independence Avenue in Washington, D.C.

United States embassy official Royce Fitche's presence was also puzzling, and Mark stated he found the Bolivian and Eastern officials' conduct equally baffling. For example, prior to arriving in Bolivia, all the members of the team agreed that it would be best to conduct the ascent "expedition style"—that is, scaling the mountain as a mountain climber would, meaning carrying all the needed food, water, shelter and equipment with them. But upon their arrival, the Bolivian government inexplicably interfered and wouldn't allow this. Without any protest from the NTSB, they were instead forced to climb under the auspices of the Bolivian Red Cross personnel, who were supposed to supply all needed services and equipment. But the Bolivian Red Cross botched everything. They had no food or water and insufficient shelter for the ascent because these essential items were placed in the wrong locations by the Bolivian porters. When they attempted to bring this to their attention, they got nowhere because none spoke English. Yet these basic components were crucial to the successful and safe completion of the ascent. In fact, many unforeseen and unplanned-for difficulties arose as a result of not having the needed, vital equipment. Eastern was also supposed to supply shovels for digging and fuel for cooking at the campsites, but these were also placed in the wrong areas. The collective result was rather than devoting their efforts to successful completion of the mission, they had to instead cope with doing without the necessary but mundane, everyday items, like water, that they had taken for granted would be there. Can you imagine having no shelter or not eating or drinking anything for an extended period, at altitudes over nineteen thousand feet? This is exactly what happened. These deliberate blunders also contributed to edema, and collectively doomed the operation.

Despite these problems, to their credit, the team did ultimately make it to the crash location. I asked if he saw any human remains. Mark Gerber replied that there were no bodies or body parts, not even any blood, other than some material on a cockpit shoulder harness that could have been blood. He added, "This was very mysterious."

From his many conversations with the others, and from the problems they encountered, he stated, "No one, not Eastern, the NTSB nor the Bolivians wanted any investigation. Even though we finally went, various parties made a mess out of it, making certain it would fail."

I also queried Mark Gerber on why he thought Judith Kelly undertook the climb. His response surprised me. "She wanted to collect more than the $75,000 insurance money, and also felt guilty because she and her husband were in divorce proceedings," he stated. Mark didn't know I had already met and spoken with Judith and, to the best of my knowledge, neither of those statements was correct. If Judith was getting divorced, why would she risk life and limb to mount an expedition? In turn, that led me to believe the divorce story was concocted, similar to the ones about Campbell's piloting abilities. I asked Mark Gerber when and where he had heard this. "It came from someone in the NTSB, but I'm not certain from whom," he replied. It was clear that the NTSB was attempting to taint the credibility of the person who had forced them to do their job.

He also corroborated the report of the U. S. military's offer of a high altitude "Blackhawk" helicopter. He was told that the U.S. Army offered it in the days immediately following the crash, but the Bolivians wouldn't allow it and United States officials didn't insist. Gerber couldn't understand that, given that some of the crash victims, including the cockpit crew, were American citizens. Just prior to the conclusion of our conversation he repeated, "There were *heavy* politics involved in this, although I don't know for what reason or reasons. Perhaps it had to do with Mrs. Davis or smuggling of some type? I don't know for certain. But aside from Judith Kelly and ALPA, it was apparent no one else wanted an investigation."

The lack of high altitude acclimation caused Mark Gerber to become ill with pulmonary edema. I asked him to summarize the entire expedition. Without the slightest hesitation he replied, "It was a three-ring circus."

He had correctly interpreted many of the otherwise inexplicable circumstances surrounding the expedition as meaning something was seriously awry. These insights proved invaluable, as they reinforced many of the same thoughts I had concerning the motivation and conduct of the NTSB, Eastern and the Bolivians.

There is no doubt that the responsibility for this failed mission sat squarely on the shoulders of the NTSB. This fact was confirmed by additional comments contained in the transcribed debriefing of all the trek participants on October 15th that I had secured from ALPA. Here are some of Greg Feith's comments contained therein.

"It was one of those trips where I still haven't really figured out why we were up there this late in the game. Um, I was brought into the picture very late, um, I was selectively volunteered for this mission because I'm from Denver, Colorado, a mountainous area, and I've done some mountain climbing on accidents that they have had out there in the high altitudes so I was probably the best candidate for the least effective high

altitude work. Um, it was eight months after this airplane crash that we
were going up there [note: the actual time was over ten months after
the crash] in ten feet of snow and it's very hard to go through, I mean
when this picture was taken there was only, you know, a few feet of snow
on top of the wreckage and we probably would have stood a better chance
of finding those black boxes in January or March or possibly even in May
than in October."

Feith's remarks showed the NTSB was withholding all information
that conflicted with their official time line. Had they released the contents
of this debriefing tape, it would have proven that many of the public reasons they gave for this expedition's failure were outright lies. Other comments confirmed this: *"For a trip of this magnitude it could have used a lot
more planning . . ." "We were basically all given three days notice . . ." ". . .
there was no lead time." ". . . the trip would have been more successful had we
had more lead time."*

The illogical, foolish and unscientific timing of an expedition after the
harsh winter, along with faulty or nonexistent planning, were the main reasons this expedition failed. And the NTSB was singularly responsible for
these calculated blunders. Of course, none of these facts were carried in any
of the formal press releases following the expedition. The official news bul-
letins simply stated that an attempt was made, but that it had fallen short.
Clearly, the federal government's spin-doctors were hard at work.

This transcript also contained a number of other statements that were
highly critical of the manner in which the expedition was handled. And
these comments laid the blame squarely at the feet of the NTSB hierarchy,
meaning then-Chairman Jim Burnett, for the many problems.

I next turned my attention back to Feith's official NTSB report. The
copy the NTSB sent me had many blacked-out sections that were redacted
by NTSB officials because in their words they represented, *". . . the personal views of the investigator"* and *"his conclusions and recommendations to
the Safety Board with respect to the conduct of high altitude accident investigations under hazardous conditions."*

I wondered what possibly could be the differences between Feith's personal views and any other "official views." Why wouldn't they be released to the general public? Lacking participation in the expedition by any other NTSB representative, Feith's opinions would represent the NTSB's only ones, and no one else would be in a position to either agree or disagree. Why were Feith's opinions viewed as unfit for the public's eyes? Who deleted them? Even more important, why? In fact, the second part of the NTSB's deletion statement contradicts the very reason for their existence. The NTSB was fully aware of Eastern's daily flights over the same routes, so this should have been important knowledge to impart to an ALPA pilot representative whose pilots were doing this flying. Therefore, I once again composed a letter to the NTSB in my official ALPA capacity and requested the deleted portions. I made my request, if necessary, under the Freedom of Information Act (FOIA). The NTSB nonetheless still denied me the information and once again invited me to go to court. I am certain that this denial was premeditated.

This gut feeling was confirmed by the contents of another note contained in the ALPA file. This memorandum contained a handwritten note entitled, *"1/6/85 Organizational Meeting."* Included in this document was the statement:

Status: All NTSB reports will be written as internal memos to protect from FOIA *[Freedom of Information Act]* and Bolivian government embarrassment.

The date on this document confirmed that a mere six days after the crash, the NTSB was already scheming to willfully withhold information through the use of internal memos, which under applicable law are exempt from FOIA requests. I wondered if the ALPA investigators were suspicious about this, so I queried Captain Bud Leppard, a pilot constituent and ALPA accident investigator involved with the Flight 980 crash. He replied that he was also concerned and was simply told by the NTSB bureaucrats that the official reason was, as stated, to preclude Bolivian government embarrassment, as information secured under FOIA could be prematurely leaked to the media before any official Bolivian crash report was issued.

This *might* have seemed plausible at the outset, but my request was made well after the Bolivians had issued their useless report, meaning there could be no "premature release of information." Nonetheless, the NTSB continued to withhold important details and facts.

There are a number of ways to insure the failure of an investigation like this one. From the contents of the aforementioned debriefing tape, it's clearly shown that a concerted effort was being made to do exactly that. But the NTSB's dereliction of duty didn't only concern the Flight 980 crash. Since Eastern was flying uninterrupted throughout South America, the NTSB now became a guilty party, on a continuing basis, responsible for any future crashes, should any occur. To state there was negligence of the highest order is the kindest statement one can make about the way federal government agencies and Eastern Airlines top management betrayed the trust of everyone who had ever boarded a commercial United States jetliner. Those who perished on Flight 980 didn't even get the benefit of an objective investigation into the cause of their deaths, and with this precedent, how can we expect to prevent a recurrence for others who might follow? Take your pick for justification the next time around; once again, national security? The fight against terrorism? We already know these items can trump lots of things, no doubt including impartial airliner crash investigations.

Based upon all the collective evidence, I concluded that the NTSB had to be involved in a cover-up to suppress what happened. It was the only explanation that fit their illogical actions.

CHAPTER FIFTEEN

In January 1986, the only "official" report on the Flight 980 crash was ultimately released by the NTSB. It was a fourteen-page Spanish language document prepared by the Bolivian Ministry of Aeronautics, dated September 4, 1985. NTSB officials initially claimed poor translation created the four-month delay. This, of course, was pure nonsense, since the U.S. Department of State Office of Language Services did the translation. I first believed that perhaps the Bolivians might be waiting for the NTSB-led expedition to conclude. But even if that were the case, Feith's commentary on the NTSB trek was issued on November 5th, still leaving a puzzling two-month intervening time period. But even then, the NTSB didn't forward the Bolivian report to ALPA until March 6, 1986, a full two months after they purportedly received it, and just coincidentally, a short time after Eastern had been handed over to Texas Air. I guess we can chalk this up to simply more "inexplicable" delays?

To an untrained eye, the Bolivian document might have seemingly unearthed some reasons for the crash. But upon closer scrutiny, it stated nothing of substance and was based totally upon speculation and conjecture. For example, in the "Conclusions" section, the report reached the determination that the crash was *"Apparently caused by the aircraft's deviation from its airway, possibly because of operational failure, aggravated by bad weather conditions at the site."* The use of the word "apparently" and "possibly" render this report useless, as there are no clear-cut reasons in the report to support any of these conclusions. That is what aircraft accident investigation is expected to be about: unmistakable and precise reasons, a "why" and "how" for everything, not "apparently" or "possibly."

There are additional statements that I believe were included only to mislead. For example, in order to lend credibility to this incompetent document, the Bolivians reference other NTSB reports. The Bolivians included statements like, *"I also wish to inform you that the Direccion General de Aeronautica Civil, exercising its prerogatives, authorizes the National Transportation Safety Board to publish the NTSB report together with the report prepared by the competent Bolivian Authority . . ."*

One major problem with the Bolivian bullshit is there never was any NTSB accident report issued, and without one, the Bolivian "findings" were based solely upon guesswork. No doubt this non-existent NTSB report was only included in an attempt to deceive and lend credibility to the Bolivian fabrications. Furthermore, why was the word "competent" included in the Bolivian document? Is that to suggest that some knowledgeable individuals might otherwise find it "incompetent?" Actually, to describe the Bolivian report as "incompetent" would be benevolent.

What follows are some noteworthy sections of the allegedly "competent" Bolivian report, which in actuality, was anything but.

> . . . the aircraft had disintegrated, presumably because of a violent impact and subsequent explosion.
>   . . . Because of the violent impact on the rocky ice on the southern slope of Mount Illimani, and the characteristics of the aircraft (pressurized altimatica cabin, etc.) it has probably disintegrated.
>   . . . Because of the violent impact against the rocky icy surface of Mount Illimani and the technical characteristics (pressurized cabin, altimatica, etc) the aircraft disintegrated completely.
>   . . . After the first and sole impact, there was probably an explosion and fire, which consumed the few remains of the aircraft.

Despite these Bolivian "findings" being couched in official-sounding governmental language [I have appended the complete Bolivian report] nothing in it was credible. For example, due to the lack of oxygen at the crash site's altitude, 19,600 feet above sea level, it would be impossible for an explosion to have taken place, at least as a result of impact with a mountain. The aircraft came to rest in an area covered with snow and devoid of vegetation. At this altitude and in that environment, the possibility of a fire is nonexistent. All prior treks failed to produce one shred of evidence to support the hypothesis that there was a fire. The climbers sent by Valdes reported the strong smell of jet fuel, but no evidence of fire.

Then there's the use of the word "disintegration." Three individuals who were at the site believed the recorders could be recovered, an impossible task if the plane had "disintegrated." To the best of my knowledge there has never been a plane crash where the aircraft "disintegrated," the Webster dictionary definition of which is to *"cease to exist."* What comes across quite clearly is that the Bolivians were attempting to say, "Don't bother to look because there's nothing there. The aircraft, passengers and recorders, were all vaporized and vanished." Yet, aircraft remains were clearly visible, even to the untrained eye. So this was just another attempt only to discourage a proper investigation. The NTSB never pointed out any of these factual errors, simply agreeing by their tacit silence.

The "explosion" statement, however, is important for other reasons. An explosion and subsequent breakup could have been caused by a bomb. But, instead of supplying evidence to support or refute that possibility, these lame statements were not backed up with any additional explanation. Or maybe tests were performed on some wreckage by the Bolivians and explosive residue was found, which they wanted to hide? Unfortunately, we will probably never know the answer to that vital question because the implications and ramifications would have been tremendous.

The Bolivian report also stated, *". . . no corpses could be found, nor were there any bloodstains or other evidence . . ."*

The Bolivians were the third party to make this statement. Blood would stand out clearly against the white snow, and because of the high altitude, there are no animals to carry off the bodies. Again, the question of how twenty-nine bodies simply vanished was never addressed. If a bomb had exploded in a different location, however, the bodies could have been blown apart and out of the plane.

But the Bolivian report *did* reveal a crucial time lag between the loss of communications with Flight 980 and the start of any search and rescue operations. The DAKON intersection, the last point reported by Flight 980, is 55 nautical miles southeast of the La Paz airport. The maximum time it would have taken a Boeing 727 to cover this distance, even at a reduced speed, would be fifteen to twenty minutes. Yet their report showed that an hour and fifty-one minutes passed before the Bolivians even placed the aircraft in the "distress" phase. Where did they think it had gone? Once again, no reason was provided for this inexplicable delay. If there were survivors—and at this point, the Bolivians didn't know whether or not there might have been—it would have been crucial to reach them as quickly as possible. But the Bolivians waited that hour and fifty-one minutes before even declaring that the plane was conceivably in trouble. An aircraft was finally dispatched to take a look, but not until a full two days later! This time lapse, however, is significant for another reason. The last radio communications between the crew of the plane and traffic control at La Paz took place at 8:37 p.m. local time. In South America, January 1st is one of the longest days of the year. If a search had begun immediately, there would have been sufficient light remaining to spot the aircraft and to rescue any survivors. At the very least, aircraft remains could have been located. Furthermore, in their flawed report, the Bolivians contend that the aircraft had exploded and burned. Thus, according to them, there would also be smoke from a fire that would have been clearly visible. Waiting that hour and fifty-one minutes, until 10:28 p.m., insured the jet would not be found, as it was dark by that time. It also sealed the fate of any passengers who might have survived. By delaying two full two days to even send a plane to investigate, the chances of finding anyone alive were zero. But once again, the NTSB never questioned this.

The Bolivian report also referred to a mysterious and secretive group of unidentified mountain climbers. The Bolivian report states: "... *According-ing to the statements by the group of mountain climbers* [who] *reached the site of the crash ...*"

Bernardo Guarachi was dispatched to the crash site two days after the plane went down. Recall that, at later dates, he also accompanied Judith Kelly and the NTSB expedition. As a result, he was at the site more frequently than anyone. This gives rise to a number of other questions. Why was Guarachi sent the first time, and who dispatched him? Was he paid? If so, who paid him? What was his specific mission? What did he discover?

Did he take pictures? Did he see or recover the recorders? Again, why didn't the NTSB demand answers to these important questions?

The Bolivians *probably* dispatched Guarachi two days after the crash, because they were the only ones to even publicly acknowledge that this expedition took place. Any knowledge gleaned from Guarachi is extremely important, because he was the first person with an undisturbed look at the area. Yet I've never seen any pictures taken by him, and nothing was mentioned about him in any NTSB documents. There was also no public record, anywhere, of anyone debriefing him.

The ALPA investigators led by Don McClure ultimately became aware of Guarachi's first expedition, and after questioning him about it, characterized his response as bizarre. At first, he wouldn't even admit he had gone until McClure threatened him with jail, although he didn't have the power to make that threat stick. But even under this cloud, Guarachi still wouldn't reveal who sent him, or what he'd discovered. Even though they informed the NTSB officials, the ALPA people received no assistance from them and the ALPA personnel were powerless to force him to answer. His evasiveness led McClure to speculate that Guarachi might have recovered the recorders. McClure believed that would explain the airline's reluctance to participate in the subsequent NTSB expedition; that is, if Eastern knew the recorders had already been retrieved, there would be no need to send anyone. Notwithstanding my high regard for McClure, I do not agree with his assessment, as many subsequent Eastern management and government actions suggest that the recorders had not been recovered, at least not by Guarachi. By way of illustration, why would Borman and Magurno have been so concerned in their meeting with Valdes if Eastern knew someone retrieved the recorders? Fear of bad publicity? That makes no sense either, because the Valdes video was only going to be shown to Eastern employees.

The Bolivian report contained numerous other inconsistencies. Their conclusions as to the possible causes and suggestions to remedy these hypothetical deficiencies weren't worth the paper they were written on. And even if they wanted to, which they did not, the Bolivians could only recommend changes to Eastern's operations as they had no enforcement power other than to deny Eastern landing rights in Bolivia, a political action that would be certain to raise the ire of the U.S. State Department.

Although the Bolivians never proceeded with an objective, step-by-step technical investigation and analysis, during the intervening year before the publication of their report, the NTSB held all interested parties at bay by stating a formal Bolivian investigation was underway. But the truth was far different. Absolutely *nothing* was being done and no new information was ever produced. They were simply buying time.

I wasn't the only one who considered the Bolivian report worthless. The ALPA accident investigators also recognized the serious flaws contained in it. Known facts were simply glossed over or ignored as though they didn't exist. The Bolivian report could have been written a week after the crash and would have contained the same pathetic information. Between the time of the crash and issuance of the Bolivian report, the NTSB's silence was comparable to the eerie hush at the crash site. And, by not subsequently challenging any of these flawed conclusions, the NTSB became a willing partner in a silent conspiracy of lies and deception.

The NTSB hierarchy knew that for those without some type of personal involvement, memories quickly fade. Indeed, the media had quickly lost interest since there had been relatively few Americans aboard and there were virtually no lawsuits pressed by family members. Kreindler & Kreindler, the New York-based largest and most experienced aviation crash litigation firm in the world, handled the few cases, and all were quietly settled.

To further demonstrate the lengths the NTSB went to quash any interest, they wouldn't even provide me with a list of the names of the Flight 980 passengers, even though I requested one in writing. Once again, I was subjected to the classic bureaucratic runaround when they claimed not to have a list and referred me to Eastern. Using the name of the local ALPA field office manager, I wrote to Eastern's legal department and asked for the names, but they didn't even bother to respond. I eventually got the list from ALPA. It was quite apparent this was one crash that all interested parties, except ALPA, wanted quickly forgotten.

CHAPTER SIXTEEN

I next turned my attention to the other possible reason surreptitiously raised to employees by Eastern management: that the crash was the fault of Captain Larry Campbell. Campbell was forty-nine-years old at the time and a twenty-two-year Eastern veteran pilot. He had flown most of his career out of the New York pilot base and we had become acquainted while flying together. He had recently transferred to his Miami domicile after a divorce.

The records indicated he had never before flown over Eastern's South American routes. His first flight into South America had departed the day before the crash, on December 31st, when he had piloted the southbound portion of the trip. Kenneth Rhodes, the copilot, and Mark Bird, the flight engineer, were also making their initial flights into South America. Mark Bird was also new to the airline.

Eastern pilots were attracted to the South American routes for a number of reasons. For example, countries like Paraguay and Bolivia were wild and exotic, and the layovers in various South American cities frequently offered unusual and fascinating sights. There was also extra hourly pay, known as "Intercontinental Pay." This amount was added to all flying done south of Panama City, Eastern's South American hub. This extra pay could produce an added monthly income of $765 for the captain, $595 for the copilot and $518.50 for the flight engineer. Since a pilot's retirement amount was based upon a percentage of his average earnings during the period preceding retirement, which then was mandatory at age sixty, for a captain like Campbell this $765 per month could have a positive impact on retirement income. In the airline business, seniority is everything and the more senior pilots normally flew these routes. Campbell's overall seniority wasn't that high, but he was within the top thirty percent of 727 captains in the Miami base, high enough on the totem pole to do some South American flying, particularly on holidays when the more senior pilots were at home. On that fateful night, the entire Flight 980 crew had zero experience flying into South America other than that performed on the same trip.

Following the crash there were newspaper reports, with Eastern as the named source, incorrectly stating that Kenneth Rhodes had South American flying experience. This was yet more erroneous information, as an April 4, 1985 NTSB memo directly contradicted it.

"Mr. Rhodes had no previous flying experience in SA." [SA stands for South America].

In the days following the crash, before a shred of evidence concerning a possible cause was gathered, unsupported rumors about Campbell began to filter down through the Eastern pilot ranks. These in-house stories mostly concerned how Campbell had failed his most recent check ride, the standard test given to all captains twice annually to demonstrate flying skills for situations not normally encountered. These accounts also described how he supposedly ran an "undisciplined" cockpit, and it was alleged these items caused the crash.

Since his piloting abilities were questioned, I went back and checked the records and discovered that, nine days before the crash, Campbell experienced a problem on a standard six-month captain checkride, with some items graded as "unsatisfactory." Management knew that difficulties like those were fairly common. Out of the approximately ten percent of Eastern pilots who experienced check ride troubles annually, less than one percent ever developed into career-threatening scenarios. Considering Campbell had just gone through a pressure-packed divorce, his case was no different than many others. In this checkride record, the "unsatisfactory" items fell into the categories of abnormal or emergency procedures. Ironically, purportedly to prevent a permanent blemish on Campbell's record, this check ride was instead turned into and officially termed a training session. In the intervening time between that check and the following one a few days later, Campbell was given one simulator practice session. Here, a different instructor graded all of Campbell's results as satisfactory, the standard grade given when everything goes normally. Then, on December 27th Campbell retook and successfully completed his check ride with another instructor. When he passed this test, he was again considered fully qualified in both Eastern's and the FAA's judgment and was immediately returned to flying duties. Despite the fact that the failed check ride wasn't even supposed to be on his record because it had been called training, immediately following the Flight 980 crash management officials dredged up this "permanent blemish," as they referred to it, no doubt hoping that this information would somehow put the blame on Campbell for "flying the airplane into the mountain."

Kenneth Rhodes was the copilot, or First Officer, a former Air Force pilot before joining Eastern in 1970. It would seem highly unlikely that a man from such a regimented background would be part of any alleged "undisciplined" cockpit. In fact, the prior quoted NTSB memorandum contained the following statement, supplied by an unidentified Eastern pilot friend of Rhodes.

"He described Mr. Rhodes as a person who was not an eager beaver but who would monitor the Captain when the Captain was flying and would quickly and politely point out any errors he observed."

This monitoring is the basis for a premise known as the "crew resource management," or CRM, which was taught religiously at Eastern's flight school. It ensures that if one crewmember errs, the others aren't afraid to speak up and call into question any actions or judgment decisions they perceive as unsafe. It's clear from both his background and his friend's comments that Rhodes possessed such discipline.

Mark Bird, the flight engineer, or Second Officer, was brand new to the airline, with no prior South American experience. He was assigned the trip because Ramon Valdes had bid off.

When I spoke with Allen Gerber, he surprised me by letting me know that people at the United States embassy in La Paz had informed him they believed there were *three* possible reasons for the Flight 980 crash: the plane being flown into the mountain, sabotage, or that the entire flight crew was high on drugs! Talk about bullshit! None of the Flight 980 pilots had a history of drug abuse and the chances of all three doing so at once were zero. I wondered who dreamed up that one.

I also questioned why management would want to blame Campbell, since I had witnessed exactly the opposite corporate reaction after other Eastern crashes. In these cases, management was concerned with the welfare of the deceased flight crew's family and attempted to do everything possible to stop any premature finger-pointing until the official cause of a crash was uncovered. It is well known within the ranks of airline pilots that many times the NTSB often "blames the pilot." But in this case, Eastern management was attempting to blame the dead pilot, but only within the ranks of his co-workers. The story put out for public media consumption was different. For these, management spokespersons openly stated that the crash was truly "tragic" and that Campbell was a fine aviator.

The job of airline pilot is definitely not the glamorous one frequently portrayed in Hollywood movies. There's an old adage in the business that goes, "An airline pilot's life is 99.999% pure boredom and .001% sheer terror." A similar expression would apply to layover time spent away from home: 99.999% unremarkably dull and .001% somewhat interesting. Although the traveling public normally equates pilot layover time in a city away from home with their personal vacation experiences, this is not the case. Depending upon how many hours were worked and the duration and location of the layover, the time is more likely to be spent watching TV, reading or sleeping. But in some cities, like New Orleans, there can be more to do. The Eastern crew layovers there were fairly long, and virtually everything of interest was within walking distance from the Marriott Hotel on Canal Street where we stayed. While reading over the Flight 980 material, I recalled the time that I had run into Larry Campbell while on a layover in the Big Easy.

It was raining quite hard that day and into the early evening. I had sprinted from the hotel to Houlihan's restaurant on Bourbon Street to dine, a distance of approximately a quarter mile or so. At the restaurant, I was informed it would be a few minutes before I could be seated, so I went to the bar to wait. Houlihan's was interesting, not just because of the food, but because it also attracted a cross-section of the different folks found in

New Orleans, and people watching was a great leisure-time activity. Before I could sit down, however, my table became available

Upon entering the crowded dining room, I saw a chubby guy with gray hair in a comb-over style waving to me from a corner table. It was Larry. We shook hands and he invited me to join him. As I sat down, I discreetly checked Larry out. The last time our paths had crossed he mentioned he was going through a divorce. I had flown with enough pilots in various stages of divorce that I had devised my own method of identifying which stage. For example, if a pilot wore his work shirt during the layover, the odds were good that the divorce was final. Larry was wearing a white shirt with epaulets. I shifted my gaze to the collar of the shirt for part two. It was worn and had little creases on the sides, a sure sign that he had ironed it himself. In my estimation, his divorce was final and there was no girl-friend.

He informed me he'd transferred from New York to the Miami base. After expressing regrets that we would no longer be flying together, I asked if he had moved to Miami, or was he commuting from his home in New Jersey? He explained that after the divorce he thought he would be able to hang on to the house, but he'd been forced to sell it and split the proceeds. He had friends in South Florida who invited him to stay with them, so he moved there. Because of the lower Florida real estate prices, he hoped to buy a place soon. He mentioned that another reason for moving to the Miami base was the South American flying. He told me that the extra bucks would add considerably to his retirement. As I dined and he sipped coffee, per the norm our conversation turned to the airline. "I'm really fed up with all the bullshit that we've had to endure," I recall him saying.

"Yeah, but for now, things seem to have turned around," I replied. "And we're part owners."

He raised his eyebrows. "Maybe. But life's too short for all the crap we've had to put up with. The past five years have taken a lot out of me and all that pressure was a major reason for my divorce. The old lady just didn't want to hear it any more. I'm gonna fly, hopefully in and out of South America, till I can get a decent retirement when I'm fifty-five, and then I'm outta here."

I reminded him, "But your highest earnings are during the last five years before mandatory retirement kicks in at sixty. Why leave early and lose the extra bucks?"

He just shook his head. "I'm out of here at fifty-five."

I still recall the irony in Larry's last statement. When I hired on, Eastern was the airline that virtually every pilot wanted to work for. But by 1984, after years of infighting, it was the airline that many of its pilots were anxious to leave for the greener pastures of retirement. It was also ironic that, in spite of the many conflicts and constant threats that many times caused divorces like Campbell's, Eastern pilots were expected to study for check rides and fly as though nothing was wrong. For years management would never acknowledge their way of doing business was causing many pilots' physical and mental problems, but I knew better because, as an ALPA rep, I heard "confession" virtually every day from the pilots I represented and sometimes their spouses, when they sometimes called. At times I felt as though I should turn in my pilot licenses and go into the marriage counseling business.

Between bites I asked Larry if he was concerned about flying into South America, because the flying was primitive, a far cry from what the he was used to. "There have been some close calls," I told him, "so be very careful. Hopefully, there will be special training or schooling to teach the pilots all the ropes and what to expect."

"Well, I ain't heard of any," he responded.

"Just be extra careful," I repeated.

"You can bet your ass on that. It shouldn't be too bad though, because I'll be flying with experienced first and second officers."

I next commented to Larry that he looked a little tired.

"It's probably the divorce," then adding on a more serious note, "I've been pushed me to my limits. When I'm fifty-five, I'm gonna stick up my middle finger at the people in the *Taj Mahal* as I waltz out the door."

We both laughed as I suggested, "Don't delay. Stick it up, now!" I urged. Larry commented that he'd love to do that to top management that very moment.

Since the rain had slacked off to an intermittent drizzle, I finished up and we slowly ambled back to the hotel, taking in the unique sights, sounds and smells of *"Le Vieux Carre,"* the New Orleans Old French Quarter. We passed by a number of places, recalling some stories, but mainly reminising about the old days at the airline, how good it used to be and how things had changed for the worse.

I never imagined when we parted company in the lobby that would be the last time I would ever see Larry, or that his death would be the catalyst for the destruction of Eastern.

CHAPTER SEVENTEEN

In the aftermath of the Flight 980 crash, but before the issuance of the Bolivian accident report, I had been researching Eastern's South American operation as unobtrusively as possible, my studies only interrupted by the contract crisis and subsequent sale to Texas Air. As part of this, I held a number of private discussions with knowledgeable individuals from the pilots' union and top management, as some of the latter were also concerned. From these conversations it became clear that there were serious South American flight safety shortcomings that needed to be addressed. But I had to wait until the Bolivian report was issued to see if any were mentioned because I wanted to see how the NTSB, FAA and top management would respond. But it turned out that the Bolivian report was worthless, meaning there was no reaction from any parties. I had compiled my data with the idea in mind that, if necessary, I would present my findings to top management and use my ALPA credentials to try to force them to take corrective actions, figuring they might listen. I was also prepared to take my case to the FAA or, if required, the public media.

An airline crash is rarely caused by a single problem. More frequently it's the culmination of a seemingly unrelated series of decisions, circumstances, events or errors, which come together on a particular flight and which are usually set in motion some time in the past. If this potentially deadly chain can be recognized and broken, the disaster can be avoided. Numerous in-flight items can affect the pilot's thought and decision-making process, making it impossible to say with any degree of certainty that, had any one decision or action *not* been changed, a crash would have occurred. Pinpointing with certainty when the chain of events is interrupted and a crash avoided is next to impossible. But when a crash does

occur, a logical, step-by-step investigation is able to reverse the process—
that is, to start at the crash and work backwards, uncovering each contributing factor.

This is why aviation accident investigators will first attempt to assem-
ble all potentially related items and determine how they might affect a specific air disaster. NTSB investigators normally perform this work by first
reading the information found on the flight data and voice recorders and
then looking into related events, eliminating some, while attempting to
uncover those that might be linked. To accomplish this in a competent
manner, the inquiry must be well defined and disciplined, following a well
thought out, step-by-step process. Since this meticulous process never took
place with the Flight 980 crash, it left me at a disadvantage. But even without the benefit of a proper inquiry to fall back on, the first question I
nonetheless had to attempt to answer was whether the crash was indeed
Campbell's fault. Or were Campbell, his crew and passengers all possibly
innocent victims of a set of circumstances that culminated in the crash? My
investigation showed that the stage was set in motion for the Flight 980
crash in 1978, when United States airlines were deregulated.

When airline deregulation became the new law of the land, it gave U.S.
airlines the unprecedented opportunity to fly to any domestic city of their
choosing. Harding Lawrence, then President of Braniff Airways, began to
expand Braniff's operations at breakneck speed, as he believed the larger
the airline, the more resources it would have to insure its long-term survival under the new rules of the sky. A very simple example of this would
be if a fare war in the deregulated American skies broke out over one
route—for example, New York to Los Angeles—a large airline would have
staying power created by raising fares slightly on its many other routes to
offset the lower fares and lost revenue on this route. Through rapid domestic expansion, Lawrence attempted to make certain Braniff would be one
of the survivors.

Braniff's South American routes were unique and extremely valuable
as they were still afforded regulated route protection, also meaning inter-
nationally agreed-upon higher airfares and little or no competition.
Lawrence believed that Braniff had the best of both worlds, a deregulated

marketplace at home with which to feed the high-earning South American routes. Although this thinking was correct, in his efforts to expand so hastily, Lawrence threw caution to the winds, and almost overnight, Braniff attempted to become a major carrier by invading a host of domestic markets. In the airline business, cash flow is the name of the game and monetary problems quickly arose that were caused, in part, by growing too rapidly. Braniff suddenly went from being the darling of Wall Street to teetering on the verge of bankruptcy. Lawrence thought that he could grow the airline even further to resolve these cash problems, but the airline's Board of Directors disagreed and fired him, and put Howard Putnam in charge.

Braniff shared its main Dallas Fort Worth hub with American Airlines. Because Braniff didn't have its own computerized reservation system, they were paying hefty sums to use American's highly sophisticated, state-of-the-art SABRE computer reservations system. No one knew at the time that American Airlines, through the use of the then-new technology contained in this system, had taken a number of questionable actions against Braniff. For example, American biased its own flights over Braniff's, or passengers were redirected to American fights. Other times, if a prospective traveler telephoned Braniff's reservations number to inquire about a flight or fares, instead of being placed on a Braniff they were bombarded with information on American's schedules and fares. At times, potential Braniff passengers weren't even informed of a Braniff flight and were instead placed on American, at a lower price. These questionable actions resulted in steadily shrinking passenger loads and revenue for Braniff. In effect, Braniff could have been destroyed in part and its passengers stolen by the very system it was paying to use. Braniff management couldn't comprehend what was happening and although they tried to attract travelers with a host of different marketing gimmicks and lower fares, these were not successful. Only after Braniff had been placed in bankruptcy proceedings and declared insolvent were American's actions discovered. This was an act so unsettling that the United States Congress subsequently passed laws to prevent a recurrence. Unfortunately, the legislation came too late to save Braniff.

Many of Eastern's domestic and international routes were flown out of its large Miami hub, as were almost all of Braniff's South American routes. Therefore, it was a natural fit for a cash-hungry Braniff to sell these routes to Eastern.

The South American routes were especially valuable because they were bestowed through bilateral treaties negotiated between the various South American countries and the United States government. Many of these nations had their own government-subsidized airlines and didn't want to lose their share of this revenue. As a result, the number of airlines that were allowed to provide service was very limited. Not only was access closely guarded, so was the number of flights, insuring high passenger loads. Very high airfares were also charged, assuring maximum profits.

There was another priceless asset that went with the Braniff routes. When Braniff merged with PANAGRA, they were also granted invaluable fifth freedom rights, the exceptional privilege of not only flying passengers between South America and the United States, but also taking on and dropping passengers off in the different South American countries. The aviation rules in the United States are very different, expressly prohibiting any foreign airlines from flying passengers domestically. So, for a fraction of their true value—a mere $30 million—Eastern picked up Braniff's routes, along with these fifth freedom rights.

There were, however, some potential snags, the most glaring of which was Eastern entered into this purchase without any narrow-bodied aircraft properly equipped to fly in and out of South America's geographically diverse areas. As a result, even though the passenger loads didn't warrant it, the routes were initially serviced with Lockheed L-1011 jumbo jets. These were utilized until Eastern retrofitted three smaller stretched Boeing 727-200 aircraft with more powerful engines. One of these was the aircraft used for Flight 980.

Top management also requested relief from sections of the Eastern pilot contract, purportedly so the new South American routes could be immediately flown, claiming there wasn't enough manpower to do the flying under the current work rules. If the pilots would agree to a relaxation of these work rules, in exchange management vowed to hire additional pilots and revert back to the prior work rules at a later date; the "carrot," and the "stick" approach. The "stick" was if the pilots didn't agree, top management threatened to sell off or even give the routes away. As a result, these contractual changes were subsequently adopted.

As I examined the ALPA crash-related materials in depth, it came into clear focus that on January 1, 1985, while the trusting, innocent passengers and crew on Eastern Flight 980 believed they were simply flying to their destinations, in reality I determined that they were caught up in a potentially deadly crossfire; a complex web involving various high ranking U.S. government officials and agencies, Eastern top management and Latin American functionaries, with a host of criminals and unsavory characters thrown into the mix. From the information I secured, it appeared as though the NTSB's lack of action was connected to the other possible cause of the Flight 980 crash: sabotage.

While developing the timeline leading up to the sale of Eastern to Texas Air and after assembling the diverse yet related pieces, I unearthed a carefully orchestrated scheme to dispose of Eastern by delivering it into the outstretched, eagerly waiting hands of a corporate raider. Under Texas Air's control, employees would be far too busy with other matters to pay attention to a crash that occurred in a strange, exotic land in which relatively few people were killed. Digging even deeper, I tried to dismiss the common denominators as being too incredible, too similar to a James Bond thriller. But there were far too many "coincidences," meaning I believe that the destruction of Eastern Airlines must have been brought about by design. The scheme had taken but one year and fifty-five days from the date of the Flight 980 crash to complete. Eastern's passing was the final step to insure that the reason for these twenty-nine deaths would never be scrutinized.

The directive not to investigate the Flight 980 crash must have had the support of, or been initiated by, some very powerful Washington politicos in order to succeed. In fact, this decision went so high up that I believe President Reagan and a few of his closest operatives were involved, that their power and backing was required to put a stop to any substantive investigation. The cornerstone of this plan could only succeed if there was no investigation of the Flight 980 crash, meaning everything leading to the demise of Eastern had to seemingly be related to labor management economic warfare. The icing on the cake would be to place as much blame as possible on the back of IAM union leader, Bryan, a misrepresentation that was widely carried throughout the media. Speaking of the media, Borman was quite adept at utilizing it to his full advantage. The press quickly grabbed at this all-too-obvious, spoon-fed information and never did the necessary digging to uncover the underlying reason for the airline's tremendous losses and its subsequent sale. Eastern went so far as to provide an office and other communications equipment for several weeks leading up to the Texas Air takeover to the *New York Times* reporter covering unfolding events at the airline. What additional perks might have been afforded other media outlets? Because of our meeting with Borman, only Copeland and I knew that the acquisition by Texas Air was finalized under totally false pretenses, as Bryan had offered to cave in to all of Borman's demands well before that night's Eastern Board of Directors meeting, without any stipulations attached. Yet Borman falsely claimed, and the media echoed, that it was Bryan's unwillingness to throw in the towel and his subsequent requirement that Borman step down that was responsible for the sale and subsequent demise of the airline.

Particularly ironic was that while Nancy Reagan was preaching the pitfalls of drug abuse to young Americans in the very same media outlets, her husband and some of his staff, through their now-documented illegal actions pertaining to the Iran Contra affair, were allowing untold billions of dollars of illicit drugs to flow freely across our borders. While she was urging young Americans to "just say no," some within the Reagan administration were "just saying yes" to the Latin American despots who, along with their relatives, trusted generals and others, were getting rich beyond anyone's wildest imagination shipping illegal drugs to America. Each part of this chain was controlled in a businesslike fashion. After the coca was grown in South America, it was manufactured into cocaine and then exported to the American market. Drug use certainly wasn't new to American society, but the sheer amount appearing almost overnight on the streets indicated the products had to be smuggled into the United States with almost total impunity and, as it turned out, with official protection.

The size, scope, and ruthlessness of the operation is well described in the book *The Cocaine Wars* by Paul Eddy, Hugo Sabal and Sara Walden (W.W. Norton & Company, New York). This book recounts the sad spectacle of this drug trafficking as it unfolded and how an aging American president, intent on "stopping communism" throughout Latin America at any price, either knowingly or through neglect, created a situation for which American society continues to pay a very high price.

CHAPTER EIGHTEEN

Following Ronald Reagan's presidential election, one of his great concerns was the perceived communist threat throughout Latin American. Many years of Castro had taken its toll on the United States and fears of yet another communist-led government established anywhere in the Western Southern Hemisphere was foremost in the minds of those in a position to influence American policy in that region. So the Reagan administration resorted to some questionable and illegal tactics to stop this perceived communist threat, beginning with the United States' government-backed attempt to overthrow the democratically elected Daniel Ortega–led Sandinista government in Nicaragua. He accomplished this by clandestinely shipping money and arms to equip a right-wing insurgent group known as the Contras. When Congress discovered what was taking place, however, and that the Contras were guilty of rape, murder, kidnapping and other hideous crimes, and fearful of U.S. involvement in another protracted Vietnam-like situation, they passed a number of measures to ban the flow of money and arms. The first of these laws, the Boland amendment, was enacted in December 1982 and followed by other versions that remained in effect until October 1986.

Congress believed this legislation would eliminate the shipments as it prohibited them outright. However, the Reagan Administration's illicit response was to "privatize" the operation. This was undertaken through the efforts of individuals such as then Defense Secretary Casper Weinberger; former CIA Director, William Casey; former National Security Advisor, Robert McFarland; retired Admiral John Poindexter; Lt. Colonel Oliver North; former General Richard Secord; and others, allegedly including then Vice President George H. W. Bush, along with a host of other sleazy characters thrown into the mix. Highly secretive, hush-hush sales of arms, including anti-tank, anti-aircraft missiles and other weapons, were made to Iran for support in its war with Iraq, with the supposed "private" profits diverted to support the Contras, in direct and clear violation of a number of U.S. laws. But this wasn't a private operation at all. Instead it was subterfuge, a clandestine federal government within the government, a CIA-run undertaking. Only a very few, hand-chosen people within the Executive Branch were even aware of its existence. It was run furtively out of the White House basement by North, who resorted to arm-twisting of wealthy benefactors to make certain the shipments continued.

One of this illicit operation's biggest logistical problems was physically transporting the large amounts of money from the arms purchases to a location where the funds could be laundered. At the outset, this was done mostly in offshore banks in the Bahamas, with private charter planes utilized. Since this was a top-secret operation, there was guaranteed entry back into the United States, with no questions asked.

Some of the disreputable characters involved in the scheme quickly realized that anything could be brought back, including illegal drugs. It didn't take long until unprecedented amounts of drugs began flooding American streets. But the goings-on became so huge that they could no longer be kept in check. A few of the people involved were finally apprehended, which put the entire operation at risk of exposure. So the use of small planes was abandoned and Eastern Airlines was chosen as the carrier of choice, with the new money routing process moving the cash from the United States through Panamanian banks. Of course, when he discovered what was taking place, then-U.S. ally Panamanian dictator Manuel Noriega cut himself in on a percentage of the deal.

Since Panama City was Eastern's hub for its South American flights, it was a natural fit, as there would be no special attention paid to large, unmarked pallets of "air freight," which were actually cash. This was facilitated even further because U.S. dollars are officially used by Panamanian citizens, meaning the expenditure of U.S. currency was commonplace in Panama, as it has no paper currency of its own. Additionally, there were no foreign exchange restrictions in place in Panama during this timeframe.

But Eastern was soon more than just the best selection for smuggling the money into Latin America for laundering. It quickly became the carrier of choice for smuggling drugs back into the States, the amounts of which were truly mind-boggling. Smugglers later admitted to drug loads worth hundreds of millions of dollars.

Like most Eastern employees, I had heard stories of enormous amounts of drugs discovered aboard our planes returning from South America, with no special measures apparently being taken to stop it. To give you an idea exactly how large these amounts were, I secured official U.S. Customs records for the first part of 1984 under the Freedom of Information Act. These records indicate there were 232 pounds of cocaine seized on Eastern planes in twenty separate incidents. At the time, these drugs had a wholesale value in excess of $2 million and a street value of over $17.5 million. And these cases covered less than one year and only represented the tip of the iceberg, since they were only the drugs that were interdicted. From mid-1984 until January 1989, a period of just over four years, official government records revealed there were 2,723 pounds of cocaine, over a ton, and 826 pounds of marijuana seized by Drug Enforcement and U.S. Customs on Eastern aircraft flying into the United States.

These numbers represent an estimated total street value of over $2 billion! At the time, officials estimated that twenty to twenty-five percent of the total amount of cocaine smuggled into the U.S. entered the country via Eastern. The numbers were so mind-boggling that when reported by the media they could no longer be ignored, with federal lawmen forced into taking action. Standard U.S. Customs procedures call for impounding the mode of transportation responsible for the importation of illegal drugs and subsequently selling them at auction. Advertisements appear in many newspapers for these cars, boats and planes. In the case of Eastern, however, although the aircraft were initially confiscated, within hours they were returned. Fines were levied, which until February 1989 amounted to over $21 million. But according to the official U.S. Customs records, of this amount, only a paltry $465,808 was actually paid. That amount equals roughly 02.2 percent of the total fines. Could you imagine being fined, say, $100 for speeding, and paying the court only $2.20? First you would be laughed at and then thrown in jail. Yet that is what Eastern got away with, and you would be astute in wondering why this was so.

CHAPTER NINETEEN

The Eastern connection to the Panamanian money laundering portion of the operation might have gone completely unnoticed had it not been for one inquisitive Eastern pilot, Jerry Loeb—the same Jerry Loeb who was assisting Schulte during the time prior to the sale of Eastern to Texas Air. Loeb was employed as a pilot in January of 1967 after having achieved the rank of Commander as a Navy pilot. At the time of the Flight 980 crash, in addition to his ALPA committee positions, Loeb was a forty-nine-year-old L-1011 Eastern Second Officer based in Miami. In this position, he frequently flew to Panama City.

Loeb had a pal who was an FBI agent. Friends since their days together in the military, his buddy had been working in the FBI's San Juan office, but had recently transferred to the San Francisco office, close to Loeb's home. After the move they got together for lunch, and the conversation got around to Eastern Airlines. The agent informed him of an ongoing FBI investigation concerning reputed money laundering and drug trafficking on Eastern's Latin American flights. This rang a bell in Loeb's mind and he related a scene he had witnessed in Panama City, something he had never before observed during his entire airline career: the off-loading of unmarked pallets of United States currency from his aircraft. One of his duties was to walk around and visually inspect the aircraft after each landing. When doing this in Panama City, on a number of occasions, he had witnessed the notes being off-loaded from his aircraft by armed guards. The money wasn't in marked and locked heavy canvas bags, as it's normally transported, but in plain cargo pallets simply marked "air freight," sometimes with a small amount of actual cargo around it on the outside. The guards doing the unloading all wore patches indicating they were from the Panamanian Defense Forces, Manuel Noriega's private army, and were placing the pallets into waiting armored cars. Loeb suspected something improper might be taking place, but had no idea what. The agent said this account corroborated other information the FBI had received.

Another FBI agent who was involved in the Eastern investigation contacted Loeb and they also met. At this meeting, Loeb again detailed what he'd observed and was asked if what he had seen might be an illegal money laundering operation utilizing Eastern aircraft. Loeb replied that he wasn't positive. He was next asked if he knew anything about drug trafficking on Eastern. Loeb mentioned drug-related accounts passed on to him by Eastern's Panamanian airport ground workers. Out of fear for their lives, these people refused to name the individual, who was simply described as a shady character, whose name *always* cropped up whenever drugs were discussed. He had allegedly embezzled forty-thousand dollars from Eastern, but the allegations were never proven, and he remained involved in the airline's operations in some vague capacity. Some Panamanian airline workers swore he was Manuel Noriega's personal Eastern connection for money laundering and was also in charge of drug shipments throughout the entire Eastern route system.

The agent requested Loeb to keep his eyes open and report back. Loeb subsequently hand delivered the agent a narrative of events he witnessed, which he suspected might be related to money laundering; accounts that were confirmed by two other, unnamed Eastern pilots.

Loeb had also seen South American newspaper articles stating that Flight 980 might have been sabotaged for drug-related reasons by Stroessner. These tabloid accounts were translated for him by friend, also named Gustavo, who worked for Eastern in Bogota, Columbia. These articles suggested a tie-in between Gustavo Stroessner, the son of Alfredo Stroessner, and an attempt to assassinate Ambassador Davis.

Since there had been no NTSB investigation, Loeb penned a letter to the FBI stating his concerns over the potential for the sabotage of Flight 980, outlining the details alleged in the newspaper articles. Even though the sabotage possibility had been publicly downplayed by the NTSB and

Eastern, Loeb began to wonder if Flight 980 had indeed been blown out of the sky. At the time Loeb wrote his FBI letter, the sale to Lorenzo was simultaneously unfolding. He had also provided Borman's name to the FBI as Eastern CEO. He had figured Borman might be aware of some additional details of the money laundering. After initially witnessing the pallets being offloaded, he had first discussed this subject with Schulte. But having heard nothing further from him, he then met privately in a one-on-one meeting with Frank Borman a short time later. Yet nothing had changed during the intervening time. I will quote only parts of Loeb's FBI report as it is quite lengthy and gets into other areas. What follows are pertinent quotes with some names deleted:

Prelude
    January 7, 1986
    Eastern Air Lines: Domestic and Foreign Allegations of Drug-Trafficking, Money Laundering and Kickback Schemes involving EAL and its employees. This bizarre case involves a varied cast of EAL characters ranging from the Chairman of the Board/CEO, to Senior Vice-Presidents, Vice-Presidents, Directors, Managers, Clerical Workers, Flight Attendants and other current or previous employees.
    As per ascending order of suspect areas of alleged illegal activities are: Cocaine and other drugs delivered to EAL Flight crews at their respective, foreign layover stations and hotels throughout Central and South America. A Senior Vice-President in charge of the Central and Latin American Divisions who is implicated in a franchise-type agreement and arrangement for kickbacks, money-laundering and drug-trafficking.

Loeb must have touched on some very sensitive concerns because, following Borman's appearance in front of the MEC on the afternoon right after Eastern's sale to Texas Air, Don Davidson proposed a surprise motion for Loeb's immediate removal from his ALPA committee position, as the first order of business. This was done without prior notice and without Loeb present to refute any of Davidson's accusations. Davidson launched into vicious personal attacks on Loeb, accusing him of attempting to have Borman replaced, and how he had also gone to the FBI with complaints of some unspecified crimes that Borman might be aware of. I thought it extraordinarily strange that *any* MEC member would bother with something as trivial following the Texas Air takeover and all of its huge, negative implications. I also thought it very odd that Loeb was attempting to replace Borman at Schulte's bidding, but that important fact wasn't even mentioned by Davidson, or Schulte. Plus, Borman had already stated to the MEC that he would be leaving.

Some debate followed, but without his presence, after Davidson's character assassination and lacking Schulte defending him, Loeb was removed. Davidson had not only jettisoned Loeb from the committee, but more importantly, also stripped away a valuable shield afforded him under the Railway Labor Act; assurance that an elected or appointed union official would be free to carry out his or her union job without fear of management reprisal. If management now fired Loeb, it would be problematic for him to claim he had taken his actions in an official union capacity, as the union had just shown its dissatisfaction by removing him. I was concerned, and called Loeb and suggested he and I meet. A few days later we had dinner at Mancini's and during dinner, Loeb related that someone in top management knew of, or was involved, in Latin American money laundering. He also told me details about the money being off-loaded in Panama City, which he had witnessed. He also revealed the crux of the conversation when he had met with Borman and reported what he had witnessed, never suspecting Borman's possible involvement.

"What did Borman *specifically* tell you?" I asked.

"He insisted that what I told him about the money offloading must stay between the two of us while he investigated further. But that was several months ago, and I subsequently witnessed the same thing on numerous occasions. Each time I saw the cash being offloaded, I checked the cargo manifests, but no money was listed. I recently tried to contact Borman again, but he refused to speak with me." He paused again, deep in thought. "Maybe he *is* somehow involved?"

Had Loeb given information to the wrong person?

Loeb continued. "Since I didn't get any assistance from Borman, I delivered another letter to the Miami FBI office outlining how I believed the operation might work. I also asked if they had made any progress, in that they had requested that I report what I witnessed to them." He also wrote that an Eastern employee was believed to be involved in a top secret, CIA-backed cocaine pipeline. Some frightened Eastern Panamanian ground-crew personnel also stated that a former Braniff worker, currently working for Eastern, had physically planted a bomb on Flight 980 in Asuncion, specifically not naming the individual out of fear for their lives.

While putting this timeline together, I realized it was soon after he delivered the letter to the FBI that Davidson's criticism and ridicule of Loeb began. Loeb couldn't understand how anyone, especially management, even knew of his FBI report since the only person he'd copied was Schulte. But during the debate over Loeb's removal, Davidson stated that Loeb had gone to the FBI and accused top management of possibly being involved in money laundering and possibly drug smuggling. I thought perhaps Schulte had informed Davidson, who in turn had passed the information on to someone in top management, but I wasn't certain.

Loeb asked, "Do you think management might attempt to fire me?" He was worried because in his letter he'd named Borman as a suspect in the money laundering, due to his inaction on what Loeb had previously reported to him.

I told Loeb that I didn't know, but related Borman's declaration that he was leaving in a few days. "With Borman gone, you ought to be safe." I then informed Loeb of Borman's refusal of the offer Copeland and I made the day before the sale. To say that Loeb was stunned would be an understatement.

"That would have saved the airline," he stammered. "Why?"

I answered his question with a question. "Why would top management be involved in something like money laundering?"

"Probably because they were told the people behind it could protect them. . . "

"Meaning they had to be very powerful." I advised Loeb to be *very* cautious.

I subsequently came to believe Borman was either asked for or volunteered Eastern's services to transport the money. A simple, private request from North or any of the other principals, perhaps even Reagan himself, would have sufficed to bring him in. As a self-professed, God-fearing, good American, who hobnobbed with Presidents Nixon, Reagan and Bush, Borman would bend over backwards to have Eastern lend its assistance in "fighting communism." The highest possible government involvement assured protection on the United States end of the transaction, meaning he was probably also promised he would be shielded if anything went awry. But the Flight 980 disaster altered all that. The entire deal could be unmasked due to the likes of Ramon Valdes, Jerry Loeb and Judith Kelly, all of whom were raising pertinent questions, especially if any investigation showed the jet was sabotaged. But, with Eastern handed to Texas Air, Borman no doubt believed he would succeed in distancing anyone and everyone from any thoughts of a further crash investigation.

CHAPTER TWENTY

As I continued developing my timeline concerning the sale to Texas Air, the related, sad saga of what happened to Mort Ehrlich surfaced.

Borman had been President of Eastern Airlines for approximately eleven years, a tumultuous period when the airline lurched from one period of internal strife and crisis to another. But fairly peaceful, brief interludes occasionally ensued, causing employees to ride an emotional roller coaster. Prior to 1984, top management had squeezed concessions from its workers a number of times, mainly through Borman's threats to file for Chapter Eleven bankruptcy protection. These difficult years were finally followed by the Employee Involvement and stock plans, during which Eastern experienced financial success and outward harmony. It was under what turned out to be a bogus veil of success that, by early 1985, Borman ordained that since he had led Eastern to its now flourishing position, he would step aside, leaving the day-to-day operations of the airline to a new Eastern President. He made it known that his chosen successor was to be Mort Ehrlich.

Ehrlich commenced his employment with Eastern in July of 1968 as the Director of Economic Planning and by 1985 he had been promoted to Senior Vice President in charge of Planning and Government Affairs, where he was either responsible for, or became involved in, virtually all of the airline's vital marketing and other related decisions.

A native New Yorker, the businesslike Ehrlich fully understood the inner workings and complexity of Eastern, its strengths and weaknesses. With some trepidation, because I didn't really know him well, I subsequently interviewed him for this book, hoping to perhaps discover why Borman had turned down our offer from a management perspective.

During the genial interview he informed me that, although not personally involved in the labor-related crises, he was well aware of the troubles and conflict they created. As a *perceived* Borman disciple, he privately worried about the labor-management friction and the toll it had taken, and was happy to experience the harmony that finally arrived in 1984. Although he embraced the Employee Involvement and stock ownership programs, Ehrlich was also aware that Borman had been forced into instituting them. This caused him some anxiety because they were not the result of good faith. Despite the airline's excellent balance sheet and outward appearance of success, he realized it would be a challenge to smooth over hard feelings engendered by so many years of in-house discord. He was also wary of the private, contradictory signals emanating from Borman about the employee programs. Negative words were dropped here and there, or sarcastic remarks made "in jest." Ehrlich believed that additional positive changes were needed in management-labor relations. He privately believed Borman should step down from involvement in the day-to-day operations, as he no longer commanded respect among the rank and file employees, something Borman ultimately confirmed.

Borman had hinted throughout the early months of 1985 that Ehrlich would be his choice to become the next Eastern president. Since Borman was also the Chairman of the Board and had filled many of the positions on the Board with his own people, when he personally confirmed to Ehrlich that he was his hand chosen successor, there was no doubt on the part of both Ehrlich and Eastern's organized labor groups that he would also be the Board's choice. Ehrlich also believed that expansion was the key to Eastern's long-term success. So, it was with growth in mind that Ehrlich began making inroads with the various union heads. He held a number of meetings to discuss ways in which labor and management might work in partnership to ensure continued stability and growth, always clearing these meetings in advance with Borman. Knowing Borman's concern for his public persona, Ehrlich was careful never to blame him for past problems. Ehrlich didn't want employees to live in the past, but rather to look to a positive future and work with new top management in making Eastern the finest airline in America. He embraced the employee programs and, as the

new Eastern president, would also be committed to providing the traveling public with safe and reliable transportation, without neglecting
employees' welfare. He wanted Eastern to flourish and its future success
would be his legacy.

The Eastern Board of Directors was scheduled to meet in May of 1985
to select the new president. The day before this meeting, Borman again
confirmed to Ehrlich that he was to be his heir, so Ehrlich invited his entire
family to Miami for a celebration of this lifelong ambition. His secretaries
planned a small office party, including a cake inscribed, "To the New Eastern President."

Just prior to the Board meeting, however, Borman hinted to Ehrlich
that his nomination might be "in trouble," mentioning that the Board "had
reservations" about him. During our interview, Ehrlich informed me,
"Only much later, after I privately discussed my promotion with several
Board Members, did I discover that Borman had been deceiving me all
along."

When the Board meeting convened, out of protocol as an inside Director and due to his impending nomination, Ehrlich did not attend. He was-
n't elected, however, and Borman didn't even nominate him! The only
position of consequence filled that day was that of Executive Vice President, putting a virtual unknown, Joe Leonard, into it.

Although Ehrlich continued his employment at Eastern until July of
1985, when he officially resigned and went to work at TWA, he never
returned to his office after that painful day. His and Borman's paths subsequently crossed twice, but no explanation of what happened was ever
offered nor requested. A short time later, the inexperienced Leonard was
appointed president.

When I asked Ehrlich if he knew why Borman had purposely misled
him, he replied, "I don't know for certain, but maybe it was because I had
more support from labor than he did? Maybe he thought I would attempt
to push him out once I was president? But I would not have. He knew this
because I personally told him so."

I wondered why Borman would deceive Ehrlich into believing that he
would be the next president and then pull the rug out from under him.

Borman could simply have told him that he wasn't his choice, unless this was part of some larger scheme designed by Borman to achieve another goal, one that only he had knowledge of. So I asked Ehrlich if he and Borman were friends or ever socialized outside the airline, perhaps with their families, figuring Borman might be more honest with him in an informal setting. He looked at me incredulously and stated, "George, I'm Jewish. Borman would never socialize with a Jew." Ironically, Borman had previously received a "Flame of Truth Award" from a Jewish charitable fund for higher education. I never realized that Borman apparently carried around with him a well hidden bagful of prejudices, not only against organized labor but others as well.

What did happen was that Eastern's labor leaders dropped their guard, believing that the trusted and respected Ehrlich would be taking over. It was, however, but a short time after Leonard's appointment as president that other mysterious and inexplicable events began happening.

My timeline showed that almost simultaneous with Ehrlich's departure, almost overnight, the airline began bleeding staggering amounts that made all the prior losses look like peanuts—and allegedly no one understood why. By the spring of 1985 all the employee programs were in place and, it would seem, working well. The passenger loads were heavy. There had been no downturn in the economy, and no large up-tick in fuel prices. The few fare wars out there had been started by Eastern, "in order to regain or retain market share." The airline was providing excellent service and its on-time performance remained top-notch. Yet huge monetary losses suddenly surfaced.

I got a firsthand demonstration of where some of the money was going while flying an Airbus jumbo jet on a New York to Miami flight. We were at the gate at LaGuardia and, due to a heavy passenger load, were running about fifteen minutes behind schedule, time we could easily make up because of favorable tailwinds. Inexplicably, a number of ground supervisors boarded and distributed refund checks to the passengers. In many cases, these checks were for amounts greater than the customers had paid for the ticket! As a result, the passengers wound up getting a free flight to Miami and some even made money in the process. I had heard of main-

taining good public relations, but this was ridiculous. I had attempted to
determine why this was happening, but when I inquired of the people
handing out the checks, they didn't know, simply stating they were "just
following orders." One flight might not seem like a lot, but if you multi-
ply this by several hundred or thousand per day, over an extended period
of time, the numbers would be staggering. During the timeframe coinciding with Ehrlich's departure and Leonard's appointment—the last half of
1985—Eastern went from having its most financially successful year, ever,
to incurring tremendous losses, supposedly once again teetering on the
verge of bankruptcy; this, according to Borman and Leonard.

However, the true reason behind the huge losses was far different.
In subsequent, sworn testimony before the United States Senate Committee on Banking, Housing and Urban Affairs, then-IAM leader Bryan
described the cause of the bulk of them. Excerpts from his sworn testimony follow:

> In the first seven consecutive months of the one-year period preceding
> the sale of Eastern Air Lines, the company showed remarkable financial
> results, with operating income of almost $300 million, far exceeding any
> prior performance by the company. Unfortunately this prosperous period
> came to an abrupt end as Eastern's management implemented a plan that
> led to the demise of Eastern as an independent company, delivering it into
> the waiting arms of a corporate raider.
>
> Only five months preceding the sale, management, without any expla-
> nation, implemented a new operating plan which severely cut back East-
> ern's utilization of its assets. They reduced their planned block hours of
> flying by 5 percent and cancelled another 3 percent, which translated into
> an annualized reduction in revenue of $400 million. This was only one of
> the many negative actions which led to the immediate hemorrhaging (sic)
> of the profits produced through the preceding seven months.
>
> Before these negative management decisions were disclosed either to
> the Board of Directors or the unions, the IAM, in an effort to give East-
> ern an additional competitive edge in the industry, proposed an agreement
> to reduce the top rates of pay in our contract by 5 percent. The IAM
> members ratified this 5 percent pay reduction on October 17.

Throughout much of the autumn of 1985, the other Eastern Board members, and Borman, also professed not to understand why the company was losing so much money so quickly. It was not until their October 1985 meeting that Bryan finally discovered the block hours, the total amount of flying performed by the airline, had been secretly cut by eight percent, with Eastern's gross revenue slashed by an almost comparable amount.

Although there was a tremendous reduction in revenue caused by these block hour cuts, the airline's fixed costs remained the same, meaning the expenditure to put one seat in the air for one mile, the Available Seat Mile, or ASM cost, was substantially raised. By then, the latest labor crises were beginning to unfold. Just like the bizarre ticket refunding I witnessed, these block-hour reductions in flying translated into huge, intentional losses.

To illustrate the actual net effect of these cutbacks, by July of 1985 Eastern had a net income of $168 million thus far for that year. For the remaining five months, with the block hour reductions in place, the projected losses amounted to approximately $165 million. Put another way, the losses from these cancelled hours equated to almost the *exact* dollar amount of earnings for the entire year. This meant, at best, 1985 would turn out to be a breakeven year for the airline. But the crucial question remained: why was this done?

Bryan's other comments to the same Senate Committee about the reduction in flying are also pertinent. He quoted a section from a report he had presented to the Eastern Board on October 22, 1985, before anyone, including Bryan, fully grasped what was happening and, more importantly, why.

This report stated in part:

> . . . As a member of the Financial Committee, I believe that the Board of Directors has a fiduciary obligation to determine how this impending disaster occurred—especially the conscious planning of significant under-fly during the 4th quarter and all of 1986. I also believe the Board should thoroughly explore the failure of the projection and planning process at Eastern. From what the IAM has been able to learn, it appears that there was a very serious breakdown in communications and coordination within

EAL. While the Board never saw Forecast 1*, and has only been presented with Forecast 2* today, we understand that departments within
the Company were producing "informal" forecasts which were in substan-
tial variance to the information the Board was being provided with. It
seems that there were actually different information projections, depending on the department involved, and that the estimates were not evalu-
ated in a comprehensive manner. They were most certainly not reported
to this Board. We must take steps to insure that this kind of "surprise"
never occurs again. . .

**Note: "Forecast 1" and "Forecast 2" are Eastern's traditional early and mid-year
predictions for the current year's results.*

Bryan then further testified:

. . . As the **management-induced** *[Emphasis added]* crisis was unfolding,
on December 4, 1985, and again on December 10, Frank Borman, as part
of his efforts to find a buyer for EAL, secretly met with Frank Lorenzo . . .

Bryan's sworn testimony clearly showed the financial crisis which ultimately led to handing the airline over to Lorenzo's Texas Air had been
intentionally created and that Borman had been secretly meeting with
Lorenzo months before the culmination of the sale. Bryan had even gone
so far as to send a letter to middle-level Eastern managers asking them to
support his efforts, ". . . *to reverse the suicidal course of action of Eastern's
current top management.*" Unfortunately, Bryan's pleas fell upon deaf ears
and he was once again attacked by Borman.

Despite my limited experience in the area, I felt that cuts of this magnitude would be made only in the event of a severe national economic
downturn or curtailments that had been forced on the airline for reasons
such as the fuel rationing that took place during the 1970s. Since I'd never
held a management position, I asked Mort Ehrlich if this assessment was
correct. As the now-former Eastern Senior Vice President of Planning, he
would have been the person responsible for scheduling and implementing
the total amount of annual block hours scheduled to be flown. This was
his area of expertise. He had devised a sophisticated computer-based

system to accurately predict levels of flying based upon advanced bookings on selected flight segments. Under Ehrlich's procedure, predictions could be made far enough in advance to shift different sized aircraft around on various routes, either adding or taking seats away, depending on the projected demand, which was based upon certain key indicators. Since the planning for cuts in service, the magnitude of which took place in mid-1985, would normally be made many months before they were actually implemented, I thought perhaps they were made while he was still in charge of that department.

I first asked Ehrlich why he believed Borman had misled him on his promotion. He slumped a bit in his chair and his reply was slow in coming. "Until this day I don't fully understand." I then informed him about the eight-percent cut in the block hour flying. He looked at me incredulously, and confirmed that such draconian cutbacks would only be made in the event of a severe downturn in the economy or a fuel shortage. A pensive Ehrlich next added, "Perhaps now, for the very first time, I grasp why Borman did what he did to me. If I was still working there, I would *never* have allowed those reductions. In 1985, business was very good and all the indicators pointed to it remaining so. The cuts in flying were tantamount to economic suicide." After a moment of silence he added, "It's as though what happened was done to purposely bankrupt the airline. Reductions of this magnitude meant huge losses would be guaranteed," he confirmed. "Whoever was responsible for this knew full well Eastern would be bankrupt in a very short period, probably within six months, but maybe even sooner. Someone set it up to fail."

I believe at that point Mort Ehrlich—the honest guy who wanted only to run the best airline in the world, and who could have—understood for the first time why he was lied to and not promoted. Not only had the airline's collapse been orchestrated, but he had been forced out in order to facilitate that collapse.

As it turned out, from many different perspectives, there were quite compelling reasons for the airline to be disposed of as quickly as possible.

CHAPTER TWENTY-ONE

Before the book on Eastern could finally be closed, a couple of meddle-some pilots had to be dealt with by Borman, prior to returning to his office "to clean out his desk," namely Valdes and Loeb. He probably believed they were working together, so top management monitored their daily activities: Loeb for of his written and verbal remarks to the FBI, and Valdes because of his continued interest in the Flight 980 crash.

Since no one had heeded Valdes' South American flight safety warnings, he attempted to resurrect ALPA interest in these deficiencies by showing his Illimani crash site video to the ALPA MEC during a meeting held in New Orleans. Afterwards, he fielded questions from MEC members and discussed management's reaction to his activities. Although the video prompted questions, and a number of MEC members wondered why there had been no NTSB investigation, no formal action was taken. But this demonstrated Valdes' continued involvement in the Flight 980 disaster to top management, and also that he wouldn't be intimidated. This prompted further action, including having him investigated by a private detective agency. When I began scrutinizing this situation in depth, I was informed by the Eastern system chief pilot, Captain Bob Shipner, that Eastern's Internal Security department had hired an outside private investigative firm named Barry Associates, which in turn had subcontracted the job to spy on Valdes to the Intercontinental Detective Agency. This turned out to be false, as Barry Associates was hired specifically at Borman's direction, who probably also directed that the investigation be handed over to Intercontinental. This came out in testimony taken at Valdes' subsequent termination hearing. William Barry, the head of Barry Associates, was asked under oath:

Question: "The decision to involve you, at least peripherally, in the inves-
tigation of Mr. Valdes and others connected to him, however, was made by
who, if you recall?"

Answer: "I would guess Colonel Borman."

Question: "Colonel Borman?"

Answer: "Yes."

The only other person Borman might have spoken with about the hiring of Intercontinental was Magurno. Since he is an attorney, these conversations are privileged and subject to lawyer-client confidentiality, so we will never know the absolute truth about who actually retained them. But the answer to this question is significant because there are some very interesting links regarding the Intercontinental Detective Agency and some of the mysterious circumstances surrounding the crash of Flight 980. The question of why Intercontinental was brought in to investigate remains.

The investigation of Valdes was given to an Intercontinental investigator named Luis Dabalsa. For a Florida State–licensed private investigator, Dabalsa had quite an unsavory background. He had been employed previously as a police officer by the Metro Dade Police Department, but had allegedly been involved in a narcotics conspiracy and was arrested. He went on trial in Federal Court, but was acquitted. Following his acquittal, the Internal Review department of the Metro Dade police investigated, determined that he had perjured himself during his criminal trial, and he was subsequently terminated. In 1984, when applying for his Florida State private investigator's license, he apparently neglected to mention his termination from the Metro Police Department and the license was issued. During his assignment to the Valdes case, Dabalsa attempted to offer a $5,000 bribe to two other investigators; this, according to a formal complaint filed with the Florida State Division of Licensing. These investigators were involved in the case in order to obtain false information about Valdes that allegedly linked him with Loeb in some undefined conspiracy, purportedly against top management. The investigators Dabalsa approached ultimately informed

Valdes of the attempt, who then filed a complaint against Intercontinental and Dabalsa, outlining Dabalsa's actions. I won't include the entire complaint here, just two of the relevant portions.

15. The two employees of Eastern, who I mentioned earlier were about to be fired for disloyalty *[Valdes is referring to himself and Loeb]*, were allegedly involved in a plot to unseat certain members of Eastern's Board of Directors. Since I have gone on record on several occasions and complained about certain deficiencies in Eastern's Flight Safety Program, I have also been a likely target of management sponsored reprisals."

[Note: Valdes was referring to his prior information sent to Eastern management on his concerns and opinions on the safety deficiencies found in Eastern's South American flight operations.]

The complaint continued:

My initiative in thoroughly investigating a tragic airplane crash in Bolivia in early 1985 has further embroiled me in controversy with Eastern management. Concerns about flight safety and the airplane tragedy are not grounds which would justify terminating a long-time loyal employee of Eastern such as myself. Only by attempting to link me with a plot by other employees against Eastern's Board of Directors would justification [be] found to fire me.

Mr. Dabalsa knew no such plot existed, yet sought through bribery and extortion to suborn perjury and provide false evidence for his client [Eastern Air Lines]. This is a reprehensible abuse of the license to perform private investigative services currently held by Mr. Dabalsa.

Other than the obvious question of why management was attempting to falsely create grounds to terminate Valdes, there are a number of other, pertinent questions raised by these actions. Why were Valdes and Loeb, two Eastern pilots concerned with different aspects relating to the Flight 980 crash, singled out by management for reprisal? Who was the executive Intercontinental was reporting to? Why would top management of a multi-billion dollar, publicly held corporation use corporate money to hire an investigative agency to attempt to falsely incriminate two pilots whose only common link was the Flight 980 crash?

In my attempt to answer these troubling questions, I discovered yet another interesting "coincidence." Intercontinental had a principal inspector, Raul Diaz, a former Miami policeman. Diaz had a particularly nasty history of alleged drug trafficking that tied in with Eastern. While Diaz was a police officer, he founded CENTAC, an elite corps of Miami police whose goal was supposedly to eradicate the drugs freely flowing into the United States from Latin America through Miami. Differing stories as to why Diaz was eventually forced out of the Miami police department subsequently surfaced, with numerous allegations of corruption. Soon after Diaz left the force, there were rampant rumors linking him with drug shipments and tying him to the CIA efforts to fund the Contras. The following is from the book *The Cocaine Wars.*

> There are officers of almost every local, state, and federal law enforcement agency in Miami, and prosecutors in the US attorney's office, and investigators for Congress, who believe Diaz was a thoroughly corrupt and corrupting cop. They believe he sat at the center of a web of corruption; that he made up his own laws and selectively enforced them, not necessarily for personal profit—though that allegation hangs in the air—but to pursue his own idea of justice, and to further his career. Since leaving the police force he has been accused of fashioning an unholy alliance between drug traffickers and the CIA in order to supply the Contra rebels in Nicaragua with funds.
>
> Nothing criminal has been proven against (Raul) Diaz, nor is there any evidence that he stole or corruptly received any money. Even so, US prosecutors are still trying to put him in jail. One of them described him as "the most dangerous man in Miami."[1]

There are a number of other "coincidences" which tied Diaz to Eastern, the CIA, and the Contra money laundering and supply efforts. Through his association with Intercontinental and Eastern, Diaz was also linked to the Ramon Valdes investigation. In addition, Diaz was suspected

1. *The Cocaine Wars.* Paul Eddy, Hugo Sabal, Sara Walden. W.W. Norton & Company, New York. pp. 80–81

of being the CIA go-between—in this case, the link between the CIA spies and the drug traffickers. This was also brought out in *The Cocaine Wars.*

> . . . Blum became convinced that he had identified not merely the game but also one of its major players: the "cut out" between those nether worlds of espionage and drug trafficking, the 'link man' between the Cartel and the CIA—former police lieutenant, Raul Diaz.[2]

Was it also purely coincidence that after Diaz' removal from CENTAC he was chosen to supervise the police force at Miami International Airport? It was also during this time that Diaz underwent divorce proceedings and worked another part-time job, allegedly to make ends meet. Again, by strange "coincidence," this other employment was at none other than Eastern Airlines. This is what *The Cocaine Wars* says about his subsequent positions.

> On December 15, 1982, almost a year to the day since CENTAC began operations, news of the two investigations and some of the allegations against Diaz were published in *The Miami Herald* under the headline, "FBI Probes Homicide Supervisor: Metro Officer Denies Corruption Allegations." The following day, Diaz was relieved of his command of CENTAC but was told he could pick his next assignment; he chose to go to Miami International Airport as commander of the afternoon watch —the equivalent of going to Siberia, which he thought appropriate.
>
> At the airport, Diaz took two jobs because he needed the extra money to help pay for his divorce. From 10 AM until 3 PM, he worked for Eastern Airlines, watching the baggage carousels to ensure that nobody stole the luggage. At three he put on his squad commander's uniform and tackled the daily paperwork, which took, on average, forty-five minutes. For the rest of his shift, until 11 PM, he would stalk the airport, greeting arriving passengers: "Welcome to Miami."[3]

2. *The Cocaine Wars.* Paul Eddy, Hugo Sabal, Sara Walden. W.W. Norton & Company, New York. p. 339

3. *The Cocaine Wars.* Paul Eddy, Hugo Sabal, Sara Walden. W.W. Norton & Company, New York p. 93

Why would Diaz choose to do work that was the "equivalent of going to Siberia"? Was he simply watching the baggage carousels or did his involvement at Eastern go deeper? His work hours there coincided with the time of arrival of many of Eastern's South American flights. Was he involved in the large-scale Eastern drug smuggling operation, which in many cases involved off-loaded, checked baggage full of cocaine? Although Diaz wasn't one of them, a number of Eastern ramp workers were ultimately indicted for unloading bags full of cocaine inbound from Latin America. For a lengthy time they avoided apprehension by simply placing the cocaine-laden suitcases on the baggage carousels from domestic flights. The bags were then picked up without having to clear Customs inspections, a simple, but very effective process.

The estimates were that Eastern Airlines was utilized for the importation of twenty to twenty-five percent of the cocaine used in the entire United States during 1984 and 1985. At the same time, the now-documented Contra-related drug shipments were flowing freely into the States from Latin America via Eastern. Were all these cocaine Intercontinental-Eastern tie-ins just happenstance? I think not.

This is what *The Cocaine Wars* has to say about that:

> Diaz said that in the War On Drugs, he had lost sight of that, [the objective being to remain in the game] and gone for overall victory, and, consequently, he had lost. He was, he said, no longer so naive: "The whole thing's a game. It's all a fucking game."[4]

I attempted to discover who at Eastern had hired the Intercontinental Detective Agency, the firm that employed Diaz, allegedly "the most dangerous man in Miami." All fingers ultimately pointed to Borman, as shown by the previously cited sworn testimony. Only Borman would have had insider knowledge that Diaz was also a player, albeit at a different level and in a different manner, in the same, clandestine, top-secret money-

4. *The Cocaine Wars.* Paul Eddy, Hugo Sabal, Sara Walden. W.W. Norton & Company, New York p. 270

laundering and "guns for the Contras" operation in which Eastern played a central role. It would make sense to hire a firm that employed a person with a clear understanding of why management needed to fire two meddlesome pilots, and that could fabricate seemingly valid grounds for their terminations.

There were, undoubtedly, specific reasons why Borman felt particularly intimidated by Valdes and Loeb. Borman feared Valdes because of his personal wealth, which he most likely equated with power, as well as his many ties to the large Miami Latino community. Some others involved in the Iran-Contra scheme were also Latino, and Borman likely perceived that it would only be a matter of time until Valdes stumbled upon what was going on.

Loeb also needed to be dealt with because of his private statements to Borman, public statements to the MEC, and subsequent letters to the FBI concerning the money offloading and possible sabotage of Flight 980. He was snooping in a dangerous area where he didn't belong. Management's campaign began by first stigmatizing Loeb with Davidson's name calling, followed by his removal from his ALPA MEC position. But the truth was far different. Loeb had enough firsthand observations and other information to provoke awkward questions about Eastern's involvement in the money laundering and the possible sabotage of Flight 980. Borman also knew Loeb was reporting his suspicions to Schulte. It turned out that at least one other person, a now deceased, former ALPA Eastern MEC Chairman, Lloyd Anderson, had also provided a copy of Loeb's report to top Eastern management. I don't know for certain how Anderson received it, but can state from past dealings with Anderson that he was clearly in management's hip pocket—and that is a benevolent portrayal.

Loeb hoped his eyewitness reports would initiate an official FBI probe. However, only much later did I discover that the FBI was also reporting his allegations directly back to top management! This was proven to be the case under sworn testimony given at the Pilots System Board of Adjustment.

Magurno, Eastern's chief legal officer testified as follows:

Question: What MEC meeting?

Answer: I believe it was a MEC meeting which took place in early February, 1986 in which allegations were made off the record by an Eastern pilot that Mr. Valdes had already discussed his investigation of me. He told pilot X he had an investigation begun on me for the purpose of determining my sexual preference, and the subject matter of Valdes' investigation was a subject matter of discussion before the MEC in February.

Question: So what you are saying is a pilot who remains unidentified . . .

Answer: Jerry Loeb.

Question: Jerry Loeb?

Question: Mr. Loeb then carried that allegation . . . ?

Answer: That is correct, Mr. Loeb then carried that allegation to, of all places, to the FBI where he had a discussion with the FBI about my alleged sexual preference; that discussion was on or about January the 3rd or 4th, 1986.

Question: So I understand, based on information that Mr. Loeb presumably obtained from Mr. Valdes regarding your sexual preference, Mr. Loeb communicated the same, according to your testimony, to the MEC during the course of a February, 1986 meeting and also to the FBI on January the 3rd, 1986?

Answer: 3rd or 4th of January.

Question: How do you know these things?

Answer: The FBI informed me about it.

Question: The FBI, who?

Answer: I don't know the gentleman's title. He was in a director capacity in the Miami office.

Question: When did the FBI inform you of this fact?

Answer: In January of 1986."

The foregoing meant a conveniently unidentified FBI Director was keeping Magurno fully abreast of Loeb's assertions. More problematic is that the FBI would even report Loeb's concerns to management when Loeb's statements involved alleged criminal activity by one or more members of top management. Why the FBI did this has never been answered.

But it was subsequently disclosed that certain high-ranking FBI officials were aware all along of the ongoing illicit money shipments and drug smuggling onboard Eastern's planes, which were taking place with the Reagan Administration's blessing. Perhaps the FBI was equally concerned with how close Loeb was to uncovering the totality of this illegal scheme, including the possible related sabotage of Flight 980—concerned enough to pass on Loeb's allegations to top management, providing the pretext for his termination.

Loeb represented a serious potential threat, not only to Eastern management, but also to the secretive U.S. government agencies clandestinely involved in the Iran-Contra conspiracy. Powerful people could go to jail. Consider the following partially redacted excerpt from an FBI report, one of the very few Loeb successfully secured under the Freedom of Information Act.

FM MIAMI (192B-134)
To: Director Immediate
Attention: Cid, Organized Crime Section
Section Chief Frank Storey
Attention: Office of Congressional and Public Affairs

BT
UNCLAS E F T O

Information Regarding Possible Allegations of Criminal Activity at Eastern Airlines
Re TELCALL ASAC William E. Perry, Miami to Section Chief Frank Storey, April 21, 1986, and Re Miami Teletype to FBIHQ January 23, 1986.

For information of FBIHQ and as reported in referenced Miami teletype of January 23, 1986, Gerald K. Loeb, Legislative Coordinator for the Airline Pilots Association (ALPA) at Eastern Airlines (EAL) *[information deleted]* appeared at the Miami FBI Office on January 8, 1986, and provided information regarding possible allegations of criminal activity by

management personnel et al. RETEL set forth a synopsis of the allegations provided. Interviews were conducted by the FBI Miami *[information
deleted]* regarding criminal activity. Investigation by FBI did not substan-
tiate criminal activity.

[information redacted]

The FBI should be alert to this and be prepared to respond to any
media attention orchestrated by Loeb. FBI Miami did not confirm or deny
that Loeb had provided allegations or what, if any, investigation may have
been conducted.

[information deleted]

Miami FBI does not intend to make any comment at this time to
EAL regarding this matter. Since at this time Miami is unaware of what,
if anything, Loeb will say to the media, no FBI comment is deemed
appropriate . . .

This heavily censored memo seemingly indicates that the FBI investigated Loeb's allegations, but found them "unsubstantiated." However, all
the corroborating witnesses named by Loeb were never contacted nor interviewed by FBI personnel. But because Loeb had provided statements to the
FBI coinciding with the labor turmoil at Eastern, the FBI seemingly had
an excuse to question what he was alleging.

Another interesting aspect of this memo is where it is stated, "...*Miami
FBI does not intend to make any comment at this time to EAL regarding
this matter.*" (note: EAL stands for Eastern Airlines.) Yet, according to
Magurno's sworn testimony, someone from the FBI, whose name he
conveniently couldn't recall, had informed him of Loeb's allegations.
According to Loeb, there were three agents who were conveying his
allegations back to top management: Special Agent in Charge F. Corliss,
Assistant Special Agent William Perry, and Special Agent Rod Beverley.

If Loeb was guilty of anything, it was attempting to accomplish too
much at the same time. By simultaneously advocating for the replacement
of management at Schulte's behest and probing the mysterious circumstances surrounding the Flight 980 crash and related money laundering,
he made himself a target. Unbeknownst to him, thanks to different individuals, probably including Schulte, Davidson, Anderson and the FBI, top

management was being kept fully abreast of his assertions on a timely basis. Through information supplied, in part by the FBI and the Intercontinental Detective Agency, management obviously felt there was enough evidence to justify the firing of Loeb and Valdes.

Since their reports are not covered under the Freedom of Information Act, I could not discover what Intercontinental manufactured or disclosed to management concerning Loeb or Valdes. Furthermore, I was also unable to determine how they either manufactured or received it, how this information was conveyed to top management, or who did the reporting. Their report was shrouded in secrecy.

Loeb was the most obvious and immediate threat because of his former union position. All he had to do was convince anyone in the media of top Eastern management's involvement in the then-unfolding Iran-Contra scandal and how this might be connected to the possible sabotage of Flight 980. With the media's access to many sources of information, any subsequent investigative reports could have uncovered the entire conspiracy and forced a full-scale, in-depth investigation that would result in a feeding frenzy that no government agency would be able to stop. The entire house of cards could collapse, including the Texas Air transaction. If proven, besides putting those involved behind bars, the President and Vice President of the United States could be impeached.

CHAPTER TWENTY-TWO

From top management's perspective, Loeb and Valdes had to be fired, and they acted swiftly to remove the perceived danger both men posed. As a member of the Eastern Pilots System Board of Adjustment, the judicial body that adjudicates various pilot grievances including firings, I knew that once a pilot is sacked, either rightfully or wrongfully, many of his fellow pilots shun him: the "guilty until proven innocent" mentality. Top management knew for these men it would, to a degree, destroy their credibility, isolate them and deny them a forum. There would be no access to cockpits, crew rooms, pilot lounges or operations offices, where they could freely speak their minds with fellow pilots. Because of Davidson's recall, Loeb would no longer be viewed as being an important MEC Committee Chairman or as a pilot eyewitness to illegal actions. Valdes would no longer be the pilot concerned with South American air safety and matters surrounding the Flight 980 disaster. Both men would be stigmatized, relegated to "disgruntled former employee" status, ex-pilots conducting personal vendettas against their former employer. Anything they said concerning Eastern top management would appear to be tainted. Management would assist in this endeavor by never missing an opportunity to reinforce this perception. Another side benefit would be that Loeb's and Valdes' challenging of their terminations to regain their jobs would keep much of their attention diverted to that singular goal. Thus, on April 21, 1986, via hand-delivered letter, management first fired Loeb.

This is the text of Loeb's termination letter:

April 21, 1986

HAND DELIVERED

Dear Capt. Loeb:

Effective upon receipt of this letter, you are hereby notified that your employment with Eastern Air Lines, Inc. is terminated.

Attached and incorporated to this letter are two hand-written memoranda entitled "EAL Management, A Tactical Plan for Incumbent Management Removal and Installation of New Management" and "Tactical Planning for Borman's Removal, a Chronological Recap of Events and Planning Phases." Both of these documents state that they were prepared by you, and they contain your signature. We have independently verified that you did engage in much of the conduct outlined in these memoranda. The actions referred to in the attached documents form the basis for your termination.

You have intentionally engaged in an outrageous course of conduct well beyond all bounds of acceptable employee behavior. For example:

1. You provided the Federal Bureau of Investigations with a "19-page report" alleging that senior Eastern management officials are engaged in "bribery," "corruption," "illegal kickbacks" and other serious felonies. Your allegations are false and groundless, and they were maliciously put forth to the FBI by you for the purpose of achieving the goal of your "Tactical Plan"—the removal of incumbent management by any means;

2. In paragraph 9 of your December 26 memorandum, you state the following:

"A look-see at the personal lifestyles of certain high-level EAL management members is already underway by several, non-related sources. This highly sensitive area is being handled by very discrete and trusted contacts."

Independent investigation has verified that senior management officials were subjected to this unreasonable deprivation of their privacy. There can be no excuse for you to engage in or condone this type of conduct;

3. You repeatedly made false and groundless accusations of sabotage involving the crash of EAL Flight 989* in La Paz, Bolivia, in January, 1985. Additionally, you have groundlessly alleged that senior Eastern management officials have attempted to cover up the alleged sabotage;

Note: the flight number utilized is incorrect, it should be Flight 980. I believe they chose to give the appearance of downplaying its importance by using an incorrect number.

4. You implemented a plan designed to effectuate the "conversion" of select incumbent EAL BOD [Board of Directors] members through persuasion of defecting from the incumbent EAL management group or risk personal, financial devastation." You have advocated a plan to coerce members of the Board of Directors into voting to remove incumbent management with threats of devastation of "their individual personal fortunes by way of multibillion dollar derivative litigation" and "prosecution of certain EAL BOD members for [alleged] SEC violations."

The excerpts referred to above from your memoranda are illustrative of the type of conduct which caused you to forfeit your right to continued employment with Eastern Air Lines. It is somewhat understated to say that your actions as exhibited in the attachments were contrary to the best interest of Eastern Air Lines, Inc. You set a goal of the removal of incumbent management, and you proceeded to attempt to attain that goal by falsely and maliciously accusing senior management officials of engaging in serious criminal activities, by invading the privacy of senior management officials by investigating their personal lives with the view to coercing some unidentified action, by attempting to coerce members of the Board of Directors to disregard their fiduciary obligations and to "convert" to your tactical plan by threats of criminal prosecution and devastation of their personal wealth, and you have made false and groundless claims that lives were lost in the crash of an Eastern Air Lines plane as a result of intentional sabotage, and that management and several governmental agencies are covering up the alleged sabotage. Each of these individual actions would justify your termination. Combined, your actions are so ruthless and disloyal and so contrary to the best interests of the airline that there is no choice but to effectuate this termination immediately.

Sincerely,

R. J. Shipner
Vice President
Flight Operations and System Chief Pilot

Two items in the letter that immediately caught my attention were the words, "We have independently verified that you did engage in much of the conduct outlined in these memoranda," and, "Independent investigation has verified that senior management officials were subjected to this unreasonable deprivation of their privacy." There is no further information on how, where and when top management *independently* verified that Loeb had engaged in "much of the conduct outlined in these memoranda." Was it the Intercontinental Detective Agency that provided this material? That question is quite pertinent because it was shown by the Valdes formal complaint that they tried to manufacture false information.

Loeb immediately realized that his greatest mistake was in the timing of his reports, as he referred to management replacement in almost the same breath as the hauntingly mysterious circumstances surrounding the Flight 980 crash. As a result, for the first time, Loeb grasped that something much larger than his dismissal was at stake. But instead of simply "going away," as management hoped, Loeb now attempted to obtain related information concerning U.S. government investigations into the possible relationships between Eastern, the Flight 980 crash, potential sabotage of Flight 980, the then-unfolding Iran-Contra money-laundering scandal and the associated drug smuggling. He felt this information might provide him with the means to go a step further and establish a link to his termination, which could then be used in his defense at his reinstatement hearing at the System Board of Adjustment. Loeb utilized the United States Freedom of Information Act (FOIA) to try and secure the needed information to establish these links. The Freedom Of Information Act is purportedly the federal law designed to make it easier for American citizens to check on what their government is doing behind closed doors. There are exceptions, like the previously mentioned use by the NTSB of internal memos during their Flight 980 crash investigation so they would not be subject to these requests. Despite what this law was supposed to represent, *every* United States federal government agency Loeb contacted denied him access to any relevant information. From the tone of the denials, some agencies seemed to be inviting him to hire a lawyer and sue them, which he could not afford to do. I became clear that Loeb had underestimated the power and interrelationship between the various government agencies and Eastern top management. Loeb wondered who the good guys were and who the bad guys were. It came as no surprise to me that Loeb's requests were met with the classic bureaucratic runaround. I had run into, and continue to experience to this day, the exact same roadblocks from the NTSB with my Flight 980 crash-related requests.

The only federal agency that supplied any information to Loeb was the FBI, and the documents they provided were heavily censored. Neither the Drug Enforcement Administration nor the Central Intelligence Agency released anything, both claiming they either didn't have them, couldn't locate them, or that they were part of unspecified top-secret records not covered under FOIA. The CIA wanted money to even check into their files to see if there was any information available.

Since the only connection between Valdes and Loeb was the Flight 980 crash, Valdes became the next target on management's hit list. His similarly worded termination letter was also hand delivered on April 24th, 1986.

As an aside, I had never before seen letters of termination hand delivered. The normal, contractually mandated procedure was to send it certified U.S. mail, return receipt requested. I believe this action further demonstrates top management's abnormally high level of concern.

The Loeb and Valdes termination letters were both signed by Captain Bob Shipner, the system chief pilot. I had known Shipner informally since he had unsuccessfully run against Captain John O'Donnell for ALPA President. He was one of the former ALPA officials given management positions. After losing, he had been subsequently offered the System chief pilot post, a high-level management position. Although he later denied it was the case, I knew Shipner had close relationship with Borman and would blindly do his bidding. Terminating a pilot was the equivalent of "capital punishment," reserved for only the most serious offenses. This made it essential that Borman have someone, like Shipner, in the chief pilot position that would not question the true motivation behind them. This was especially important, because upon closer examination it was clear that even if the charges in the letters were factual, neither Loeb nor Valdes was guilty of anything warranting termination.

Shipner subsequently revealed to me that he hadn't written either termination letter. He simply affixed his signature to them after they were written by Magurno, also claiming that he was "forced" to sign them, without further explanation of what would have happened if he didn't. But, the worst that could possibly happen would be that Shipner would be relieved of his chief pilot position and returned to line flying as a captain, since he was on the Eastern pilots' seniority list. I believe Magurno wrote both termination letters at Borman's behest. I do not believe that Shipner knew the true motive behind why Borman wanted Loeb and Valdes fired, although Shipner did know Loeb had gone to the FBI with information concerning money laundering and drug trafficking on Eastern, along with his belief that Flight 980 might have been sabotaged. From his union background, Shipner also knew that since Loeb had been removed from an important union position, he was vulnerable. Since the Railway Labor Act guarantees protection for a union official to carry out his or her duties without fear of reprisal, if a union person is fired, a good labor attorney like John Loomos could make a compelling argument for immediate reinstatement, with most arbitrators giving the benefit of the doubt to the employee. But I believe that Davidson's recall of Loeb was carefully orchestrated to prevent Loeb from utilizing this defense.

After learning of Loeb's sacking, since I was now an ALPA MEC delegate, Copeland and I telephoned other MEC members, soliciting each to join with us in calling a special meeting to address Loeb's removal from his committee position and subsequent dismissal. With Loeb present, after in-depth deliberations, it became crystal-clear that Davidson's basis for Loeb's removal was not credible. I proposed a resolution directing that ALPA National pay Loeb his full pilot salary (he was now a Boeing 727 captain) pending the outcome of the hearing disputing his dismissal. There was a small amount of resistance from some MEC members who had initially voted to remove him, but I countered these arguments by explaining that Loeb had been operating with Schulte's full knowledge. I also played on their guilt by stating that by voting to remove Loeb they might have inadvertently assisted management in upholding his firing. Over Davidson's vociferous protests, and despite Schulte's telling silence, the majority voted to have ALPA pay Loeb his full salary until a decision was rendered. This agreement also stipulated that if he won reinstatement with back pay, he would reimburse the money. At least Loeb wouldn't starve.

From informal discussions I also learned that some MEC members had only heard management's side of Valdes' termination. They were told that Valdes had hired a private investigator and was out to destroy top management and also determine Magurno's sexual preference, which would somehow allegedly do immeasurable harm to the airline.

In the airline industry, the Railway Labor Act mandates a trial-like hearing for employee grievances, including terminations, by the aforementioned System Board of Adjustment. The Board was comprised of two members representing ALPA and two representing management. If these four people deadlocked, as would undoubtedly happen with Valdes and Loeb, a fifth, neutral person would be called in to reach the final determination.

Under the Eastern pilot contract, both Valdes and Loeb had the right to bypass the four-member Board and proceed directly to the five-Member Board, which is what Valdes chose to do. His hearing commenced in Miami on January 27, 1987 and continued until January 30th. Mr. Louis Crane was the fifth and final authority. The decision was rendered on April 20, 1987. The final Award paragraph of the nineteen-page decision read:

> The Association's motion to dismiss is granted. Ramon Valdes' discharge is therefore set aside, and he is hereby reinstated with full seniority rights, and with the pay and benefits he lost as a result of his discharge.

Valdes had been vindicated and reinstated with full back pay, and I was elated. However, after much deliberation he decided not to return, as he was pretty worn out after the legal battle. Plus, he wanted to take care of his spouse, who was ailing with cancer that ultimately proved fatal. So after receiving his back pay and benefits, he opted for early retirement. By doing so, he inadvertently accomplished one of management's goals; no longer actively employed, he would have no further involvement with any South American flight safety items or Flight 980–related activities.

Allow me to digress to underscore top management's treatment of yet another Eastern pilot, as their actions clearly demonstrate their inordinate fear of *anything* that any pilot uttered in connection with Eastern and drug smuggling. Unfortunately, for this particular pilot, it was a matter of mistaken identity.

As a member of the Eastern System Board, I had arbitrated cases which ran the full gamut, from minor contractual disputes to termination cases. I knew from experience that Eastern *normally* only fired pilots for serious offenses. In July of 1987, I was requested to hear the concluding testimony in the dismissal of another Eastern pilot, Edwin Korczynski, which had been continued from an earlier date. This was the second time that the Chicago-based Korczynski had been fired. In a prior case, a different arbitrator had overturned Korczynski's discharge and ordered him reinstated. But before his return to duty could be accomplished, Shipner fired him again. This time it was for allegedly improperly attempting to get reduced rate transportation.

I was aware that Shipner detested Korczynski for unspecified reasons, and believed it likely that he had taken out his wrath by firing Korczynski not once, but twice. I immediately became suspicious of the motivation because I knew from similar situations that when an employee had abused reduced rate travel privileges, the usual punishment was to suspend the benefit for a specified period of time and have them pay for the flight in question—not to fire the person. I concluded there had to be another reason.

During the closing portion of this case, after hearing the testimony, I sensed that things were not going well for Korczynski. Although I picked up the case during Korczynski's testimony in defense of his actions, it was clear from the tone of the neutral member's remarks and probing questions that he had doubts. I related this concern to John Loomos, who was representing Korczynski. Loomos was also worried, because after his first victory, Korczynski came off as arrogant, confident of also winning this case. After Korczynski finished testifying, Loomos told the Board members that he had one more witness to call the following day and informed the Board that it would be him. This was highly unusual, and although allowed under the Board's rules, I had never before seen an attorney take the witness stand on a client's behalf.

When his testimony began, I was surprised. To paraphrase what Loomos said under oath, over vigorous but failed objections by Eastern's attorney, Korczynski was terminated because in1985 he had been mistakenly identified by top management as having gone to the Drug Enforcement Administration asserting that Eastern crewmembers were bringing drugs into the U.S. on flights from South America. As a result, the DEA threatened to launch a full-scale investigation, with some members of management the specific targets.

Loomos discovered there was a DEA agent with a Polish last name that sounds very similar to Korczynski's and that he was peripherally involved in an investigation of drug smuggling on Eastern. When Shipner had heard the similar-sounding name, he immediately, and erroneously, assumed it was Korczynski. This turned out to be yet another case where management concocted an underhanded plot to terminate an employee they believed, in this case erroneously, had reported drug smuggling on Eastern, with the firing done under the guise of "pass abuse."

I attempted to learn if management had also retained the Intercontinental Detective Agency as part of its investigation of Korczynski, but couldn't get a definitive answer, although indications pointed in that direction. This case clearly demonstrated the lengths management would go to silence any pilot they perceived as concerned about drug smuggling on Eastern. If there was nothing to hide, why use such measures?

Back to Loeb. While his termination case was pending, he was subpoenaed and in February of 1988 gave sworn testimony before U.S. Senator John Kerry's United States Senate Subcommittee on Terrorism, Narcotics and International Operations. As word leaked out about the drug smuggling on Eastern, this Senate Subcommittee wanted to know why and how this was happening right under the noses of the government persons who should have been interdicting the shipments and apprehending those responsible. Loeb testified how he had witnessed the cash shipments being offloaded from his Eastern flights in Panama, and also brought up an Eastern "Frequent Flyer," a fellow he dubbed "Fast Eddie" [his true identity

remains unknown]. "Fast Eddie" always accompanied the money shipments to Panama, showing up at the last possible moment, undoubtedly
after having witnessed the money safely stowed onboard. Loeb nicknamed
him Fast Eddie because no matter where he was seated, he was always the
first to deplane. He would then stand on the ramp, a supposedly restricted
area, and supervise the money being off-loaded into the waiting Panamanian Defense Force's armored vehicles.

* * *

One evening, a Panama-to-Miami return flight was cancelled for
mechanical reasons. The entire crew, along with Fast Eddie, went to the
airport hotel and Loeb ran into him in the bar. The guy became inebri-
ated, and Loeb asked him what was in the pallets. Fast Eddie confirmed it
was money and informed Loeb he was working for Eastern in some vague
capacity. Loeb didn't know whether to believe him because, although he
did produce valid Eastern ID, from their discussion it became obvious he
knew nothing about the airline's operations other than the money shipments.
A few months later, Fast Eddie mysteriously vanished without a trace.

Additional witnesses also offered sworn testimony before Senator
Kerry's Committee that verified Loeb's accounts concerning the money.
Ramon Milian Rodriguez, born in Havana, Cuba, at the time was incar-
cerated for 43 years in the Federal Corrections Institution at Butner,
North Carolina, for violations of the criminal Racketeering and Influence
Corruption (RICO) laws. Specifically, he was jailed for crimes of illegal
money laundering and transporting cash to Panama. I won't go into all of
his testimony, only excerpts confirming what Loeb had witnessed.

> Mr. Rodriguez. "Anyway, the money was packed in these boxes which
> were very official looking . . . and transported to an air freight facility . . ."
> Senator Kerry. "When we say 'air freight' did we use commercial air-
> lines at the time? Were you using those?"
> Mr. Rodriguez. "Yes. The reason we . . . "
> Senator Kerry. "Did you use Eastern Airlines?"
> Mr. Rodriguez. "Yes. The reason we . . . "

Senator Kerry. "Was this money literally put on pallets and palletized?"

Mr. Rodriguez. "Yes."

Mr. Rodriguez. "Yes. What you do is you put your money in the middle and you put cargo on the outside. You strap it, and you ship it on a commercial flight . . ."

Senator Kerry. "Was this money met on arrival in Panama?"

Mr. Rodriguez. "The money was met on arrival . . . An armored vehicle with a Panamanian Defense Force detail."

Senator Kerry. "Was the Eastern station manager . . . on the payroll of the [Medellin] cartel?"

Mr. Rodriguez. "No Sir. The Eastern and Braniff people were Noriega men."

Senator Kerry. "They were Noriega people?"

Mr. Rodriguez. "Yes sir."

Senator Kerry. "Were they part of the drug process, laundering?"

Mr. Rodriguez. "I do not know all of General Noriega's endeavors, but for some personal reason he maintained a very tight control over the airlines that landed in Panama, a control to the extent that he always was sure to name the [airline's] station manager dealing out of Miami."

Senator Kerry. "How much money did you begin to handle?"

Mr. Rodriguez. "Well, towards the end of my career I was handling $200 million a month."

Senator Kerry. "Was there a central collection point?"

Mr. Rodriguez. "In Miami. . . we would put it on the pallets and ship it out of Miami."

There was additional testimony given to the same Senate Committee from a Panamanian, Floyd Carlton Casides who was in the Federal Witness Protection program. He was thoroughly familiar with the Noriega-related money laundering operation and how it worked. He testified with a black hood over his face and what follows is a relevant excerpt from his testimony:

Senator Kerry. ". . . You became familiar with the money laundering operation that took place in Panama. You knew how it worked."

Mr. Carlton. "Yes, that is correct."

Senator Kerry. "Now, you know also that some money that came in to be laundered came in on commercial airliners; is that accurate?"

Mr. Carlton. "Yes sir."

Senator Kerry. "Do you know which airlines were involved?"

Mr. Carlton. "Air Panama, Eastern Airlines. . ."

Although I won't quote them all, there were a number of others who also confirmed the Eastern connection to money laundering, which was exactly what Loeb had reported witnessing to both Borman and the FBI, and for which he was fired.

A decision on Loeb's case was ultimately rendered at the System Board of Adjustment by Neutral member Ralph Baird, just prior to Eastern closing its doors and going out of business, and it went against him. Once again, Schulte never testified on Loeb's behalf that he was working for him in attempting to have Borman removed, which could easily have changed the final outcome. However, at that point reinstatement was a moot point because there was virtually no Eastern to return to. For this reason, Loeb decided not to put much effort into his case or to pursue an appeal. At least Loeb suspected why he had lost his job. There were eventually approximately forty thousand other Eastern employees who lost their careers, with absolutely no clue as to why the airline had crashed and would never fly again.

CHAPTER TWENTY-THREE

Based upon the evidence I accumulated, I believe it clearly shows that the very top U.S. government officials and other operatives, along with highest level Eastern management, concocted a sinister plot that was so inimitable and Machiavellian, yet so diabolically simple that no one ever saw the scheme for what it really was, as the reasons behind it were totally masked. The goal was to deliver what *appeared* to be a financially ailing Eastern Airlines to the Texas Air Corporation. Texas Air would then sell off or transfer the profitable parts, insuring the Eastern's ultimate destruction. This would remove, forever, the fear that the Flight 980 crash would ever be properly investigated.

In order to get the scheme to work, however, the conspirators needed to cultivate trust in the employee ranks—the one missing but crucial element—to get workers to drop their guard. That trust was infused in early 1985 with the assistance of innocent, unknowing employee leaders. Since worker morale was greatly improved, any skeptics were silenced. What better way to gain the needed trust than to seemingly embrace a union-inspired idea? Borman went so far as to personally take to the airwaves in televised commercials, surrounded by legions of smiling employees, touting the programs, proclaiming the airline's superlative service and the resultant profits that meant that Eastern was "zooming." But all the while, his Washington top-level comrades and he were plotting its demise. A potential catch-22 surfaced when the new programs worked better than anyone had expected. The sizeable profits meant there had to be larger than anticipated cuts in the block hours, leaving the door ajar for early discovery. Had employees still been distrustful of Borman, Mort Ehrlich's departure also would have caused alarm, which in turn might have led to the entire plot being unmasked. But instead, this was viewed as discord amongst top management. With Ehrlich gone, no one was in a position to recognize what was happening in time. As a result, the plan went forward, uninterrupted.

Because of what happened with Mort Ehrlich, signs point to the Texas Air takeover initially being set in motion following the Valdes expedition. Judith Kelly provided the icing on the cake, proving to the entire world that the Flight 980 wreckage was not inaccessible, as had been falsely asserted by the NTSB, or disintegrated, as the Bolivian report later falsely claimed. If sabotage was proven, it would take but a short time to uncover the entire stinking affair.

The next phase of the scheme was somewhat more difficult to achieve, as Borman still wanted to extract his pound of flesh from the one person who had been the single biggest thorn in his side, the man who demanded answers: Bryan.

To demonstrate his good faith and belief in the employee programs, Bryan agreed to put the voluntary five-percent contractual wage reduction to a membership vote, as a way to demonstrate the IAM's commitment to seeing Eastern prosper. Although this cut amounted to millions in IAM-represented workers' pay annually, Bryan was confident that his members would recoup it through the higher value of the common stock they held and via the profit sharing. So, he encouraged his members to vote for it. The timing of the secret block hour reductions was excellent because although it appeared to Bryan that something might be wrong, he didn't quite yet have a grasp on exactly what. Who would even suspect that a CEO might knowingly create a money-losing situation? Bryan discovered the cuts just prior to the membership vote on the five-percent wage reduction and probably could have immediately communicated with them to defeat it. But he didn't. He believed the other Eastern Board of Directors members would be convinced that the flying hours needed to be restored or increased further, as cutbacks of this magnitude were a form of "corporate financial suicide." As a result, the pay cut was overwhelmingly approved by the IAM membership.

The majority of the Eastern Board, however, ignored Bryan's red flag, even though he produced figures showing what would happen. This dealt him an unexpected blow. Only much later did Bryan discover Borman had secretly informed some Board members that Bryan would say something to make him look bad, and that Board members should ignore him. So his ominous alarm went unheeded and caused no immediate negative reaction from other employees, as in the midst of the most successful year in the history of the airline, most refused to believe yet another crisis was in the making.

Once the NMB's Walter Wallace agreed to speed up the pilots' contract negotiating process, the airline immediately entered a deadly nosedive, from which there was no recovery. All the time, Lorenzo and his minions waited patiently in the background salivating over Eastern's valuable assets.

With the luxury of my timeline, it's clear there were a number of key elements to the scheme. No doubt everything would have gone exactly as planned with no one the wiser, except that, by unexpectedly surrendering, Copeland and Bryan threw a potential huge and unanticipated monkey wrench into the entire scheme. But Borman also knew that Copeland, a man of his word, couldn't relate Bryan's offer without doing potentially grave damage to the IAM contract. In fact, we told him exactly that during our meeting. Consequently, the carefully prepared script, as dirty as the grimiest back alleyway in Washington, went forward unimpeded, assisted by the power of the federal government.

* * *

Arthur Davis remained as the U.S. Ambassador to Paraguay and, no doubt with bittersweet feelings of revenge, assisted in toppling the Paraguayan "President For Life" Alfredo Stroessner in a CIA-backed coup; this coming after a thirty-five year uninterrupted reign. But this amounted to only half of Davis' retribution. His next stop was as U.S. Ambassador to Panama, where for some time he was unable to complete the remaining part. But as the saying goes, everything comes to those who wait. His patience finally paid off when, on December 20, 1989, the George H. W.

Bush Administration invaded Panama in "Operation Just Cause," forcibly removed Noriega and put him in jail, "in order to preserve democracy in Panama," as the line we have all heard before—and since—went. Mr. "Pineapple Face" Noriega served out his seventeen-year U.S. jail term for shipping cocaine to America, but then was shipped off to France for yet another trial for drug money laundering. He was also convicted there, and sentenced to seven years, but was extradited back to Panama before this sentence was served. In Panama, he had been convicted in absentia for embezzlement, corruption and murder. It seems highly unlikely that he will ever again see the light of day, meaning that no additional evidence will be forthcoming concerning the connection between him; clandestine, top-secret U.S. government operations and operatives; and Eastern Airlines. But Arthur Davis made one important mistake by only looking south for the responsible parties. Oh, they were guilty, but there were plenty of equal or greater culpability right in his backyard—in the CIA, State Department, White House and Eastern Airlines. Although not guilty of sabotage, they set up a situation that could have led to it. But it would have been extremely difficult for Davis to exact similar revenge on them. So, in order to alleviate his suffering somewhat, more convenient and visible targets were offered up as sacrificial lambs.

PART IV

SUBSEQUENT, RELATED EVENTS

CHAPTER TWENTY-FOUR

Due in part to "national security" measures imposed by the Federal Court, assisted to a certain extent by the irrelevant, mainly political concerns of the Congressional Counsel made under the same pretense, the most serious charges were dropped against the Iran-Contra principals who actually went to trial. Others, who were convicted despite the withholding of information by the Executive Branch on the same, false grounds of national security, were pardoned by President George H.W. Bush, who was vice President under Reagan during the time the sordid affair took place. Even Oliver North's convictions were ultimately overturned, as his prosecution and subsequent conviction were based in large part upon his testimony before a Congressional committee that had granted him immunity as a condition to get him to talk. As a result of this travesty of justice, which came to be known as the Iran-Contra or Contragate scandal, corrupt CIA operatives were allowed to continue peddling officially sanctioned illicit narcotics to the American masses that had no clue that it came from the very people associated with their own government. Other than Senator Kerry's hearings, none of the Eastern-related disclosures were ever placed under a microscope as they should have been.

I'm of the opinion that Borman most likely initially perceived that allowing Eastern's planes to be used for the money shipments was simply the duty of a "loyal American," standing by his friend, President Reagan, and his ideals. Although I do not believe there is any evidence that shows Borman was part of the Eastern drug-smuggling operation, as president of the airline, he certainly knew it was taking place. Hell, Loeb told him.

After the Flight 980 crash and the Valdes and Kelly expeditions, Borman's probable perception was that he was trapped and possibly risked prison if Flight 980 was proven to be brought down by sabotage and the trail was tracked back to the money laundering. As a result, *everything* related to this tragedy was never properly investigated, odds-on as a result of a direct presidential request or dictate to Burnett. Judith Kelly's TV appearance was eventually followed by an accident investigation that really wasn't one and a plot that was constructed to destroy *all* the evidence, in this case meaning Eastern Airlines. It would look even better for Borman if the blame could be placed on a union's shoulders for the airline's demise. Borman subsequently utilized many public media outlets to try to do exactly that: blame the IAM's Bryan for the airline's downfall. He went so far as to author an alleged autobiography with the assistance of a ghost writer to accomplish that goal. Recall that Copeland and I made our offer to Borman at approximately 4 p.m. on the afternoon of February 23rd. In his book, Borman related that most difficult time in his life was between the time the Eastern Board of Directors recessed their meeting that same afternoon and driving from his home in Coral Gables back to the recon- vened Eastern Board meeting. I can picture the false sniffles, and I do mean false, because this was the *exact* date and time when Copeland and I met with him. Yet there is absolutely no mention of the almost-2-billion-dol- lar offer we placed on the table, including Bryan's capitulation. I presume that is called selective amnesia? Rather, Eastern's demise is a story built upon man's timeless and never ceasing inhumanity and lust for ego, money, and power—until the very real fear of being caught sets in. Throw in some 1980's anti-union sentiment for good measure and to some, maybe Bor- man and his political henchmen might even appear to be the ones wear- ing the white hats.

Although he subsequently seemingly vanished into obscurity for a time, Borman walked away a wealthy man, with his million-dollar golden parachute in addition to any other retirement earned at Eastern. The for- mer was no doubt a reward from Texas Air for the bargain basement price they paid for all the valuable Eastern assets. When these were sold off or transferred, it enabled Continental not only to survive but prosper, ulti- mately merging with United Air Lines. This was accomplished at the East- ern workers' expense, with untold numbers of lives forever shattered.

Apparently still unable to totally extricate himself from the airline business, Borman remained a member of the Texas Air Board of Directors for some time. Perhaps still seeking public limelight and acceptance, he sometimes makes television or video appearances, in which he puffs his credentials as a former astronaut or airline CEO, in the latter case continually misstating the true reasons for Eastern's demise. The most recent attempt that I witnessed was in 2013 when he appeared in a video contained on the Merrill Lynch website entitled "An American Icon—Still Soaring at 84." In this video he appears with his wife and two men who presumably are his Merrill Lynch financial advisors. In it, he gives his purported reason why the airline was handed to Texas Air. "You get to the point where you have to do something for the shareholders," Borman declared. Do something for the shareholders? He again conveniently fails to mention that all stockholders' equity was ultimately wiped out by the Texas Air transaction as a result of all the labor unrest Lorenzo brought with him. He also apparently "forgot" that Solomon Brothers refused to render a fairness opinion on the sale stock price, or that Merrill Lynch replaced them as the investment banker for the deal, which no doubt made the latter quite a few bucks. The end result is that the misrepresentations continue in a feeble attempt to absolve Borman and government cronies of culpability. Just like when he also seemingly "forgot" to mention the meeting with Copeland and me. Makes me wonder if he still wears his bulletproof vest. Not working full time for the government meant Borman didn't have the protections afforded others or the almost-guaranteed pardons that followed for many. So instead, the power of his government cohorts was brought into play, most clearly demonstrated by the lack of any appropriate response from the NTSB to the Flight 980 crash.

This brings me back to the NTSB and Mr. Burnett. Soon after resigning from Eastern, I flew with a pilot at my new airline, and the cockpit discussion got around to the NTSB. Without going into detail, I mentioned the Flight 980 crash and the lack of a timely investigation while Burnett was chairman. I was surprised when he stated that his spouse was employed at the law firm where Burnett currently worked.

"Would your wife ask Burnett to speak with me about NTSB matters during his tenure as chairman?" I asked, also requesting he not mention Flight 980. His wife subsequently inquired, and Burnett readily agreed. I called, and we chitchatted cordially *until* I raised issues surrounding the Eastern Flight 980 crash, and the lack of a timely and proper investigation. At that point, his entire tenor changed, and he brusquely informed me that he was "awaiting a federal judicial appointment from President George H. W. Bush," had nothing further to say, and hung up! He was never appointed by Bush, but his reaction said it all.

I also subsequently spoke with a former NTSB investigator in an informal setting and specifically inquired about the Flight 980 crash and Burnett's role. Rolling his eyes, he stated, "Burnett would do whatever he was told to do by his boss, the president, no questions asked." Burnett passed away in 2010 and a statement by the Republican Party of Arkansas contained in his obituary in *Newsday* stated, "Jim was a national leader on transportation safety issues." If you believe that, then I have a bridge to sell you in Brooklyn.

You might wonder about the FAA. They too wouldn't push for an investigation. If you were responsible for allowing a major airline to use an untested VOR, and permitting the use of inferior on-board equipment when there was much better available, would you want to be subjected to the intense scrutiny of an accident investigation?

The rubber stamping of the Texas Air purchase of Eastern by a number of federal agencies quickly followed the buyout. The Reagan Department of Justice had absolutely "no problem" with the antitrust implications of the Eastern sale, even though Eastern and Continental, now both owned by Texas Air, at the time would control approximately twenty percent of all the available airline seats within the United States domestic air transportation system. Perhaps those in charge at DOJ already had the word that Lorenzo would dismantle and then tank Eastern?

Likewise, the U.S. Department of Transportation under Elizabeth Dole also gave its official stamp of approval to the acquisition, with its only concern being the lucrative northeast Shuttle market, this prior to the time when Texas Air sold the Eastern Shuttle to Donald Trump. Texas Air was ultimately forced to relinquish takeoff and landing slots on those routes to another airline, but one of its own choosing. Texas Air chose the financially weakest carrier, Pan American World Airways, which subsequently folded. Interestingly, in 1985, Dole's Department of Transportation also withheld the Labor Protective Provisions granted in prior airline mergers, so the precedent had already been set for the Eastern employees to get nothing, which is exactly what they received.

The Reagan-appointed Department of Labor also offered no resistance to the acquisition. This federal agency claimed that the Eastern pilot contract contained strong and clear Labor Protective Provisions, which "guaranteed" job protection for the Eastern pilots. But this never materialized, as Texas Air refused to abide by or even recognize them. The DOL insisted that all Eastern workers were similarly protected under the terms of the United States Airline Deregulation Act. These supposed "guaranteed job protections," however, also never materialized or resulted in one Eastern pilot or other worker either getting their salary or gaining employment at any other carrier with their seniority intact, as also falsely promised by the Airline Deregulation Act. Obviously, the skids were well greased for the smooth transfer of Eastern and its valuable assets to Texas Air, without Texas Air having to worry about any of the Eastern workers' rights.

After gaining all the needed approvals and removing two pesky pilots, Borman eventually did depart Eastern for greener pastures, mostly removed from the public limelight, as was no doubt strongly suggested to him, believing that he was free from the stigma associated with any part of the entire stinking Flight 980 affair, his name sullied only by his failure as a businessman. But even on that count, he continually attempted to shift all the blame onto Bryan's shoulders.

There were also two subsequent, related and crucial items that took place. While "The Gipper" chucked a final pass to see the Eastern sale received all the necessary government approvals, his successor and former head of the CIA, George H.W. Bush, perpetuated the deceptive actions concerning Eastern Airlines. He had no choice but to do so, because Ramon Rodriguez's statements in front of John Kerry's Senate Sub-Committee also implicated the CIA, meaning Bush, its former head, in the money laundering and arms deal for the Contras. Just prior to the March

4, 1989, IAM strike deadline, then-President Bush received a strongly worded recommendation from Walter Wallace, at the time still the National Mediation Board Chairman, requesting that Bush immediately convene a special Presidential Emergency Board to defuse the Eastern labor-management situation and prevent a devastating strike. But in an unprecedented move, one-termer Bush refused to do so. Once the strike began, it took but five days for Eastern to be placed into Chapter Eleven bankruptcy proceedings. Contrast Bush's action to those of President Bill Clinton, when in February of 1997 he intervened to prevent a strike by the American Airlines pilots. He sent the pilots back to work and empanelled a three-member Board to successfully resolve the differences between the parties.

After more than eight months after the IAM strike began, the Eastern workers could still have obtained a reprieve, again, but for Bush. Both Houses of Congress passed resolutions forming a bi-partisan, four-member Blue Ribbon Commission to probe the ongoing Eastern's labor troubles. Only eighteen minutes before it would automatically have become law, without a plausible explanation, Bush vetoed the bill, with no time for an override that night. The House of Representatives subsequently attempted an override, but fell short by a meager twenty-one votes. Just like the eight-percent cut in block hours could be falsely attributed to a "poor business decision," the Bush veto was simply put down under the heading of "politics."

I will never forget the night the aforementioned resolution was passed. I was living in a pilot commuter apartment, when I received a phone call from Skip Copeland, who at the time had been elected as the Eastern ALPA MEC Chairman.

"We got it!" he excitedly announced.

"Got what?" I innocently asked.

"The Eastern Blue Ribbon Commission was passed by both Houses with bi-partisan support. Bush *can't* veto it," Skip eagerly added.

At that time, Copeland didn't know what I had uncovered. I didn't want to rain on his parade, but I informed him, "Skip, he *has* to veto it."

This veto meant that, just like the Flight 980 passengers, the Eastern workers would never get the benefit of an impartial investigation into what actually happened to their airline. No doubt this commission would have gone back, as I did, and scrutinized the origins of all the problems that began with the Boeing 727 crash on that bleak South American mountainside. The rest is history.

Paradoxically, the phony Bush refused to aid Eastern's workers at the very same time that he openly supported and embraced the highly visible Polish Solidarity labor leader, Lech Walesa, and his ideals. In part because of Bush's veto, to this very day many Eastern workers have no clue as to what occurred, other than their lives were forever shattered. While it's true that every airliner crash alters a number of destinies, at least all other U.S. airliner air disasters were properly investigated. But for Eastern Flight 980, the same institutions made certain that important evidence remained buried on that remote South American mountainside, along with the hope of *any* justice for those left behind. But the conniving by those who had no regard for the safeguards built into our system resulted in an attack on the very system they purported to be "protecting." Ponder what these actions portend for you, or me, and everyone else who might follow.

CHAPTER TWENTY-FIVE

No doubt the lingering question in this chronicle is: Who or what caused Eastern Flight 980 to crash? Was it unknowingly flown into the mountainside, or was it blown out of the sky? After all the pieces are assembled, I believe this catastrophe was the genesis of a series of events that not only caused the Flight 980 disaster, but ultimately brought the entire airline down. We may never know that answer as to the exact cause, although the extent of the official cover-up indicates those in power at the time truly believed and, as important, *continue to believe,* that the flight was sabotaged. And, if this were substantiated, their entire conspiracy would have been laid bare.

Borman had to shoulder a good portion of the responsibility no matter what the cause, something he was unwilling to accept. So, with the hushed assistance of his inner circle of powerful Washington politicians, who were only interested in covering their tracks to make certain they could never be held accountable, he assisted in keeping the cause hidden, forever. Such is the awesome, sometimes corrupt power of the United States government.

The entire plot to obscure the absolute truth probably would have worked, except for the likes of Ray Valdes, Jerry Loeb and Judith Kelly, who are the real heroes of this painful and sad saga. They were the ones who first raised the still-unanswered questions.

CHAPTER TWENTY-SIX

On August 9, 1990, Frank Lorenzo announced he was selling his stake in both Continental Airlines and the Texas Air Corporation (by this time renamed Continental Airlines Holdings) to the Scandinavian Airlines System consortium, and leaving the airline business. His dirty work was done at Eastern and there weren't many tears shed. But there were definitely large numbers who simply said "good riddance" to a mean-spirited, vindictive individual and the mayhem he wrought on a once quiet, gracious industry, dragging it down into the gutter. He subsequently attempted to start up another airline, but the DOT, under President Bill Clinton, banned him for life from the industry.

After serving as ALPA MEC Chairman, in November 1986, Larry Schulte was elected to a four-year term as ALPA National Secretary. In this position, he comfortably sat out most of the Eastern IAM strike that was backed by the Eastern pilots, and the subsequent bankruptcy proceedings, with full pay and benefits paid by ALPA. He was up for re-election in November of 1990, but decided to step down. He then flew for another large airline, with his hand still in some ALPA business while there. No doubt he will be one of the beneficiaries of the various parties' revisionist history.

I discussed this book with Judith Kelly on a number of occasions, years ago, but felt as though she never really opened up. She did her crying alone, and I can certainly understand and respect that. I also had a gut feeling she might still be attempting to cope. Could you ever really picture yourself in a position where you suddenly lose the person you love and then have to climb a nineteen-thousand-foot mountain just to say your final goodbyes because your government refused to lift a finger? Her trek no doubt did bring some closure and constitute a farewell of sorts. I wish her peace.

Ramon Valdes retired and now resides in western Florida. But one nagging question must have continually surfaced, "Why not me?" On that fateful night, Eastern Flight 980 was supposed to be his flight. Like any other destiny-altering event, the effects are felt forever. Nothing can be the same again.

Since Jerry Loeb was being paid by ALPA National, he toiled to the very end as a member of the Legislative Affairs Committee for the National organization. He remained in that position until Eastern closed its doors, and then returned to his native California where he worked in real estate and later taught children with Attention Deficit Hyperactivity Disorder (ADHA) and Asperger Syndrome. He also published a novel and released two CDs as a symphony violin player, a gifted and talented individual who got a raw deal.

Charlie Bryan remained in his IAM position until 1992, when the president of the larger national IAM unit eliminated District 100 where he was in charge. He subsequently retired and although he was an invited guest speaker at some business seminars held at various universities, he tried to put Eastern and the airline industry completely out of his life. I interviewed him for this book several months before he passed away, and asked how he was affected by Borman's claims that he was the person responsible for Eastern's demise. He claimed he wasn't surprised at all, stating that Borman *always* looked for a fall guy, and had publicly threatened to "tell the world" that Bryan was to blame. But Bryan was merely an all-too-convenient scapegoat. I got a bit closer to the personal truth when the unpretentious Bryan admitted that he had "spent untold numbers of sleepless nights" trying to fathom the true reason for Eastern's demise. I never informed Bryan what I had discovered, and asked how he personally felt about Borman. He sighed and declared, "He did what he did for reasons known only to him, and he has to live with the knowledge of the thousands of lives he destroyed, for the rest of his days."

Charlie Bryan's actual legacy should be showing what positive results can be achieved when all workers collectively toil toward a singular goal, as demonstrated by Eastern's economic results in early 1985, and not the bogus smears and venomous vilifications Borman placed at his feet. I only wish that he had lived long enough to read this book.

Skip Copeland was subsequently elected to the top Eastern ALPA MEC Chairman position and toiled for the Eastern pilots in that position until the very end. However, by the time he assumed that role, the airline's assets had been stripped bare, Eastern a mere shell of what it once was and already doomed. Full-time ALPA work took a steep toll on both his health and marriage. Like the other pilots who remained to the bitter finale, he lost most of his pension. But Copeland is, and always will be, a fighter. So when ALPA's national leadership ultimately decided not to attempt to enforce the labor protective provisions contained in the Eastern pilot contract that would have entitled the remaining Eastern pilots to transfer to Continental with their seniority intact, he and other Eastern pilots filed a duty of fair representation lawsuit against the union. Sadly, that suit was time-barred by the Federal Court. A few years later, ALPA offered membership back into the ALPA union fold to the Continental pilots that most likely would not have been approved had ALPA protected the Eastern pilots. What that meant was that for the ALPA hierarchy it all boiled down to money, rather than doing what was contractually and ethically correct.

ALPA's shameful actions were subsequently proven true in another case, when the former Trans World Airline pilots sued ALPA after they were sold out when TWA was taken over by American Airlines. The American pilots are in the different union, the Allied Pilots Association, and ALPA betrayed the TWA pilot members in a futile attempt to get the American pilots back into the ALPA fold. In that case, however, the TWA pilots sued ALPA in a timely manner, and after many years of litigation, won in court. ALPA subsequently settled that case for $53 million. I think it is pretty evident where ALPA's loyalties lie.

To this very day, Copeland is still owed over a quarter of a million dollars by ALPA for his time as MEC Chairman, and he has never been compensated a single dime.

But even after the whine of the engines is silenced and the smell of kerosene is gone from the clothing, after hanging the uniform in the closet after the final flight, in Copeland's case, one thing will never change; he will *always* remain a man of the highest integrity. Sometimes in a situation such as this, some individuals might look back and wonder, *Could I have done something differently?* In this case there was nothing left, as devious events at the highest levels, first engulfed and then destroyed the airline that touted itself as "The Wings of Man." No one could have stopped it, and God knows Copeland certainly tried his very best. I will always look up to and respect him for the person he is, what he did and, more importantly, attempted to do.

* * *

I finally said a personally painful goodbye to an emaciated Eastern several months after my term of office ended, approximately one year prior to the start of the IAM strike, and over two years after the Lorenzo takeover. Skip Copeland and I had spent two years and a huge amount of energy struggling to put together an employee buyout, but came up short for a variety of reasons. Although I knew it was coming, I nonetheless felt bewildered and saddened witnessing what Texas Air did to the airline. No matter how hard I tried, I just couldn't see any future for Eastern, particularly after experiencing firsthand the disdain in Texas Air management's treatment of the Eastern employees, particularly the pilots and IAM workers. Despite the fact that it had been stripped bare and become a mere skeleton of the airline I loved, no one from any federal government branch or agency lifted a finger to stop what was conspicuously taking place.

I originally thought I would be fortunate to be able to fly out the remainder of my career at another large carrier, one that had a reputation of providing for its employees. But fate once again intervened, and that airline also underwent a transformation that Lorenzo would have been proud of, ultimately going through the throes of bankruptcy twice and in due course emerging. But it was never the same there, even before the changes. I had to start all over again at the bottom of the seniority list, which although expected, was tough. More importantly, it was a far different place, with a totally different spirit, and pilots who were far different from the ones I flew with and respected at Eastern. I became just another one of the thousands of former Eastern employees whose lives were forever altered.

The final nail in the financial coffin for the Eastern workers, the pilots in particular, came when it turned out that their defined benefit pension was grossly underfunded, thanks to three funding waivers granted by the IRS during Borman's years at the helm. It was with this in mind, after Texas Air acquired Eastern, Congress passed legislation which made employee pension liabilities flow through to all the subsidiaries owned by a parent corporation. This meant that the unfunded Eastern pilot pension liabilities, over $700 million, had to be made up by Texas Air's other airline, Continental. As the MEC Chairman at that time, Copeland had a handshake agreement with Continental's top management that they would repay this obligation in full. But they instead opted to file for their second Chapter Eleven bankruptcy protection several days later in an attempt to escape that obligation. And the bankruptcy Court let them off the hook. As a result, the Pension Benefit Guarantee Corporation (PBGC) took over administration of the Eastern retirement and the pilots received a mere pittance compared to what they were told they had earned, and were entitled to. The old expression that "shit flows downhill" once again proved true. Not only did many Eastern employees get far less pension money than the amount they were entitled to, but some, the pilots in particular, were also forced to repay money the PBGC had paid to them in the mistaken belief that Continental would be forced to ante up the shortfall. This was made even more painful in light of Borman's million dollar golden parachute. There were also problems with the other Eastern pilots' defined contribution plan, known as the "B" plan, as much of it was invested in non-liquid real estate, which also took a large hit right around that time.

Of course, it is much more difficult, indeed impossible, to quantify the *silent* suffering and anguish of many Eastern workers. In addition to a large number of divorces, there were thousands of dislocated and shattered families, lost homes and a number of suicides. Many suffered total financial ruin and lost all their worldly possessions.

The sordid Eastern story continued to the very end. Its Chapter Eleven bankruptcy proceedings dragged on for well over a year, until on April 18, 1990, Bankruptcy Court Judge, the late Burton Lifland, at long last removed Lorenzo and his henchmen from having any further involvement with the airline. The appointment of Bankruptcy Court Trustee, the late

Martin Shrugrue, to run Eastern, gave rise to renewed hope that the internal and external strife might cease, that the airline just might pull itself up from the ashes. But it turned out to be too late; the most valuable assets were gone, with the Eastern carcass plucked clean of those assets by Texas Air, with only a skeleton remaining. Shrugrue was stuck with trying to accomplish the impossible, against insurmountable odds—attempting to undo all the harm that Texas Air had inflicted.

On July 26th, 1990, in what would come as the final curtain call for Eastern, a number of the airline's top maintenance managers were indicted by a New York Federal Grand Jury for knowingly falsifying aircraft maintenance records. Much of the traveling public is frightened of flying to begin with. Need I say more?

But the Eastern deal was particularly good for Lorenzo's Texas Air Corporation. During the time they owned and ran Eastern, my calculations show that they siphoned off virtually every valuable Eastern resource. The Air Shuttle, Latin American routes, Miami and LaGuardia terminals were all sold for hard cash, while numerous aircraft with the most favorable financing were shifted to Continental. As previously mentioned, Texas Air also took possession of Eastern's state of the art reservations system. Taken collectively, these assets totaled over $2.5 billion dollars. It was only through these types of transactions that Continental Airlines was able to survive, meaning the entire scenario played out exactly as Copeland and I had predicted on the day of our ill-fated meeting with Borman.

With Eastern at less than a third its former size, with its darkened Miami headquarters and system-wide terminals more closely resembling ghost towns, and with virtually all of its valuable corporate assets stripped away, the airline's chances of survival weren't slim; they were zero. America lost a historic treasure in Eastern Airlines. But the American people also lost much more: the ability to trust those in power who would do whatever it took to ensure that the truth never surfaced.

*　*　*

Eastern Airlines finally closed its doors and passed into history on January 19, 1991, at one minute past midnight.

APPENDIX A

Here is the complete text of Feith's report as ultimately forwarded to me by the National Transportation Safety Board:

Date: November 5, 1985
To: Chairman
Thru: Chief, Denver Field Office GRB 11-6-85
         Director, Bureau of Field Operations
         Director, Bureau of Accident Investigation
From: Gregory A. Feith, Air Safety Investigator

Subject: After Action Report—Mount Illimani Expedition

This report is a simplified account of the expedition that took place on Mt. Illimani in Bolivia. It also contains my thoughts about the planning and execution of the expedition.

On September 25, 1985, I was selected to retrieve the cockpit voice recorder and flight data recorder from the Eastern Airlines Boeing 727 that crashed January 1, 1985 at the 19,500 foot level of Mt. Illimani, located near La Paz, Bolivia. I immediately began researching information about high altitude mountain climbing so as to be well informed on the physiological factors associated with the high altitude and lack of oxygen. I contacted Al Errington from Boeing Aircraft Company, and a member of the investigation team, and we discussed the various aspects of the Illimani climb. He informed me that he and Jim Baker, the second Boeing team member, as well as Mark and Allen Gerber, the Airline Pilot's investigation team members, were on a prescribed drug called Diamox. The drug Diamox is a potent carbonic anhydrase inhibitor that catalyzes the reversible reaction involving the hydration of carbon dioxide. It is used to reduce the likelihood of edema (which is altitude sickness). In addition, Al told me that

they were also taking a second drug called Decadron which is an anti inflam-
matory. I obtained a prescription for Diamox and began taking the drug on October 2. I did not take Decadron. I read a couple of books that discussed the
various types of edema and the symptoms associated with each so that I could
monitor myself and recognize any abnormalities. I also read several books that
described Mt. Illimani and previous climbs (not associated with the accident).
I also researched the type of equipment needed for a climb of this caliber and
was informed by Mr. Sundeen and Mr. Hendricks, that I had to provide my own
equipment and should be self sufficient because equipment and food could not
be guaranteed in Bolivia.

I arrived in Washington at NTSB headquarters on Tuesday, October 1, for a
planning meeting with the investigation team members, Al Errington and Jim
Baker from Boeing, Allen and Mark Gerber and Don McClure from the Airline
Pilot's Association, Barry Trotter from Eastern Airlines, John Young (Ed. Note:
I believe this is Jack Young, the NTSB Investigator-in-Charge of the Flight 980
crash) and Rudy Kapustin from the NTSB, and Judith Kelly. While I was in Washington I attempted to obtain a cash travel advance of $2,500.00 because I was
told that the Bolivian economy was too unstable to use credit cards. I was only
able to receive $600.00 cash because amounts over $300.00 had to be applied
for several weeks in advance. Unfortunately I only had three working days notice
prior to our October 2 departure date. There should be a way of obtaining sufficient travel funds on short notice because credit cards are not always
accepted.

The investigation team departed for La Paz on October 2, via Eastern Airlines. The team spent four days in La Paz (12,500 foot elevation) acclimating
to the altitude. During the four days, we had several meetings with Royce Fitche,
the Consul General in La Paz, our mountain guide Bernardo Guarachi and Rene
Quinsanilla, the Red Cross Coordinator in which we discussed the logistics of
the climb. As part of our acclimation, we went to Chocultiya, the highest ski
area in the world at 16,500 feet. We climbed the slope to the summit which
is at 17,400 feet. Everyone in the team completed the climb with no ill effects.
The team was in good physical condition on Monday, October 7, when we
departed La Paz. We were transported by a small bus called a Micro to the
base camp at Mt. Illimani; we drove approximately 65 miles in 4.5 hours.

We began the climb on Tuesday, October 8, at 0800. The first leg of the
climb was done on shale rock and snow that had a vertical slope of 10 to 35
degrees. We ascended 3300 feet to our first base camp located at the 17,800

foot level, arriving at approximately 1600. When we arrived at the camp, we were surprised to find none of our equipment that the Red Cross and porters had carried up the mountain for us. After some discussions between Royce Fitche and Renee Quinsanilla via two-way radio, we learned that the equipment had been moved up to our second base camp at 19,500 because it was thought by Renee that we were capable of a 5000 foot ascent the first day. During this portion of the climb, Jim Baker had developed a severe cough which was to be a result of the very dry air. Renee was requested by Royce to bring tents and cooking supplies down to our camp because we were not able to continue the ascent. After approximately 2 hours of waiting, several Red Cross people arrived with two tents but no stoves or fuel. Because of darkness, it was not possible to retrieve any further equipment and with the equipment we had available we were able to melt enough snow to make one pot of cold noodle soup that allowed each of us one cup. The two tents that had been brought down were two-man tents, there were seven men. Al Errington, Jim Baker, and Bernardo Guarachi agreed to bivouac which allowed myself, Allen and Mark Gerber, and Royce Fitche to share the tents. At about 0130, Jim woke us and told us that Al Errington had developed signs of pulmonary edema and that he was on oxygen. Jim said that he would monitor Al and if his condition became worse they would attempt to return to the low base camp that night. As it turned out, Al held his own through the night and at 0630 Jim and Al left the team and returned to the base camp.

The remaining team members, with the aid of several porters to carry our equipment, completed the second leg of the climb to our base camp at 19,500 feet. This portion was done on a snow slope that ranged from 25 degrees to 45 degrees. During this portion of the climb, we encountered only one problem. Royce had a crampon (spikes used for walking on ice) come off which caused him to lose his balance and fall over the side of the hill that we were climbing. We retrieved Royce, fixed his crampon and continued the climb, arriving at the base camp shortly after noon. The decision was made to remain at this base camp the remainder of Wednesday and Thursday so that the team could be well rested and fed before the final leg of the climb which would be the most difficult. In addition, we also used the extra day to allow some of our equipment that would be needed at the accident site to be brought up from the low base camp.

We began the final leg of the ascent on Friday morning at 0915. This part of the climb was done on a snow and ice slope ranging from 20 degrees to 60 degrees vertical. We encountered extremes in weather conditions, i.e., starting with a bright sunny day and warm surface temperatures, changing then to overcast, cold, blizzard conditions, then back to warm temperatures. The weather was constantly changing. We had two slight problems during this ascent, first, Royce fell into a crevasse while attempting to cross an ice bridge over it; second, I had a crampon come off while walking along an ice ledge which eventually collapsed due to the weight of me and my back pack. I had to leave my pack behind so as to complete that portion of the climb. We reached the accident site base camp at 1730, 8.5 hours after starting. During this portion of the climb, Mark Gerber began showing signs of pulmonary edema. His condition deteriorated during the evening and he was sick throughout the night. Saturday morning Mark's condition had deteriorated to the point that his balance and equilibrium was significantly effected (sic) and his thought process and speech was slow and inconsistent.

At approximately 0800, we began the process of locating and digging up wreckage in an effort to locate the cockpit voice recorder and flight data recorder. The aircraft wreckage was covered by snow ranging in depth from 5 to 12 feet. We used light weight aluminum grain shovels to move the snow.

The following portions of the aircraft were located and uncovered for examination:

1. An eight foot by five foot section of the left forward upper fuselage skin and window frame. The fuselage skin had a part of Eastern's logo painted on it. This part of the aircraft was buried to a depth of approximately five feet.

2. The vertical stabilizer with the upper and lower rudder, the "bullet" and a portion of the left horizontal stabilator was uncovered. A hole of approximately ten feet had been dug to reveal the lower portion of the vertical stabilizer. No. 2 engine compartment components were located as well as passenger cabin, galley and lavatory items. Various paperwork from the cockpit was also found in this hole. No evidence of the CVR or FDR was found.

3. Small incidental pieces of wreckage were found in a crevasse that runs through the wreckage path. I identified a deflated life vest, a part of a seat back, electrical wiring, and plastic pieces that looked like the overhead storage bin in the passenger cabin. I recovered a set of shoulder harness that was attached to a cockpit flight crew seat. The metal buckles had what appeared to be blood stains on them.

4. A section of the fuselage that I identified as the aft stair area where the FDR and CVR would be mounted. This section measured approximately four feet by five feet and was covered by approximately seven feet of snow. Again, no evidence of FDR or CVR.

5. In an area adjacent to the fuselage section described in No. 4, a portion of the fuselage was found that measured approximately ten feet long and five feet wide and covered by seven to eight feet of snow. A portion of this fuselage section was uncovered and several lizard skins that were being carried on the aircraft were found frozen to the metal. This section of fuselage appeared to be a portion of lower fuselage skin possibly near a cargo door.

6. There were numerous minute and undescribable pieces of aircraft wreckage uncovered, none of which could be readily identified or used to find the FDR or CVR.

At 18:30, the digging efforts were terminated because of adverse weather and darkness. In addition, I discussed with Royce Fitche the health of the team members and because of my concern for Mark Gerber's, as well as Royce's poor physical condition, I decided to terminate the on-scene investigation and begin the descent as soon as possible. Mark and Royce both used oxygen periodically throughout Saturday evening.

We started the descent on Sunday morning. We were planning to complete the descent in two days but again the Red Cross changed plans without consulting us or even telling us. I was able to complete the descent in one day. Royce also completed the descent in one day with only minor problems. Mark became temporarily incapacitated by the edema and had to be carried down the upper part of the mountain. It took nine hours to transport Mark down to the 17,800 foot base camp. It was decided that Mark, Allan and Bernardo would spend the night at the base camp and complete the descent on Monday. Again, communication with the Red Cross seemed to lose something in the translation because when it was decided that part of the team was staying on the mountain, the Red Cross was required to shuttle equipment (fuel for stoves and food) up from the low base camp to the camp at 17,800 feet. The Red Cross people arrived at the camp with two gallons of Kool-Aid and extra clothing. Mark, Allen, and Bernardo were able to make due (sic) with what they had which got them through the night.

Mark, Allan and Bernardo arrived at the low base camp at 14:00 on Monday. Mark had recovered slightly from the edema and was able to complete the descent under his own power with help from Allan and Bernardo. The entire team, with the exception of Jim Baker, who was admitted earlier in the week to the hospital in La Paz with a lung infection and blood clots, returned to La Paz Monday evening to recover and deacclimate.

The only health-related problem that I experienced occurred after I returned to La Paz and the States. I had problems with hyperventilation and low blood pressure which have since returned to normal.

On Thursday, October 17, myself, Mark, and Allan Gerber departed La Paz for our home bases in the States. Al Errington remained in La Paz with Jim Baker who was still in the hospital recovering. They both returned to Seattle on October 26.

In retrospect of the Illimani expedition, and because an expedition such as this is a possibility in the future, I feel that the Board should be aware of the problems that we encountered, so that future missions will not be hampered by these problems. (Inserted here in this report was the following statement):

[Portions of page 5 and 6 of the attached report have been deleted. This information represents the personal views of the investigator and his conclusions and recommendations to the Safety Board with respect to the conduct of high altitude accident investigations under hazardous conditions]

I would also like to express my thanks to the Chairman, the Managing Director of the Bureau of Accident Investigation and the Bureau of Field Operations for selecting me for the mission and providing me with essential logistical support while I was in Bolivia.

Signed
Gregory A. Feith

*Note: I wonder what "essential logistical support" Feith is referencing. When you read the Gerber brothers comments later in this book, you will see that the NTSB did more to doom the mission than anything else.

APPENDIX B

The following is the complete text of the fourteen-page Bolivian crash report on Eastern Flight 980. It was written by the Bolivian Ministry of Aeronautics and translated by the United States Department of State Division of Language Services. It began with a cover letter by Captain Walter Ballivian, Bolivian Director of Civil Aeronautics.

Republic of Bolivia
Ministry of Aeronautics

La Paz, January 2, 1986

Mr. Walter West
Counselor for Economic and Commercial Affairs
United States Embassy
La Paz

Dear Mr. West:

I am replying to the request from the National Transportation Safety Board which you forwarded to our ministry.

I am happy to send you the final accident report prepared by the Comision Investigadora de Accidentes e Incidentes de Aviacion (Board of Inquiry on Aviation Accidents and Incidents) of the Direccion General de Aeronautica Civil (Civil Aeronautics Bureau) concerning the accident involving the Eastern Airlines Boeing 727-200, Registration No. N-819 EA together with the NTSB report on the accident.

I also wish to inform you that the Direccion General de Aeronautica Civil, exercising its prerogatives, authorizes the National Transportation Safety Board to publish the NTSB report together with the report prepared by the competent Bolivian authority, noting the fact that, since the CVR (cockpit voice recorder) and FDR (flight data recorder) could not be recovered because of bad weather conditions and the inaccessibility of the terrain, the conclusions of this report have not been fully confirmed.

Yours truly,

Captain Walter Ballivian C.

Director of Civil Aeronautics

Republic of Bolivia

Ministry of Aeronautics

REPORT

To: Director General of Civil Aeronautics

From: Comision Investigadora de Accidentes e Incidentes de Aviacion

Ref.: Accident involving Boeing 727-200, Registration No. N-819 EA, class International Air Carrier of passengers, mail, and cargo, owned by Eastern Airlines, Inc., which occurred on January 1, 1985, on Mount Illimani (Eastern Cordillera of the Andes), Murillo Province, Department of La Paz.

The investigation in the field was not conducted because of the topography of the terrain and insufficient resources.

I. The Facts

1.1 Description of the Flight

The Boeing 727-200. Registration No. N-819EA, with flight plan Asuncion, Paraguay (SGAS), La Paz, Bolivia (SILP), took off at 2257 hours Greenwich Mean Time (GMT) (1857 local time), carrying 10 crew members, 19 passengers, and 9,815 lb. of cargo.

The translated transcript of the magnetic tapes from the Santa Cruz and La Paz control centers, reproduced from the ESELA notification point, FIR Bolivia limit, read as follows:

Part One: Santa Cruz Control, flight 980, route UA-320, frequency 123.7 MHz

Time: 2346 hours GMT (1946 hours local time)

EA980: Santa Cruz radio, this is EA980, flight level 350 approaching ESELA.

Control: EA980 confirm your estimate to CAMIRI point.

EA980: Yes, we should be passing ESELA 50, flight level 350.

Control: Understand your estimate ESELA 50, flight level 350, is that correct?

EA980: Yes, that is correct, and our next point will be CAMIRI 0002.

Control: Understand your estimate to CAMIRI point 0002, is that correct?

EA980: Yes, that is correct.

Control: Roger EA980, report point ESELA on this frequency.

EA980: Roger, thank you.

Time: 2350 hours GMT (1950 hours local time)

EA980: EA980 passing ESELA at 50 estimating CAMIRI 02 flight level 350.

Control: Roger EA980, ESELA 50, CAMIRI 02, report CAMIRI point on this frequency.

EA980: Roger, EA 980.

Time: 0001 hours GMT (2001 hours local time)

EA980: EA980 position.

Control: EA980 Santa Cruz, go ahead.

EA980: EA980 over CAMIRI on the hour, flight level 350, estimate SUCRE at 15 past the hour, next is DAKON.

Control: EA980 estimating position SUCRE at 15 past, report SUCRE on this frequency.

EA980: Roger EA980.

Time: 0005 hours GMT (2005 hours local time)

Control: EA980, Santa Cruz.

EA980: EA980, go ahead.

Control: OK, EA980, the Santa Cruz controllers wish you a Happy New Year, and also your crew and airline. Over.

EA980: OK, thank you, and Happy New Year to you.

Control: Thank you . . . illegible . . . Santa Cruz.

EA980: Good-bye.

Control: We hope that some day Eastern will fly into Santa Cruz.

EA980: We really hope . . . illegible.

Control: Illegible.

EA980: I believe so, we can hope.

Time: 0025 hours GMT (2025 hours local time)

EA980: La Paz control, EA980. Over.

Control: EA980 go ahead.

EA980: EA980 estimating DAKON 37, maintaining flight level 350, we want
  to start our descent.

Control: La Paz, roger EA980, authorized VOR la Paz, no anticipated delay,
  descend and maintain flight level 250. For your information, weather
  forecast La Paz 080/12 unlimited, 3SC500 iCB750-3AS2400-07/04
  QNH millibars 1034 inches 30/53. Cumulonimbus SE of airfield. Report
  leaving flight level 350, and report DAKON position. Over.

Time: 0026 hours GMT (2026 hours local time)

EA980: OK, EA980 leaving flight level 350 for 250 at this time. We
  will call at DAKON.

Control: La Paz, roger, EA980 leaving 350, report DAKON, over.

EA980: Roger.

Time: 0037 hours GMT (2037 hours local time)

EA980: La Paz control, EA980 DAKON now.

Control: Roger EA980 report which level you are leaving.

EA980: We are holding 250.

Control: Roger, authorized to descend 18,000, report leaving 250.

EA980: OK EA980.

Time: 0038 hours GMT (2038 hours local time)

EA980: La Paz, EA980 leaving flight level 250 for 18,000 at this time.

Control: Roger.

After this transmission the aircraft was to call on the tower frequency
(118.3) at the estimated time of arrival (ETA: 0047 hours GMT), but there was
no further radio communication with the aircraft.

Time: 0051 hours GMT (2051 hours local time)

The Air Control Center (ACC), after contact with the stations at Arica (the
  alternative airport for flight 980), Lima, Antofagasta, and Santa Cruz,
  attempted to establish communication with the aircraft on frequencies

123.9 and 118.3 MHz, together with Eastern airline agents who were waiting for the flight, but without success.

Time: 0228 hours GMT (2228 hours local time)

The aircraft was declared in the DETRESFA phase, and the appropriate coordination with the specialized agencies of the Bolivian Air Force for the SAR (Search and Rescue) operation was begun. The SAR operation could not be conducted until January 3, 1985, because of bad weather conditions in the probable area of the crash. On that date some parts of the aircraft were found on the southern slope of Mount Illimani, at 19,600 feet, but unfortunately, no survivors were found.

According to the statements by the group of mountain climbers reached the site of the crash, the aircraft had disintegrated, presumably because of a violent impact and subsequent explosion. It was not possible to retrieve the remains of the crew and passengers, because no corpses could be found, nor were there any bloodstains or other evidence within a radius of approximately 600 meters of the site of the crash. The accident occurred at night at 0040 hours GMT (2040 hours local time)

1.2 Personal Injuries

Injuries	Crew	Passengers	Others
Fatal 10	19	—	
Serious	—	—	—
Light/Unhurt	—	—	—

1.3 Damage to Aircraft

Because of the violent impact on the rocky ice cap on the southern slope of Mount Illimani, and the characteristics of the aircraft (pressurized altimatica cabin, etc.) it has probably disintegrated.

1.4 Other Injuries

There were no injuries to third parties.

1.5 Information on Crew

Name of Pilot: Lawrence T. Campbell
Date of Birth: August 28, 1935

Type of License FAA 1461240—Type AT
Issuance Date No reference
Authorized for: B-727, DC-9, L-11 F/C
Medical Exam: December 3, 1984
Valid until: April 30, 1985
Model Experience: 4,725 hours
Total Experience: 14,436 hours.

Name of 1st Officer: Kenneth R. Rhodes
Date of Birth: January 25, 1942
Type of License: FAA 1576309—Type CO
Issuance Date: No reference
Authorized for: B-727 F/S/O L-188 F/O
Medical Exam: September 24, 1984
Valid Until: September 30, 1985
Model Experience: 2,247 hours
Total Experience: 5,941 hours

Name of Systems Opr: Mark L. Bird
Date of Birth: November 24, 1953
Type of License: FAA 2131151—Type Co and FE
Issuance Date: No reference
Authorized for: No reference
Medical Exam: August 31, 1984
Valid until: August 31, 1985
Model Experience: 55:44 hours
Total Experience: 55:44 hours

Check-in Captain: Joseph B. Loseth, Jr.
Purser: Haywood Hargrove, Jr.
Flight Attendants: Pablo Adler
                  Pablo Letelier
                  Marilyn McQueen
                  Roberto O'Brian
                  Paulina Valenzuela

1.6 Information Concerning the Aircraft

The Boeing 727-200, registration No. N-819EA, is a Scheduled International Carrier of passengers, mail, and cargo, owned by Connecticut National Bank, and operated by Eastern Airlines Inc.

According to the information furnished by the Eastern regional office in La Paz, the last major inspection of the aircraft occurred on December 20, 1984.

Aircraft Data:
Aircraft: Boeing 727

Model	Serial No.	Total Time
B-727-225A	22556	8,613 hours

Jet Engines: Pratt and Whitney
(1) JT8D-17R 707255 99:00
(2) JT8D-17R 707256 99:00
(3) JT8D-17R 707261 99:00

1.7 Weather Information

Hourly meteorological data for the date of the accident are enclosed (Annex No. 2);

1.8 Communications

In both directions from DAKON notification point (geographical coordinates: 17 degrees, 07.1' South and 67 degrees, 31.0' West (Annex No.1).

1.9 Airport Information

Not applicable.

1.10 Information on the Remains of the Aircraft and the Crash

Because of the violent impact against the rocky icy surface of Mount Illimani and the technical characteristics (pressurized cabin, altimatica, etc.) the aircraft disintegrated completely.

1.11 Fire

After the first and sole impact, there was probably an explosion and fire, which consumed the few remains of the aircraft.

II. Analysis

The pilot Laurence T. Campbell, First Officer Kenneth R. Rhodes, and Systems Operator Mark L. Bird were found to be duly licensed for that type of aircraft and in possession of valid medical certificates, as were the flight attendants: Haywood Hargrove, Jr., Paul Adler, Pablo Letelier, Marilyn McQueen, Roberto O'Brian, and Paulina Valenzuela.

The Boeing 727-200, Registration No. N-819EA, was inspected on December 20, 1984, as the Manager of Flight Operations and Maintenance for Eastern Air Lines Inc. noted in his report.

According to the transcript of the tape from the Santa Cruz and La Paz Control Centers, the aircraft was in a normal flight pattern and reporting from the points specified in its flight plan. The aircraft reached DAKON point, which was reported at 0037 hours Greenwich Mean Time (GMT) (2037 hours local time); one minute later the pilot of the aircraft reported that he was leaving Flight Level (FL) 250 for 18,000 feet.

After this communication, the radio signals stopped completely, and all attempts to reestablish contact with flight 980 failed.

At 0228 GMT (2228 hours local time), the aircraft was placed in the DETRESFA phase, and the appropriate coordination was initiated with the specialized agencies of the Bolivian Air Force for the SAR (Search and Rescue) operation, which were responsible for this operation on direct instructions from the Minister of Aeronautics.

The wreckage was found on January 3, 1985 on the southern slope of Mount Illimani, on radial 108 degree radial (VOR)/La Paz at 26 MN (Nautical Mile) at an altitude of 19,600 feet.

An analysis of the crash site and the last point reported by the aircraft (DAKON) established that for reasons unknown, the aircraft had deviated 26 degrees to the right of the scheduled airway (UA-320).

With the cooperation of experts on B-727 equipment and on Omega navigation (from LAB [Bolivian Air Lines]), the following possible causes of the deviation were analyzed.

1. Involuntary deviation from the estimated course of the aircraft.

2. Adverse weather conditions affecting the estimated course of the aircraft.

3. Confusion in introducing the coordinates into the Omega navigation system of the aircraft.

III. Conclusions

The Cimision Investigadora, on the basis of the previous analysis and the report by the National Transportation Safety Board, concluded that the accident was apparently caused by the aircraft's deviation from its airway, possibly because of operational failure, aggravated by bad weather conditions at the site.

Because of the bad weather conditions and the inaccessibility of the terrain it was not possible to reach the site of the crash or to recover the Cockpit Voice Recorder and Flight Data Recorder, which imposed limitations on an exact evaluation of this accident.

IV. The Comision Investigadora de Accidentes e Incidentes de Aviacion suggests the following:

One: It recommends that all crews assigned to International Air Carriers operating in the cordillera areas and especially at El Alto International Airport [Note: this was formerly the John F. Kennedy International Airport, but was renamed in 1999] should be properly trained and licensed for this type of operation.

Two: It recommends that, when the weather is bad at the terminal areas and en route, Bolivian and foreign airlines and operators should request information and advice from the appropriate offices of the Servico de Transito Aero [Air Travel Office] (ACC La Paz, Santa Cruz), following international rules and recommendations as published in AIP-Bolivia.

Three: It recommends that operability of aids to air navigation be checked periodically according to existing regulations.

Four: It recommends that a map of the area be prepared (to supplement the existing ones in AIP-Bolivia), which would include the most prominent obstacles, duly indicated.

We submit this report to you for your consideration.
La Paz, September 4, 1985
Signed by Bolivians in various official capacities

APPENDIX C

What follows next is the complete text of Captain Don McClure's important flight safety report, which outlines some of the problems he experienced when he personally flew over the exact route that was taken by Flight 980 when it crashed. The first day he flew from Miami (MIA) to Guayaquil (GYE) to La Paz (LPB) to Asuncion (AUS) as Eastern flight #987. After laying over in Asuncion, the following day, he flew Eastern Flight 980 from Asuncion (AUS) to La Paz (LPB) to Lima (AIM) to Guayaquil (GYE) to Miami (MIA). This was over *nine* months after the crash and Capt. McClure's critical comments are quite telling. Where some explanation of the airline phrases is needed, I added comments contained in the brackets.

Captain Don McClure's report:

Flight 987 MIA–GYE

(1) Upon arrival at the aircraft, both the [Miami] ramp service supervisor and the red coat [higher-up supervisor] attempted to get the captain to take more cargo and passengers respectively that the max allowable gross weight of the aircraft would permit.

(2) Departure fuel was 52,500 lbs. projected arrival fuel GYE 13,300 lbs. All these airports are one runway airports, this does not provide for much fuel to go to alternate, either Quito or Cali. Due to vectoring altitude and restriction by MIA [Air Traffic] Departure Control and high gross weight 183,000 lbs. at takeoff burn off 1,500 lbs. more these flight plan then would put us at Quito [the flight's alternate airport] with about 6,000 lbs.

Alban intersection JEP [this refers to Jeppesen navigation charts] & company Flight Plan lat & lon [latitude and longitude numbers] differ; which is right?

GYE–LPB

(1) Dispatch release calls for V-5 [maximum] on fuel out of GYE. Be careful to check LPB approach climb weight limit usually less than certified max landing weight, therefore you may want less fuel than max for flight plan altitude. If this is the case, and LIM is LPB IAA [alternate airport] than maybe not enough fuel for LIM IAA. Must use Santa Cruz.

(2) Between LIM VOR and LPB VOR see present NOTAM [Notice to Airmen] about using old LA [Latin America]-13 chart and UA320 (LIM 111 degree radial to AYA VOR) vs. new chart UA320 to AYA & RBCN's [radio beacon] UA304 LPB. This trip LIMA [Air Traffic] Control wanted GATUK intersection estimate even though ICAO flight plan and EAL [Eastern] computer flight plan agreed the route was the old UA320 i.e. the LIM 111 degree radial.

LPB–AUS

(1) By going to Best angle of climb speed about 10 DME [miles] before reversing course to 090 degree heading to intercept LPB 134 degree radial (DAKON 1 SID [standard instrument departure] you will pass abeam Illimani at Flight Level 240 [twenty four thousand feet] (154,000 lbs. TO [takeoff)].

(2) LPB [VOR] DME [Distance Measuring Equipment] was lost southbound at DAKON intersection at FL 280 [twenty eight thousand feet] plus.

(3) (Make) Sure Rbcn. VOR; CAMIRI Rbcn. [Rbcn=radio beacon] FILADELFIA Rbcn: positions all disagree with OMEGA by 3–5 miles. Suspect that either the radio facilities are not located where they are shown or the coordinates on the charts and flight plans are wrong.

9/9 22 980 ASO–LPB–LIM–GYE–MIA

ASO–LPB

[Note: this is portion of route where Flight 980 crashed.]

While northwest bound UA320 OMEGA continually tracked to the right of course, this coincided with off-set Southeast bound from night before. Over SUR Rbcn. VOR radial 241 read 143 DME [nautical miles] not 147 as published on

Chart. Crossing AISRO intersection VOR 205 degree radial read 134 DME not 137 as charted. All the navigation facilities on this route are so weak and unreliable that there is no good way to cross check the OMEGA. The OMEGA tracks approximately 4 miles offset to the NE [northeast] both NW [northwest] and SE [southeast] bound between LPB and ASU. This sort of inaccuracy is intolerable when flying over this terrain.

LPB–AIM

As on the southbound leg there is a discrepancy between what MIA [Miami] thinks we should fly and what LPB CTL [La Paz air traffic control] thinks. ICAO flight plan is via UA-320, both LPB and LIM CTL expect us to fly this routing, however computer flight plan has us going over an unpublished route, also there is no NOTAM [Notice to Airmen] northbound as there is southbound. During letdown into LIM ATC (Air Traffic Control) was good about not clearing us lower than minimum safe altitude, however area chart with 10, 20, 30, and 40 mile rims v. [versus] safe terrain altitude provides crews with profile.

LIM–GYE

(1) On push-back LIM senior F/A [flight attendant] advised of sick passenger who passed out. Pulled back to gate. Bolivian Dr. on board, didn't speak English. Summoned airport doctor (Peruvian) spoke fair English. Good medical care by both for epileptic with seizure. Also station manager coordinated with LIM port authority to remove passenger if need be or even to return to LIM after departure if illness reoccurred. Our Latin American flight attendants are good during crises. They are also invaluable as a translator. Ground personnel will work diligently, but must be directed. They take little initiative. Keep LIM in mind if medical assistance is needed en route.

(2) When departing LIM, especially to the North, it will be difficult to be above FL 250 [twenty five thousand feet] north of SLS. At climb at 250–260 IAS [indicated air speed in knots] at max continuous power will make it. If unable FL 250 at SLS request UA436 BTE direct FALON FPR to GYE.

(3) Be careful letting down into GYE, 10 miles north of MHL OK down to FL30 [three thousand feet] but tall mountains 22000 ft. just 20–30 miles east of course.

GYE–MIA

(1) Don't make right turn out too quick as 1600 ft. hill 5 1/2–6 nm [nautical miles] west.

(2) Incorrect ICAO flight plan routing after GCM en route to MIA.

9/9/85 Sequence 33
Observations

1. OMEGA is barely adequate for navigation in S.A. [South America]. However, it is essential as the VOR's and RBCN's [radio beacons] are so weak and unreliable that some form of precise navigation must be on board.
   Recommend: Add one INS [Inertial Navigation System] to the L.A. [Latin America] aircraft both 727 and L-1011. Make the INS the primary nav. [navigation] equipment with ONS [OMEGA] and radios as backup and cross check.

2. The distance between usable airports south of GYE is so great and MEA's [minimum en-route altitudes] so high that careful consideration with regard to fuel, oxygen, and diversion plan in the event of engine failure, decompression, elec. fire & smoke, landing gear problems must be given.

3. Fuel conservation in the terminal area must no longer be the prime concern. Early slow down and configuration of the aircraft is essential to facilitate let down and provide terrain clearance.

4. Medical assistance for passengers may be a long way off if airborne 2 hours plus.

5. Attempts by ground personnel in MIA [Miami] i.e., ramp service and passenger agents to get captains to fly aircraft over weight must stop!! The subject shouldn't even be broached; careful coordination with captain regarding the use of children weight is a must to prevent an overweight TO [take off].

6. Flight plan discrepancies between LIM and LPB must be straightened out immediately as we appear non-professional by providing position reports and estimates for fixes that are nonexistent and not on current chart.

7. A comprehensive discussion and presentation of airway chart legends is a must for ground school, ie., DAKON intersection in name vs. actual location on chart.

8. It is a must! to develop an attitude of distrust on the part of the flight crews for all aspects of this operation, ie., flight plans, ICAO's [flight plans] will be filed incorrectly, aircraft overloaded, NAV aids inop or weak, communications poor or nonexistent, weather information sketchy or nonexistent, improper coordinates on computer flight plans. Cast a jaundiced eye towards everything.

9. Oxygen mask usage and communication procedure into and out of LPB [La Paz] is poor at best.

Recommendations:

1. A different more comfortable [oxygen] mask would be desirable at least make sure rubber cushions on Puritron masks are soft and pliable.

2. A switch on the oxygen mask panel or audio panel should be provided to make oxygen mask mike hot at all times for intra cockpit communications. Thus mike selector switches could remain on the appropriate radios as the PTT [push to talk] or yoke switches activated to provide radio transmissions.

BY DON McCLURE

* * *

Although some of these items could very well turn into life-or-death situations, there was no action that I'm aware of that was ever taken on any of McClure's recommendations or criticisms.

EPILOGUE

After resigning from Eastern, but prior to the completion of this book, I doggedly continued to try to secure as much information as possible on the Eastern Flight 980 crash. I felt that with the passage of time, perhaps some new facts might have been unearthed by the NTSB that they would be willing to share and which would shed further light on what happened. With this in mind, in 1991, I authored the following letter to Jack Young, who was the NTSB Investigator in Charge of the Flight 980 crash and endeavored to appeal to him on a humanitarian level to find out what, if anything, the NTSB actually knew. What follows is the text of that letter, which included my home address, and was mailed to the NTSB's office:

August 23, 1991

Dear Mr. Young:

As a former Eastern Air Lines pilot at the time of the crash of EAL Flight #980 outside of La Paz, Bolivia, in January 1985, now with another airline, I have long puzzled over NTSB's role in the aftermath of that disaster.

Now that Eastern is history, and its management scattered to the wind, a few of us who were friends of Larry Campbell (the ill-fated captain of Flight #980), have gotten together to see if perhaps we can tie up some loose ends. As a former ALPA official, I have been asked to contact the NTSB officer in charge of the 980 investigation.

I suppose what is most troubling about the crash aftermath is the way the matter was handled—or wasn't handled. A jetliner with 19 passengers and 10 crew simply disappears and is never seen or heard of again until ten months later when an NTSB team makes it up to the crash-site—by which time most of the bits and pieces have been buried in tons

241

of new snow. Even more troublesome, no bodies or body parts were ever seen by the various parties who made it to the crash site.

So allow me to ask the following questions:

1. It has been said that the demise of #980 was the first in the history of the NTSB and predecessor agencies never fully looked into for cause. True or false?

2. NTSB investigators had flown down to La Paz the day after the crash but no NTSB investigators even went up the mountain. The only people who went up were a group of Peruvian mountain climbers who returned with part of the wreckage but no photographs. Under NTSB procedure, only Board investigators are to handle such wreckage. Who authorized them? And why did the NTSB sit this one out?

3. A few months later, a second team—hired by another EAL pilot who knew some of the cabin crew—went up the mountain and filmed the wreckage. Then in June, Judith Kelly, the widow of one of the dead & missing passengers, with a trained mountaineer-guide, made it up to the crash site and also shot pictures. Yet the NTSB persisted in maintaining the site was "inaccessible". Comments?

4. ALPA has in its possession documents in which Gregory Feith, the NTSB investigator heading the October 1985 expedition, is quoted as saying he wanted to return to the crash site, perhaps to try and recover the flight and voice recorders. However, no further attempt was made, and I wonder, why wasn't there?

5. Is it possible those recording devices might have been retrieved earlier, by "parties unknown"? (See Question 2) Did anyone from NTSB question the Peruvians?

6. In the absence of any explanation for the aircraft's demise, how did (or does) NTSB account for the loss of the 727-200 with nineteen passengers plus crew of 10? "Cause Unknown"? Has it ever reached such a conclusion in any other airline disaster?

7. How would you, as a seasoned crash investigator, account for the total absence of bodies, body parts, bloodstains on the snow? The altitude was too high to sustain predator life. No bones were found by the October 1985 search team. What happened to the doomed passengers?

8. In the absence of any formal explanation by Eastern, what does your "gut instinct" tell you about this disaster? For a while EAL publicists hinted at "pilot error" but then wisely backed off when asked for evidence. At this point, even a calculated guess might provide some comfort to Larry's friends.

9. Did NTSB make any sort of "after-action report" to the FAA following its November 1985 attempt to reach the crash-site? This is assuming the FAA was even curious.

Mr. Young, we would truly appreciate hearing from you, officially or otherwise. The death of our colleagues remains like an open wound that might begin to heal with answers pointing to "probable cause". So far, the information given out by the Government has been less than forthright.

Cordially,
George Jehn

Young never responded to that letter, so I followed up with another on October 19, 1991. The text of this letter follows:

October 19, 1991

Dear Mr. Young:
As the official NTSB Investigator In Charge, of the Eastern 980 crash, I sent you the attached letter (copy enclosed) on August 23, 1991. As of this date almost two months have passed and I have received no reply to any of the questions raised.

Just to reiterate: the questions included in my August 23rd letter, as they relate to the crash of Eastern 980 on January 1, 1985, are important. If for some reason you are unable to answer any or all of them, it would be appreciated if you would let me know this, along with the reasons why this is so. Official silence or simply ignoring my requests will not be deemed an appropriate response.

I look forward to your earliest reply.

Sincerely,
George Jehn

To this day I have received no reply to either letter.

* * *

Since this book was to be published years after the fateful Eastern Flight 980 disaster, prior to its final completion I thought it would be thought-provoking to once again speak with some of the people involved who might have perspectives and opinions on the crash and the subsequent NTSB Illimani expedition, based on information and thoughts accumulated over the intervening years. By now, some were deceased and there were others I did not want to speak with because I felt as though any information they conveyed would only be bogus or misleading. But the latter was certainly not true for all.

I began by attempting to contact the leader of the failed NTSB, October 1985 expedition, Gregory Feith. I emailed him, informed him I would like to discuss the Flight 980 trek [I had never told anyone, including Mr. Feith, about the particulars of this book] and asked for a phone contact where I might reach him. His response was swift and provided his office and mobile phone numbers. I called the very next day, but I only got his voice mail on both numbers. I subsequently attempted to phone him numerous times and left messages each time, but my phone calls were never returned. Likewise, all my ensuing emails went unanswered. I had come to the conclusion that Mr. Feith had nothing to do with any prior NTSB decision not to investigate, and still consider that to be the case. However, when attempting to inquire about various details and perhaps get answers to some troublesome questions I had (that he might also have) he avoided me. He is no longer employed by the NTSB and his behavior remains an enigma. This was a major disappointment and only further intensified the mystery surrounding the Flight 980 tragedy. The particulars of the Flight 980 crash, or rather the lack thereof, on the NTSB's official government website go hand-in-hand with Mr. Feith's snub. If a person went to: www.ntsb.gov/aviationquery/AccList.aspx?month=1& year=1985, the Flight 980 crash is second from the top under the heading of "Foreign" with the location of LA PAZ, Bolivia, listed. However unlike the other crashes that are itemized on that page and all others, when you clicked on the Flight 980 crash, you were not able to view *anything*. You instead received a cryptic message that reads, "Server Error in '/Aviation Query' Application." This is followed by "**Description:** An application error occurred on the server. The current custom error settings for this application prevent the details of the application error from being viewed remotely **(for security reasons)** *[Emphasis added]*. It could, however, be viewed by browsers running on the local server machine."

Please note the term, "for security reasons." Here it is, almost thirty years from the time Flight 980 crashed, an air disaster that the NTSB didn't want to investigate or find a probable cause for, yet they are claiming nothing is available on their website "for security reasons." Yet, apparently the second portion of that same message, which states, "It could, however, be viewed by browsers running on the local server machine," means that the internal NTSB computer did have additional material on it. I could find no other crash that contained this statement not even for the terrorist attacks of September 11, 2001. In those cases, the NTSB made the curious statement that, "The terrorist attacks of September 11, 2001 are under the jurisdiction of the Federal Bureau of Investigation. The Safety Board provided requested technical assistance to the FBI, and this material generated by the NTSB is under the control of the FBI. The Safety Board does not plan to issue a report or open a public docket."

No such statement could be placed in the record for the Flight 980 crash, as it would have led to questions that could not be logically answered. So one can only assume that the whitewash, cover-up and deception on the NTSB's part concerning what was or wasn't done on the Flight 980 crash as it pertains to the public accessing any NTSB information continues to this very day, for reasons known only to the NTSB senior executives.

But hold on a minute! Shortly before the publication of this book the information on the NTSB's website pertaining to the Flight 980 crash was inexplicably altered! Instead of the previously quoted statement, it now stated:

NTSB Identification **DCA85RA007**.

The docket is stored on NTSB microfiche number **29062**.

Accident occurred Tuesday, January 01, 1985 in LA PAZ, Bolivia

Aircraft: BOEING 727-225, registration:

Injuries: 29 Fatal.

This is preliminary information, subject to change, and may contain errors. The foreign authority was the source of this information.

Please also take note of the NTSB's disclaimer above that the information is "preliminary" (after almost thirty years!), "subject to change, and **may** *[Emphasis added]* contain errors." Talk about government doublespeak!

After reading this latest NTSB posting, I wanted to know what was contained in the microfiche, so I wrote the following letter to the NTSB and mailed it via certified mail [this letter also contained my home address, which I omitted here], requesting this crucial information. I also received confirmation of delivery.

July 3, 2013

National Transportation Safety Board
Record Management Division
490 L'Enfant Plaza East, S.W. 6th Floor
Washington, D.C. 20594

Dear Sir or Madam:

I am requesting under the Freedom of Information Act (FOIA) the complete NTSB file, docket Identification: **DCA85RA007** that is currently stored on microfiche number **29062** on Eastern Boeing 727-225 flight 980, which crashed outside La Paz, Bolivia on January 1, 1985.

Please let me know if there is any expense associated with sending this material to me and I will remit a check to you.

Thank you for your prompt attention to this matter.

Sincerely yours,
Signed: George Jehn

I waited until August first for a response, but none was forthcoming. So I wrote yet another letter reiterating my request under FOIA and again sent the second letter with my original attached to the NTSB via certified mail. Once again, I received proof the NTSB received this second letter, which follows:

August 1, 2013

National Transportation Safety Board
Record Management Division
490 L'Enfant Plaza East, S.W. 6th Floor
Washington, D.C. 20594

Dear Sir or Madam:
I wrote the attached letter to you and sent it certified mail on July 3, 2013 concerning Eastern Air Lines flight #980 that crashed outside of La Paz, Bolivia. I subsequently received confirmation of receipt. However, as of this date I have still not received any response or correspondence from anyone in your office.

    Therefore, I once again request the information contained in my July 3rd letter under the United States Freedom of Information Act (FOIA). A timely response on your part would be appreciated.

Sincerely,
Signed: George Jehn

This letter also contained my home address, but once again I heard zilch from anyone at the NTSB. So much for the Freedom of Information Act! To this very day the NTSB's only response has been complete and total silence. If there is nothing to hide, then why does the cover-up continue?

I also re-interviewed the ALPA participants in the Illimani expedition, brothers Mark and Allen Gerber, and they were once again tremendously helpful. I spoke with and emailed both men and they provided valuable information that I was previously unaware of.

Pertaining to the October 1985 expedition to the crash site, Allen Gerber informed me, "I tried to get information on the crash from the NTSB before we left for Bolivia, but they provided nothing. Then, our entire mission was inexplicably rushed. There was plenty of time, but for reasons unknown, we were whisked off to La Paz, had several meetings with the consulate there and three days later were headed to the base camp at thirteen thousand feet. This was done despite the fact that my brother and I strongly suggested that we needed time to acclimate our bodies to the high altitudes, in order to ward off pulmonary edema, which can be deadly." Mark Gerber subsequently did contract edema. Allen continued, "The entire thing didn't sit right with me back then and still doesn't to this day. I often wonder why that plane crashed and what subsequently really went on within the NTSB hierarchy. Inexplicably, when the NTSB finally decided to go, the entire expedition was done on a bare bones budget and needlessly rushed." Allen further related that he felt they were simply "run through hoops, for show purposes." The handling, conduct and reason for the expedition remain questionable in his mind.

I also spoke with Al Errington from Boeing, who is now retired, and he too was very helpful. At the time of the Flight 980 crash, he was a Boeing engineer, as well as a crash investigator and high altitude Alpine climber. He confirmed everything the Gerber brothers had related, further stating, "The problems encountered were due to the rapidity of the ascent to altitude. If we had a week or ten days to acclimate in La Paz there would probably not have been any medical problems. The entire expedition was dangerously accelerated." Al also contracted pulmonary edema.

In response to another question, he affirmed that none of the aircraft debris was returned to be tested for explosive residue, even though one possible cause could have been sabotage, a fact well known to the NTSB.

Allen and Mark Gerber confirmed this last element by stating that the NTSB team frequently discussed the possibility of sabotage. What's more, he stated that, at one meeting in the U.S. Consulate in La Paz, U.S. representatives stated that the jet could have been sabotaged, as there had been death threats made against Ambassador Davis. "Watch your backs in La Paz because we believe someone, maybe the Bolivian mafia, is shipping cocaine on Eastern. These people do not want you to make it to the crash site," they were told.

If you think about this, why would anyone be concerned if they made it to the crash site, *unless* the jet had been sabotaged? Yet despite this, the Gerber brothers also confirmed that no pieces of the wreckage were returned for explosive residue testing.

Al Errington added that he also thought it was curious that, "there were no prior *public [Emphasis added]* efforts to retrieve the recorders, especially as the tail section had broken loose and was intact." He informed me that he had volunteered to go to the site of the crash immediately and that Boeing wanted to do the expedition right away, as they felt the recorders could be recovered without major difficulty. The Boeing people pushed for that and thought it was curious that the NTSB didn't want to make the effort. He ultimately relegated the NTSB's lack of action to "bureaucratic slowness."

Allen Gerber added, "I don't know for sure what was behind the initial decision not to investigate, but when they finally decided to make the attempt, the NTSB did a half-assed job and bungled it, badly." Allen went on to state that suddenly, the trek described by the NTSB for many months as "mission impossible" overnight became "mission possible," except that all of the overwhelming obstacles they encountered were created by either the NTSB, the Bolivians or Eastern, making the mission impossible description the accurate one.

I also inquired of the Gerber brothers about oxygen packs that are frequently used in high altitude mountain climbing. Here is Mark Gerber's e-mail response:

> Considering the time limiting and cheapness of the NTSB, I don't remember any of the ALPA or Boeing climbers ever seriously considering the subject of using oxygen bottles. From the get-go, we were told to plan for self-sufficiency. Period. O.K., so we had to bring our own gear, understandable. But, heck, we had to buy our own food, and I do not remember ever being reimbursed. And I do not remember being reimbursed for a very expensive climbing rope that was stolen off Allen's pack upon arrival in La Paz.
>
> Given the time constraints that we had to work under, ferrying oxygen bottles was out of the question (weight, bulk and thus increased time and

energy expenditure). Besides, none of us had a stash [of] expensive personal oxygen bottles. We, the ALPA and Boeing climbers, were all well versed in how to acclimate for altitude, so we planned to do our best in light of the time restrictions imposed upon us.

Now, given all the preceding, imagine our surprise when we were told after our arrival in La Paz that the Bolivian government wanted to get in the act and required us to use Bolivian porters!! They could have ferried oxygen bottles for us, if the NTSB had provided some support in this regard.

But . . . in hindsight, the porters were less than helpful. The problems that we did have with altitude sickness could very well have been attributed to the poor management of the porters; the big-lunged, altitude adjusted porters bypassed our first high altitude camp site and dropped our gear at the next higher camp site, leaving us without any water or the means to melt snow and ice for water on our first night on the mountain. All we had was what was left in the bottles we had used that day. Dehydrated, we were set-up for failure once again. Only this time it was an obstacle that we could not recover (from) and overcome. I well remember trying to sleep that first night, deeply dehydrated, and heart racing at 120+ beats/minute laying in my sleeping bag. My normal resting pulse had always been 45–50!

Mark

P.S. More about those "porters": I think all of us had various pieces of equipment stolen by the porters, none of which was reimbursed."

Mark's comments pretty much sum up everything pertaining to the use of oxygen and the NTSB's bizarre behavior. In both men's opinion, the most devastating impediment was the NTSB having waited so long and then forcing them to rush once they were in La Paz.

Both men summed up their feelings by stating that almost thirty years later, they too still had numerous, lingering questions—but no answers—pertaining to this crash and many aspects of the expedition. They certainly weren't alone in that regard.

* * *

I had been introduced to former NTSB Member and current aviation expert and consultant, John Goglia, at an aviation attorney seminar a few years prior to the completion of this book. Since Greg Feith wouldn't return any of my calls or emails, I called Mr. Goglia to see if he knew any additional information about the Flight 980 crash. My first attempt resulted in one-word, for the most part yes or no replies, which led me to conclude that he didn't want to discuss it. However, to my surprise, approximately two weeks later, I received an email asking me to phone him. I did so the following morning, but our discussion added only more lingering questions. He informed me that after our brief conversation, he had spoken to Feith "as a friend" about the Flight 980 expedition. According to Goglia, Feith related that the Gerber brothers were responsible for cutting the expedition short and for its failure. I was skeptical because the Gerber brothers wanted to first acclimate to the high altitude, but had been rushed into the expedition by the NTSB and U.S. Embassy officials. Here were two men who had volunteered to try to unearth the causes, yet now they were being maligned by the person in charge of the Flight 980 expedition. That didn't sit well with me at all. Goglia also told me that time was very important to the expedition. I asked him, if time was suddenly so important, then why did the NTSB wait until ten months after the crash to conduct the operation? The response to that question was total silence.

Next, I was taken aback when Goglia stated that Feith had informed him that the members of the expedition could clearly see the flight and voice recorders at the bottom of a crevasse at the crash site, but couldn't recover them because of the poor health of the climbers. If true, this was *extremely* important information. The very next day, I again contacted Mark and Allen Gerber, informed each individually of Feith's claim that they had doomed the expedition, and repeated his claim that the recorders were visible. Mark Gerber was astonished and told me that he had never before even heard that. "If the recorders were visible, which they were not, either we or the guides could definitely have retrieved them," Mark Gerber declared.

In a separate conversation, Allen Gerber confirmed this by stating,

"Not once did we ever come across the recorders. If we had, we could have retrieved them fairly easily."

Al Errington also subsequently corroborated that no recorders were ever visible.

The Gerber brothers also found Feith's claim that they had doomed the mission to be outright deception, as it was the NTSB that did not give them enough time to acclimate. So here it is, many years after the crash expedition, and an individual who, at the time, worked for the NTSB is still spreading falsehoods.

At this point, you might be asking, "Okay. But why go back? Why dredge up the past?" The answer is that something—no, many things— that happened ought not to have regarding this crash and Eastern Airlines. To this very day, the foundation of our entire aviation flight safety system is based upon complete trust; confidence that if a United States airliner disaster does occur, any and all needed resources will be swiftly called upon to independently, objectively, truthfully and accurately determine the reason or reasons for it. These causes will then be examined in a timely, impartial manner and corrective actions instituted. But in this case, none of that ever took place; there was no timeliness, no objectivity and no remedial measures. Add to that the over forty thousand Eastern employees, many of whom lost everything of value. For many of these individuals, to this very day, there is still no closure, and no way to quantify their silent suffering. Then, you can add to these reasons the searing fire that burned in my belly all these years, knowing that many things weren't right and didn't add up pertaining to the manner in which this crash was handled, or mishandled, along with the needless sale and subsequent destruction of Eastern.

Then, there is this item to consider. I first completed this book in 1991, just prior to Eastern closing its doors. At the time, I had only written a number of newspaper and magazine articles. When I completed the initial draft of this manuscript I called a New York publisher, reached one of the editors, informed him who I was, and provided a brief outline of this book. He replied that they might be interested in publishing the manuscript, but that I needed to obtain a literary agent to represent me.

I asked if he knew one and he gave me the name of the person he considered to be the best, the late Robert Ducas, who had represented a number of successful nonfiction authors. I phoned Ducas, gave him a brief rundown, and he replied that he could possibly represent me and asked if I would mail him the manuscript. A few days later he buzzed back, saying I definitely got his attention. We met for dinner, hit it off well, and signed a representational contract that very night. He wanted me to rework the first hundred pages or so with a ghostwriter, which I began doing. A few weeks later, he phoned and requested me to come to his office. I assumed he had sold the book. But upon arrival, with the ghostwriter present, Ducas slid my manuscript across the desk, indifferently informing me, "I can't represent you on this book." He then produced another document terminating our relationship, which we both signed.

I was dumbfounded and simply muttered, "I'll get someone else to represent me."

"You can get anyone you want to represent this book, George. But if I were you I wouldn't do that," he cautioned.

I was puzzled, but he dismissed me with a wave of the hand. On the long and stressful train ride home I was troubled, pondering his actions that lacked any logic. It wasn't until a couple of days later, when Ducas again phoned, that it all came into focus.

He first asked, "Did you get another agent?"

"Not yet," came my icy reply, so cold it could have originated from Antarctica.

"George," he muttered, "I didn't want to say anything in front of anyone else the other day, but your book goes against some of the most powerful people in the world. I was delivered a clear and unequivocal warning not to help you publish it, or suffer undisclosed, but serious consequences. I'm only telling you this because I like you. However, this information must stay between you and me. If you repeat this, I will deny it."

I was stunned by this revelation. As a young father, I pondered the potential cost of going forward at that time, now knowing there were people who held the most trusted and powerful positions who not only allowed, but enabled this, in order to ensure there would be no way to hold them accountable for their loathsome actions with regard to the Flight 980 crash. Because of the potential impact on my and my family members' lives, I put the book aside and waited until now to reveal these facts.

What I had first assumed, perhaps naïvely, would be a personal probe of an airliner accident investigation that never took place turned into something much, much more.

And now, the entire wretched affair that began with that tragedy in the bleak, cold and harsh South American Andes Mountains has been told. The fire burning in my belly for so many years still isn't completely extinguished, but has been reduced to the smoldering embers of questions still unanswered and disdain for those responsible. I'm aware that you *have to* let go and *must* move on. But I, and many others, still grieve for Eastern Airlines, its workers and their families who lost such an important part of life—all for this.

The twenty-nine souls on board Flight 980 paid the highest price. This book was written for them, for those who perished on that desolate Bolivian mountainside, in a place whose name they had probably never heard of. And also for the many thousands of Eastern employees who never knew of or understood the complexity of events swirling around them, but nonetheless also paid dearly.

The route taken by the expedition to recover remains of Flight 980 (right).

Looking down on Puente Roto base camp from rocks above.

Villagers hired to help cook and carry loads higher up into the mountain (above).

Local villager carrying equipment up the west ridge (right).

Photo of Allen Gerber as the expedition departs Puente Roto base camp (left).

The team of six, with Red Cross members, ascending the west ridge (below).

Taking a break from the effects of the altitude (right).

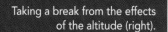

Stopping along the climb to camp at Nido de Cóndores (Condor's Nest) at 17,880 ft.

Bolivians on the way up to saddle at 20,100 ft carrying snow shovels and snow probes (right).

Descending the west ridge at about 19,200 ft.

Coming back down to the west ridge from crossing saddle at 20,100 ft (left).

Climber in harness and ropes being lowered on steep terrain after crossing saddle at 20,100 ft (right).

Digging around the tail section of Eastern 980 (right).

Tail section of Eastern 980 that should have held the Flight Data and Voice recorders (below).

Using metal probes to find wing of Eastern 980 (3 feet of snow had to be removed to expose the wing).

Taking a break from the effects of the altitude at 19,600 ft.

Uncovering as much of the tail section as possible after a few hours' work (Greg Feith, NSTB, in blue, with camera).

Part of plane in crevasse.

Another shot of the tail section.

Bolivian Red Cross members uncover another piece of Eastern 980 (above).

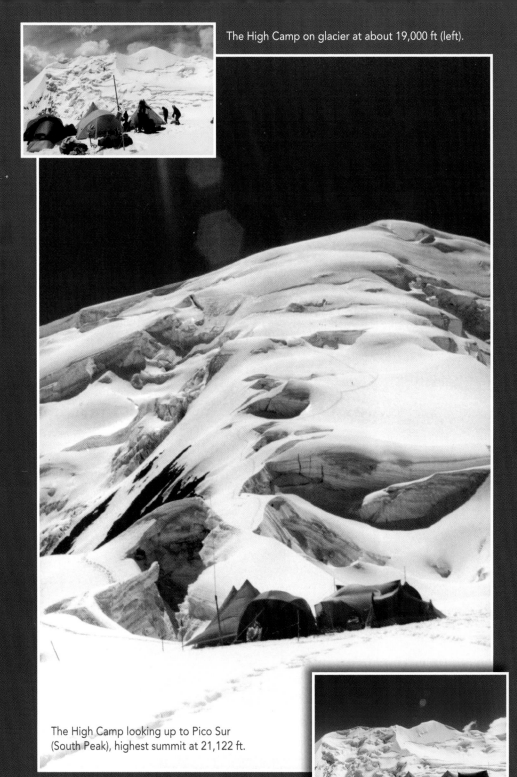

The High Camp on glacier at about 19,000 ft (left).

The High Camp looking up to Pico Sur (South Peak), highest summit at 21,122 ft.

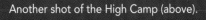

Another shot of the High Camp (above).

Climbing route on south summit.

Illimani shrouded in clouds.

Pico Sur (South Peak) from our camp at Eastern 980 crash site, at 19,600 ft.

Resting at camp lower down on west ridge (left).

Team members review photos of crash site taken by Bolivian Air Force two days after the crash to determine possible locations of wreckage now covered by snow (left & above).

Leaving crash site at 19,600 ft to go up to saddle at 20,100 ft (above).

Members of the team with snow probes and photos trying to pinpoint location of the plane's tail section (left).

Descending down west ridge to Puente Roto base camp at 14,437 ft.

ACKNOWLEDGMENTS

There were many individuals who, although they weren't even aware of it, through the horror stories related to me about what took place at Eastern and in their lives after I had departed, became the sole reason why I had the resolve to finish this book. These people are too numerous to mention. The untold number of heartbreaking, personal, truly sad stories of what happened to them and their family members as a result of Eastern's needless demise would represent a book in itself.

Special recognition is extended to Mark and Allen Gerber, Jim Baker and Al Errington. They volunteered and put it all on the line in an attempt to get to the truth behind the crash of Eastern Flight 980. The same goes for Judith Kelly. If it weren't for her perseverance and climb, the National Transportation Safety Board no doubt would never have even made their cursory attempt. I would also like to thank the Air Line Pilots Association Air Safety staff personnel, who, unlike the National Transportation Safety Board, readily provided me with much valuable Eastern Flight 980 information that I otherwise would not have been able to secure.

The Eastern 980 crash also cost Ray Valdes and Jerry Loeb dearly in their quest to uncover the truthful explanation of what happened. Then there are the twenty-nine who perished on board Flight 980—gone but never forgotten.

There is also my close friend, Skip Copeland, who paid very much, both personally and professionally, but never once wavered from the traits that I have always admired and respected in him so much, and which have guided him throughout his entire life: truth, honesty and a never-ending commitment and devotion to the Eastern Airlines pilots.

I also want to thank my wife, Lorraine, who first led me into the light—
that is the true meaning of love—and for also enduring all the days and
nights when I was away from home flying for Eastern, working for ALPA,
and, once back home, working on this book. The same applies to the other
"lights of my life": Lorrainie, Christy, Matthew, Matthew, Matthew (yes,
there are three of them), Rain, Olivia, Sara, Juliet, Rocco and Alice.

I also want to acknowledge the invaluable assistance of my sounding
board and confidant, Andrew "Duke" Maloney, the best attorney—ever.
Duke is a former Federal prosecutor in the Southern District of New York
and now a partner at the world's largest aviation litigation law firm,
Kreindler & Kreindler. Special gratitude goes to him for both his friendship and expert legal advice.

Special recognition is also extended to Neal Holland and other hosts
of the Eastern Airlines Radio Show who, to best extent possible, have put
in much time in an attempt to keep the unique spirit and essence of Eastern Airlines and its employees alive through their weekly radio show.

I also want to express my gratitude to Francesca Minerva from Changing Lives Press, who immediately grasped the importance of this book and
encouraged me throughout this long process.

Many thanks are also extended to fellow Mystery Writers of America
member, friend and novelist, Peter James Quirk, who quietly assisted me
throughout this long and sometimes arduous process.

January 6, 1984:

> *"Go back, George. It's not your time yet."*

Now I know why.

> *"The dead cannot cry out for justice.
> It is a duty of the living to do so for them."*
> — LOIS MCMASTER BUJOLD

ABOUT THE AUTHOR

George Jehn, after receiving his pilot certificates, first flew as a flight instructor and charter pilot, then as a captain for a commuter airline. He subsequently was hired by Eastern Airlines, and for approximately eighteen years—from 1970 until 1988—flew the Boeing 727, Douglas DC-9 and Airbus A-300 jets. When it became apparent that the airline was doomed, he left Eastern to work for another large airline until his retirement.

While at Eastern Airlines, George spent six years as an elected pilot Master Executive Council Representative from Eastern's New York pilot base and was simultaneously a six-year Member of the Board of Directors of the Air Line Pilots Association (ALPA), the large union that represented the Eastern pilots. He was also a Member of the Eastern Airlines System Board of Adjustment, the judicial body established under the Railway Labor Act to adjudicate pilot grievances. Additionally, he was the sole pilot Member of the Eastern Airlines Employee Involvement Committee for approximately two years until that committee was disbanded soon after Eastern came under the control of Frank Lorenzo's Texas Air Corporation.

George also founded and was the first editor of *In Range,* an ALPA magazine publication for the Eastern pilots. His writing credentials also include a popular novel entitled, *Flying Too Close to the Sun,* published in 2012 by Ring of Fire Publishing. Additionally, he has written a number of aviation op-ed pieces for *Newsday,* and has also had numerous articles that were published in *The Fisherman, Salt Water Sportsman* and *Sport Fishing* magazines.

In addition to his writing, he also works part-time as an expert witness for a number of aviation law firms.

You may reach George through his website, www.georgejehn.com.